The Slattery Media Group
140 Harbour Esplanade, Docklands
Victoria, Australia, 3008
visit slatterymedia.com

Copyright © The Slattery Media Group, 2010
First published by The Slattery Media Group 2010

National Library of Australia Cataloguing-in-Publication entry: (hbk)
    Author: Waterhouse, Gai, 1954-
    Title: Gai – In My Words / by Gai Waterhouse.
    ISBN: 9780980744736 (hbk.)
    Subjects: Waterhouse, Gai, 1954-
        Racehorse trainers--Australia--Biography.
        Women in horse racing--Australia--Biography.
    Dewey Number: 798.40092

Group Publisher: Geoff Slattery
Editor: Stephen Howell
Cover and page design: Alison Wright
Creative Director: Andrew Hutchison
Photo editors: Natalie Boccassini and Ginny Pike
Production Manager: Troy Davis
Production coordinator/typesetter: Stephen Lording

Printed and bound in Australia by Griffin Press

IN MY WORDS
Gai Waterhouse

To my darling husband, friend and supporter Rob.

The magic of Gai

BY ROB WATERHOUSE

There is no doubt whatsoever – Gai is an extraordinary person with a rare and wonderful aura. When Gai enters a room, the whole area lights up as people are drawn to her. Her charisma is irresistible. I should know, as I still succumb to it every day.

I am also inspired by Gai's enthusiasm and passion for life, as well as her humanity and her sense of compassion for others. Gai's charisma proved irresistible when, as a naïve 21-year-old, she went to London pursuing her dream of a career on the stage – against her parents' wishes and without any training or experience and not even any patronage. She miraculously landed her first role and then was constantly on the stage, a rare feat in the acting world. I still think there is no one better 'on a stage' than Gai.

Gai's success in the theatre was gained playing opposite household names such as Patrick Cargill (of *Father, Dear Father* fame) and touring Canada with Trevor Howard (who appeared in more than 80 movies). And there was Gai the family's favourite appearing in a *Doctor Who* series as a Gallifreyan (from the Doctor's home planet).

Back in Sydney, when Gai and I met and fell in love, she was still the effervescent actress. I was immediately smitten and after just two weeks asked her to marry me! A decade later when she decided to take out her own trainer's licence, granted in January 1992, I was supportive, but no one was more surprised than me by her incredible skills in training horses.

Against the odds, she broke records, from winning four Group 1 Doncaster Handicaps in a row (1994-97) to being the only trainer to trifecta the Group 1 Golden Slipper (2001) to twice training 11 Group 1 winners in a season (2004-05, 2006-07), and in 2002-03 she equalled the Sydney record of 156 wins in a season set by her legendary father, TJ Smith. And what a marvellous trainer she has become – to my mind the most extraordinary horse trainer in the country today.

Gai also is a "National Living Treasure" of the National Trust and was the NSW Businesswoman of the Year in 2000.

And then there is Gai's totally consuming work ethic. When people ask me about Gai, they are fascinated by the long days she puts in, especially with the 2.30am starts. I don't know anyone more passionate about her calling than Gai. She also has spades of good old common sense. It is this down-to-earth approach of 'tell it as it is' that is so endearing with Gai in this frank book of home-grown wisdom.

Inspired by the adversity of equine influenza in 2007, which brought the racing industry to a standstill, Gai wanted a way to communicate with her owners and all racegoers, and used skills honed earlier as a newspaper columnist to write online. No one could have foreseen the widespread response – and her blog is now one of the most widely read in the racing world.

It is Gai's good old common sense, her zest for life, personality, charisma and, yes, some of that aura which shines through in every page of this captivating book. A great insight into the magic of Gai.

Rob Waterhouse

The Lady Trainer, a national treasure

Gai – In My Words was born as a blog in the dark days when equine influenza struck the vastness of the Australian horse industry. Writing a daily diary for her corporate website has become a passion for Gai Waterhouse, exposing her driven personality with a joyful frankness. **Stephen Howell** describes her remarkable record and love for her job.

Gai Waterhouse has always been a performer. As a young woman she had a successful career as an actor; now, as one of Australia's greatest horse trainers, she performs at another level – not just pushing horse flesh to produce its maximum potential, but marketing the sport as one of involvement, joy, family and community. As she explains on her website *www.gaiwaterhouse.com.au*, "racing should be great fun, and we work hard to ensure our owners are involved and informed every step of the way".

That mission statement is exemplified by the circumstances that have led to the publication of this book. It is, in one sense, another level of performance for Gai, this time as a creative, extremely frank, funny and purposeful writer, one who arrived at the craft through unfortunate circumstances.

When equine influenza struck the thoroughbred industry in NSW and Queensland early in the 2007-08 season, Gai's first instinct was to ensure that everything that could be done would be done to nurse her ill racing stock, her "four-legged babies", back to full health. Her next was to keep her owners rapidly informed as, day by day, the circumstances changed, most of them out of the control of owners and trainers. The industry was in standstill.

The day EI hit was the day the telephone stopped ringing. "The place was like a morgue," said Gai. Her husband Rob added with a wink: "And you thought they liked you for yourself."

Gai has always acted instinctively. Always the epitome of the modern girl, she created a blog, building on her occasional writings on *www.gaiwaterhouse.com.au* and, like everything else she has done in her life, she went at it with gusto. This is not just some afterthought, a time-filler when things slow down; it has become her passion and there is rarely a day without an entry, not all of them about racing. This is a remarkable thing to consider, as she blends training, running a huge business, sleeping little, acting as a loving mother and wife, while making every effort to cook the nightly meals. At one of our first meetings, Rob explained her capacity to fit the words into this agenda: "I think she loves the blog more than she loves training horses!"

This blog has become so much more than a communication device for owners; it has become Gai's personal diary, committing to public consumption her inner thoughts on a vast array of matters – some political, some private, some just joyous exultations of life. Put together in book form, these spontaneous journal entries have become her autobiography, as so often her words refer not just to the moment, but to the influences that have made her the person and the professional she is today.

Her website provides the basic outline of her approach to whatever she does: "Gai has successfully combined tradition and innovation to establish herself among the world's most respected trainers. Dedication, determination, devotion and discipline – the famous 'four Ds' that enabled Gai's legendary father TJ (Tommy) Smith to break world records as a trainer – are the hallmarks of Gai's approach." The blog expands on that formula in detail.

It is not unusual for the child of a great leader to continue the tradition, but following in the footsteps of Tommy Smith was no walk in the park.

Smith won 33 Sydney premierships on end from 1952-53 to 1984-85 and a 34th before Gai took up the reins. Since she was granted a licence in January 1992 (after a long battle with racing authorities), she has won seven Sydney premierships. She explained her methods as a little bit of her father, and a lot of herself. "There are so many things he (TJ) taught me," she writes, "and I have blended his incredible legacy with my own style. I think my record is a tribute to the philosophy of combining the best of both worlds."

Her father trained an Australian record 282 Group 1 winners over more than 50 years. To August 1, 2010, Gai has trained 98 in nearly 19 seasons. She sits fourth on the all-time winners' list with the late Colin Hayes behind her father, Bart Cummings (260) and Lee Freedman (125), recently overtaking John Hawkes (97). Her success and her style have seen her named as a "National Living Treasure", one of about 100 nominated by the National Trust of Australia.

Gai – In My Words clearly shows that training racehorses at the highest level is not just about the personality, drive, enthusiasm or innovation of the leader; it is, like any business, one that thrives when the leader's work ethic is imposed on the staff, and all parts of the organisation are expected to contribute to its ultimate success.

Gai Waterhouse involves all her staff in all parts of her operation. She employs about 90 people – coming from many and diverse cultures – to care for the 130 horses usually in work at Randwick. For Gai, who often refers to herself as *The Lady Trainer*, it is a labour of love, one that is constantly fulfilling: "I love the mateship, I love the teamwork," she said. "I love making the horse, turning a sow's ear into a silk purse. I love winning races."

How long will she do it?

"Until the day I roll over to get out of bed at 2.30 in the morning and roll back to give Robbie a cuddle."

Stephen Howell edited more than 400,000 words
written over three years to create this manuscript.

CHAPTER 1

Horses coughed, and racing stopped

On August 24, 2007, an outbreak of equine influenza (EI) sat racing in Australia, especially NSW and Queensland, on its ample derrière. It was sudden. It threatened my livelihood, my life with horses and with horse people. It shut down racing and it could have set back the racing industry irrevocably.

On that date, a veterinarian reported to the NSW Department of Primary Industries that he had observed sick horses at Centennial Park in Sydney. The report followed an outbreak in Japan of EI (a highly contagious influenza strain that can bring on fever, coughs and runny noses in horses) and the import of breeding stallions from Japan into quarantine and reports that some of these stallions at the Eastern Creek Quarantine Station in Sydney were showing signs of the illness. About midnight on August 24, when EI was confirmed at Centennial Park, racing stewards locked down nearby Randwick racecourse. On August 29, EI was confirmed in horses trained at the track.

It turned out that, apart from one in-house meeting at Warwick Farm on September 8, racing did not resume in Sydney until December 1. Owners could not come into my Randwick stables from August 25 until October 21, when I reopened Tulloch Lodge for its famous "pleasant Sunday mornings".

What was I to do to cope, to get around the quarantine that isolated my stables and the beautiful horses in them from the rest of the world, especially my owners? An online diary reporting all the comings and goings of the stable – and me – was one way of keeping in touch.

Keeping the stable clean is the priority. The horses' feed bins are scrubbed twice daily. The partitions between boxes are limed and tarred and then the boxes themselves are limed (as is the norm) to kill bacteria and reduce odour as the poor darlings have nowhere to go.

On the whole, the horses look remarkably healthy and appear not to have lost their appetite, but it is the most contagious influenza I have come across in all my years in racing.

My main job is keeping up the morale of my staff and owners, and I hope reporting daily events will help. I spend my days inspecting each horse, but, as you can imagine, things are dreadfully quiet.

WEDNESDAY, SEPTEMBER 5

The Lady Trainer feels more like Florence Nightingale. We're all working our hardest to keep the horses as happy as possible. A new routine is in place as of this morning, with only three horses not showing symptoms. All the others are box-resting, being groomed daily, having their boxes changed twice a day and having short periods in the sand roll just to keep them mentally fresh.

Steve Dennett (supervising foreman) has organised staff rosters, making sure every horse is thoroughly checked. Tania Rouse (assistant trainer) is assisting Dr Leanne Begg (veterinarian) and keeping an up-to-date chart of the temperatures, taken twice daily.

Yesterday I spoke to Ollie Tait, managing director of Darley Stud, and asked if Darley's veterinarian based in the UK could give us some advice as to how and when to ease the horses back in to work. The reply he provided was: "For the first fortnight after the signs have abated, little, other than trotting, is undertaken; and for the next two weeks, no more than hacking or easy cantering. Fast canters or 'work' would not generally be tried in the first month."

THURSDAY, SEPTEMBER 6

We were able to trot and canter one horse who is not showing symptoms of the EI virus, on a deserted Randwick. It was an odd feeling walking on to the track with no jockeys' cars parked in their usual places, no strappers leading their charges around the tower, warming them up before the gallops begin. A ghost track.

Back at the stables (where work has been going since 3am) the tempo is constant and, believe me, it is a job-and-a-half getting around our 100-plus horses. After a 7am meeting with Leanne Begg, treatment of the horses with a temperature starts.

Rosters have been made up in every stable[1] to ensure each horse is in a sand roll for some time during the day, as the combination of boredom and not feeling well can make the horse appear depressed. I believe this approach is working and the horses are responding when treated with the anti-inflammatory Phenylbutazone (Bute).

The cut-off temperature point is 39 degrees, so any horse with a reading above that figure is treated with Bute to control the fever. If the horse spikes a temperature for a third time it commences treatment with the antibiotic Triprim for three days. We have spreadsheets of all the horses, and record all temperatures above 38.5 and all treatments. We also have a worksheet of all the horses that are coughing and whether they have a dirty nose. This stringent procedure is repeated morning and afternoon.

We don't administer Bute ourselves. Our horses are examined and, if necessary, treated by Leanne, as this virus is very vicious, very contagious and new to us all.

I know there is light at the end of the tunnel and if we just hang in there I feel that the horses will come right remarkably quickly. I know mine will, anyway.

Begg described the treatment for the benefit of our owners:

Phenylbutazone (Bute) is an anti-inflammatory/antipyretic which gets the temperature down and makes horses feel better. It is given to any horses with temperatures greater than 39C. If they get a second spike above 39, they are given Bute again. These two spikes are most likely related to the virus. If they spike again above 39, then this is most likely due to a secondary bacterial infection, especially if they have really snotty noses – which most have – and so are usually given the antibiotic Triprim.

Once a naïve (non-vaccinated) horse contracts EI it will excrete virus from its nose for about 10 days. The virus attacks the lining of the airway and it takes at least three weeks for this damage to heal. Virus has been recovered from lungs for at least three weeks post-infection, hence the recommendation for hand-walking exercise only for three-four weeks. Once a naïve horse is infected it becomes immune and has solid immunity for at least one year.

Shedding is where the horse is excreting live virus from its nose. Horses will shed while incubating the virus (over one to three days) and the naïve horse will continue to shed for up to 10 days. The vaccinated horse will shed while not showing signs of disease and continue to shed for at least 10 days and maybe

---

1 Gai has four stables: the main yard, Tulloch Lodge, is in Bowral Street just over busy Doncaster Avenue that runs next to the Randwick course; Bounding Away and Tempest Morn, both on Doncaster Avenue, back on to the course; and Chiltern is the holding stable at nearby Newmarket. (Gai gave up Chiltern in April 2008 and added Desert War, which is on the High Street side of the course, in September of that year.)

longer – it probably depends on the type of vaccine used on the horse and how long ago it was given.

MONDAY, SEPTEMBER 10

It tears my heart out to walk through the stables and hear the horses barking like dogs. On Friday you could not hear yourself think for the resounding noise of the horses coughing.

We have now been living with the EI lockdown since August 25 and with the virus affecting our horses since August 29. We are in full hospital mode. Every horse is, in different degrees, affected by the influenza, just like humans would be. Some are very bright and coping well despite having elevated temperatures; some have lost considerable muscle tone; and others are suffering from a form of depression.

A few horses have developed some tricks to pass the time, with the Stravinsky colt Music Maestro deciding the best cure is sleep. He is happy to lie down in his box and sleep through the day. Even if he is tied to his feed manger, he sleeps. The Danzero colt Pelikaan Straat has a box with a view. He has found a ledge and props himself up to watch the schoolchildren playing next door. He finds it quite amusing, just as we do, when we catch him in the act.

Our main chance for the Melbourne Cup this year, Tuesday Joy, is not enjoying her confinement. She lives for the outdoors and does not like the hours spent in her box. She is being cheered up with lots of massage and some quality time in the sand roll to give her a change of scene.[2]

At 6pm on Saturday I received a phone call from AJC track manager Dave Hodgson wanting to know if it was a good idea to open the track for gallops. My response was, "Gallop what?" Dave had been told that this flu was only really very minor and hadn't affected the horses that badly. This is just not so. In my time in racing I have never seen complete yards brought to a standstill, as we are seeing now. It is the volume that one is seeing that is so overwhelming.

TUESDAY, SEPTEMBER 11

It is amazing to think that only 48 hours ago more than 80 horses were on some form of treatment – on Bute because of high temperatures and on Triprim for snotty noses and recurring temperatures. Today we were have about half that, with 47 treatments and six temperatures.

---

2 Tuesday Joy did not get to the Cup because NSW horses were not allowed into Victoria, which remained EI free, during the crisis.

The two-year-old filly Thissideofparadise (by Platinum Scissors) makes life hell when the vet appears. She gets ready to strike with both forelegs and basically says, "Get out of my territory." The four-year-old Lion Hunter gelding Endangered, on the other hand, is a real sook. He can't bear the sight of needles. He is like a child. And, not unlike myself, he has to look away when Leanne administers the medication.

WEDNESDAY, SEPTEMBER 12

Today the overall picture is definitely improving. There were no temperatures at Chiltern (our holding stable in nearby Newmarket) this morning and even though one horse had the runs and a couple still have snotty noses, they were all bright with plenty to say.

Back at Tempest Morn Lodge, Geffen (by Flying Spur) is a two-year-old colt who has done particularly well. As foreman Mel Norton reports: "He's a very playful type who believes he is the stable star." He hasn't taken any effect at all from the virus since he spiked only the one temperature last week.

At Tulloch Lodge, all the colts went into the yard this afternoon, as has been the routine since EI started. Foreman Steve O'Halloran says: "Even though they are sick they show no signs when they get into the yard – all love to jump and buck their brands off. At least they're able to stretch their legs for a little while, which helps them a lot."

THURSDAY, SEPTEMBER 13

This week we had 20 tonnes of sand delivered. This has been shovelled into the sand rolls so that the horses have a safe and comfy playpen. It is beach sand and the horses really love jumping around in it. It's a pleasure to see them kicking up their heels.

About 15 horses were able to walk this morning, which was the first time any have had a walk since the stable was struck with EI. To do this, the horses must have had five days or more without coughs, runny noses or spiked temperatures. As you can imagine, they were really full of themselves. They are only walked for 10 minutes and will be eased back into exercise very gradually.

FRIDAY, SEPTEMBER 14

Some horses have responded really well, with some 25 being hand-walked this morning, one strapper a horse. But a couple who I thought were over the virus have fallen flat again. One is Warring, a five-year-old gelding by General Nediym. He was going brilliantly, coping with the EI, but yesterday he spiked another temperature, which has caused him to lighten up in condition.

An owner, Peter Horwitz, asked: "Does everything in Randwick have EI?" My answer was: "Yes. It is an extremely contagious virus and has moved through the horses rapidly." Another frequently asked question was: "Will all the horses have to be spelled?" Well, no, not necessarily. The safest way to make this decision is to monitor how the horses are coping as they are eased back into light exercise. Many will go to the paddocks once the movement restrictions are lifted, but I'm confident quite a number will come through unscathed.

MONDAY, SEPTEMBER 17

With the stable being a quarantine zone I thought the best way for owners to see their horses on Sunday at Tulloch Lodge was to bring them up to the front gate. It was a bit like visiting a detention centre, as we were on one side of the gate and the horses on the other. Everyone seemed to enjoy it and it was great to see how good most of the horses looked.

The powers that be at Racing NSW believe we will be back at Royal Randwick to enjoy the summer carnival. This is unofficial, but let's hope I am getting the right mail.

TUESDAY, SEPTEMBER 18

Three days with no temperature (the horses, not me). The majority of the horses are now out hand walking and, believe you me, there have been sparks flying with plenty of impressive acts.

We had a rodeo this morning. The ponies (used for leading the racehorses) were the first to contract EI and they have now recovered and have been fighting with each other for the past few days. There have been some serious stand-up fisticuffs in the pony yard at Bounding Away. So this morning they were ridden in the sand roll and it was like something out of the Royal Easter Show, with them bucking when the saddles went on. They loved going out under saddle and in the foreseeable future the racehorses will be doing the same.

We are spending a bit of time painting and spring-cleaning the stables as it is very important to kill any bacteria or germs. If you stand still for long enough in the yard you are likely to get white-washed.

THURSDAY, SEPTEMBER 20

I will have a figure like Linda Evangelista from all the walking I'm doing accompanying the strappers around the bullring, located behind the 600-metre mark at Randwick. It's a good way to hear their feedback and monitor the horses as they stride out.

SATURDAY, SEPTEMBER 22

Shock is the only word to describe the feeling I had when I arrived at Bounding Away and was told the Rosehill races were off and Warwick Farm had been closed down by the dreaded EI – two horses from Clarry Conners' Warwick Farm stable have the virus. I feel very sorry for the trainers and owners of horses there as I know what they will have to cope with over the ensuing weeks and months, dealing with sick horses and monitoring their condition. (The Rosehill meeting, the first scheduled there since the outbreak of EI, was to have been for horses trained at the track and at Warwick Farm. Two weeks earlier a closed meeting was held at Warwick Farm for horses trained there. The public was not admitted.)

Leanne Begg reported on progress:

We are still taking daily nasal swabs from Dance Hero and Where's That Tiger because they have been requested by the DPI (Department of Primary Industries, which is paying) to try to work out when the vaccinates have stopped shedding (spreading the virus). On the latest results, I have Dance Hero as still shedding. They need this information to decide when it is appropriate to test the whole of Randwick. As I understand it, at that time, they will take blood samples from every horse on Randwick and do nasal swabs on every horse. If the blood results are all positive (indicating that every horse has been exposed to the virus) and the nasal swabs are negative (indicating that horses are no longer shedding the virus) they will most likely introduce some sentinel horses that do not have EI. They will nasal swab these horses every day for approximately 14 days and, if they stay non-infected, they may lift the quarantine on Randwick, although this may not mean that they allow horse movements.

THURSDAY, SEPTEMBER 27

All horses are weighed every Monday. Fillies Lieserl, Fleur Royale, Montana Sunset and Esprit D'Amour are having three feeds a day to gradually build up their condition. They are also getting molasses in their water, which is quite salty and makes them thirsty so they drink more and re-hydrate, which stimulates their appetite.

The biggest problem – if I can call it that – is the freshness of the horses we are handling, especially the colts and the two-year-olds. Of course, this means they are now getting better. So they don't injure themselves, or their handlers, I send them to the three AJC sand rolls, where they can roll. If they are under saddle, they can go around in the deep sand, which also works well.

My stable has a set routine now as we are only walking horses. The first lot go out from Tulloch Lodge at 4am to exercise while it's very quiet. By 4.30am Tempest Morn and Bounding Away stables have saddled their ponies – they will lead numerous horses from their stables to the bullring and sand rolls. The procession of horses and handlers remains steady until nearly 7.30am.

WEDNESDAY, OCTOBER 3,

Endangered thought he was in seventh heaven when he was led off Stinky the pony for the first time. He kicked his heels up all the way around the cinders. He looked like a jackass. Gosh he made me laugh. With all the wellness there comes injury, mainly tiny nicks and cuts, but you accept that because horses are not meant to be boxed up.

All the shenanigans take place among a chorus of kookaburras. The mornings have been absolutely glorious, beautiful clear days and amazing sunrises. If that's not incentive to stop sleeping in, I don't know what is.

I took some time the other day to walk the Randwick course proper. It certainly feels different with all the rubbish gone after a "dethatching." The Kensington track looks amazing. Track manager Dave Hodgson and his team are doing a fantastic job and I can't wait to get out there on race day.

THURSDAY, OCTOBER 4

Star sprinter Dance Hero is shooting the breeze and is a very happy chappy. He can't wait to get out and do some pace work. These elite athletes just have a different attitude to any other. They want to get on with the job and compete and this EI confinement period has been painful for them.

FRIDAY, OCTOBER 5

Most horses are over the virus, but some are still shedding. The warm weather is helping as the virus cannot survive for long in sunlight.

We now have a permit to move horses from Chiltern to Randwick for the first time since EI erupted late in August. These horses contracted EI last and have only been up and walking the past 10 days. They came to Randwick by float this morning. The manoeuvre went smoothly. As you can imagine they were very poppy-eyed and fresh. These horses can now resume trotting. I haven't rushed them back on to the track because they were the last to get the virus.

There also is movement at the wider station – horses from one infected area can move to another, and in the next two to three weeks the stables at Randwick will be disinfected, then the flow of horses into Randwick will begin. There's a lot to do in a short time, but it's certainly pleasing to see the end of this confinement is near.

When I was much younger I rode out for my dad, TJ Smith. George Johnson, the course manager, a man I thought was very fearsome but was not at all, would call out to me, "That Smith girl – don't wear sleeveless shirts here ... pull your stirrup irons up". Dad's riders Kevin Langby and Bobby Pearse had great fun riding up behind young Gai and calling out to make my horse go faster. I was not a very strong rider – game maybe. These antics always got the desired results. Mr Johnson would call out as I passed through the gap, "Don't ride horses you can't hold, young lady".

MONDAY, OCTOBER 8

I spoke to Blake Shinn before last weekend to see how he was faring down south. After joining the stable with another Victorian jockey Nash Rawiller in March 2007, Blake went back to Victoria to ride during the equine influenza closure in Sydney, and he sounded very down in the dumps. I find young people often need lots of motivation. Blake is one of the most talented riders I have seen in Australia, but only recently he lost his father, the former jockey Gerald Shinn. Blake has moved back to Kilmore (where his step-father Lee Hope and mother Carol Shinn have stables) and is doing it tough picking up quality rides. As I said to him, "Pick up the phone, call (leading trainer) David Hayes and get into Flemington."

Postscript: Mission accomplished – Blake rode three winners on Sunday at Benalla!

TUESDAY, OCTOBER 9

A pea-souper morning. I can see only silhouettes from my perch at the half-mile and have to rely on my riders' feedback and what I see when the horses walk past me at the stalls. The hustle and bustle that you associate with the training session has disappeared. It's very tranquil these days, mainly because there are not many horses working, no jockeys and no pressure for the horses to be off the track to get away to races or trials.

Great talent surrounds me. Many of the young people I work with leave school at an early age, never gaining the people skills and education that some of us have been fortunate enough to have. Ronnie Nunn was having difficulty when he was filling the role of race-day foreman, not coping with emotion from the owners. He was taking it personally when they made a comment if their horse was beaten.

Recently appointed to the position of stable foreman, he found dealing with the staff a pain. I looked into a course at NIDA (National Institute of Dramatic Art) and Ron has been attending classes. Don't fear Mel Gibson, Ronnie's not going to take your role, but the classes have given him people skills. He described the experience:

> Today we taped me and my teacher acting out scenes where I'm the foreman and he's an owner or a staff member. He would act differently each time we taped. I just had to be myself and see how I would react to each scene. After we would shoot a scene we sat down and watched it. Then we would pick out the things I was doing wrong, or might give the wrong impression, and we started taping again until I got it right. We were working on my body language, eye contact and the tone of my voice. I was really getting the hang of it by the end of the session.

I like to give everyone every possible opportunity. Tomorrow Scott Martin boards a plane to the US to take his holidays and enjoy some work experience with Bob Duncan – that's 'Barrier Bob' who came out and worked with my horses. Bob is the chief starter in the state of New York, which encompasses the Saratoga, Belmont Park, Finger Lakes and Aqueduct tracks. He's a superb horseman, a lovely guy and has kindly asked Scotty to join him. Scott can't contain his excitement. The last time he was on a plane was when he flew from Auckland to Sydney more than 10 years ago, so he had to get a passport. I look forward to him coming back and giving us great assistance with the youngsters at the barriers.

Trainer Neville Voigt walked past me on Saturday morning with his arm in a sling. He was standing on a rail watching his horse and when he stepped down his ring became caught in the wire meshing and tore his finger quite badly. Neville rode for TJ (Smith) and he booted home Oncidon to win the 1973 Villiers Stakes first-up for first-time owners Avril Sykes, daughter of Dr Percy Sykes, and Gai Smith, TJ's offspring. Dad and Percy purchased Oncidon for a pittance. I think it was around £10, or it could have been dollars as decimal currency was introduced in 1966. I nearly blew the win as I was so excited. I rushed to Neville as he dismounted, laying one mighty kiss on his cheek. It was against the rules, and still is, to touch the jockey until he has weighed in. The stewards were very understanding of the young owner's enthusiasm and turned a blind eye.

THURSDAY, OCTOBER 11

Trucks come and go in regular procession, taking the horses from the stables to paddocks that are infected. These are the only places that Randwick horses are permitted to spell. Because the horses have had EI, they are now immune to the virus for the next 12 months.

Weeks are shortening to the kick-off day some time in December, I'm informed, for racing to resume. I've set myself a goal to train the card.

FRIDAY, OCTOBER 12

Jodie Liakousis, who knows Dance Hero really well and has attended to his every need for the past four years, said our champ has never looked better. I am delighted with the way he's eating. Because he is so strong he drags Jodie around in the afternoons, so this morning I put him to work over two laps of the dirt with Josh Parr aboard. He bowled along at a strong canter, and he bowled around again. He'd already walked for 40 minutes. Dance Hero is a very competitive gelding and can't bear just sitting around. I know someone very similar.

MONDAY, OCTOBER 15

All the horses are going back to the mile-and-a-quarter (2000 metres) entrance to work each morning to get more miles under their belts. Remember, they have to be fit by December kick-off time.

My assistant trainer Tania Rouse had this to say about the quickening pace at Tulloch Lodge:

> After spending the past two weeks with most of the horses completing their trotting and canter laps on only one lead leg at a time, they are now beginning to settle down and my life insurance premium has been reduced! The horses that are staying in work all look good and are handling their canter work well, building their fitness levels nicely. They have started swimming at the pool – both the horses and staff in great form now we can see light at the end of the tunnel. The warmer weather is certainly a help with the horses changing in their coats and getting a real gleam. With a few empty boxes waiting for horses to come in we are busy cleaning and disinfecting everything that does not move, and even a few things that do move, i.e. the cat (poor thing) and a goat or two.

Illume (Flying Spur-Silenty Yours) came to mind on Saturday when, between watching the excitement of the Caulfield races on television, I started reading a magazine article on the singer Stevie Nicks. Stevie, through her representative in Australia, Andrew McManus, purchased Illume, bred by Jim Fleming, from the Tyreel Stud draft. My husband Rob heard Stevie interviewed on radio when she was touring 'Down Under' a couple of years ago and she mentioned how much she would love to own a share in a horse. So when Rob told me this I immediately rang Andrew and, voilà, Stevie bought the colt. She requested he be named after her album *Illume* and the rest is history. He's a gorgeous colt and one for the black-book.

TUESDAY, OCTOBER 16

The Westbridge gelding Southwestone is a bit of a fat elephant at the moment. Owned by David Hains, of Kingston Town fame, this home-bred still doesn't know a lot, so today he was lunged for the first time. He's been hitting his hind legs (and remember they wear steel shoes) so I suggested he don a pair of Yorkshire (or brushing) boots. These are made of various materials – I even saw a pair in denim this morning! Lisa Ho, eat your heart out. They are wrapped around the horses' hind fetlocks so that when they walk it causes them to throw their legs out. It's a tried-and-true way of stopping a horse cutting or hitting himself behind.

All the horses at the stables are bedded on straw. Why? It's warmer in winter, cooler in summer; it insulates. Horses rest better on it and most of mine lie down, whereas they won't on shavings, not as regularly anyway. Straw is expensive, especially with the drought, so you won't see it in many other stables.

The horses get a scrumptious boiled feed three mornings a week, Tuesday, Thursday and Saturday. It consists of linseed oil, honey, bran, corn, molasses and a bit of magic. Each stable has a slightly different recipe and, boy, do the horses love it!

We have continued to receive terrific feedback and encouraging emails from owners. I certainly enjoy reading these positive messages and so do my staff, who have never wavered during this difficult period. This email is from owner Ron Bell:

> Absolutely loving the diary. The best thing to happen out of the EI disaster. Feels like I'm right there in the midst of all the feverish activity and enjoying all the excitement. Keep up the good work. The rewards are going to be worth it.

FRIDAY, OCTOBER 19

The Department of Primary Industries is to inspect stables on Friday to determine whether outside horses can return to Randwick. The horses are fresh and ready to go, so to keep them stimulated I have been schooling them over the jumps. There are some beautifully balanced youngsters among them and they really appear to enjoy the exercise.

Dance Hero is trotting well. This multiple Group 1 winner usually shuffles out for jockey Mark Newnham. Today he's fresh and bright. Mark waves to me as he rides past. I've never known a time where the people around the horses seem happier. It's a good sign.

It's funny with the strappers – something can bug them and I'll never know why, only that their attitude or personality changes. That's why I'm always talking with them, asking them questions. Today Jodie Liakousis was walking very slowly with one of her charges. I asked her had she lost interest in her job. "No Gai, my feet hurt," was her reply. She's been shipped off to leading orthotics designer Michael Kinchington. Hopefully, properly shod, I'll see a happier Jodie.

My star boarder, Jock Rorrison, has been a bit sick the past few days and when I returned home last night he was no good at all. I called son Tom, as he and Jock have developed a lovely 'grandfather-grandson' relationship, although they are not related. Tom talked to the old man about their times together – the games of cards that Jock always let him win, the ice cream that his mum was not keen on him having …

The 'ambos' know our home, having called a number of times over the years when Mum and Jock have broken down. When they arrived this time, they asked Jock when was he born. Quick as a whip, he said, "1906." And how old are you, Jock? With a twinkle in his eye, he replied, "101." They said they've never met anyone so mentally alert at such a grand age. They waved their goodnights and came back this morning to take Jock to hospital for a couple of days to be stabilised.

It's amazing what the power of love can do. We think Jock's on his last legs and, because he doesn't want to disappoint Tom, he finds an inner strength to keep on keeping on.

While visiting Jock in Mosman Community Hospital, a lovely patient there introduced herself to me. "My brother Graeme Weaver has a horse with you, but, like me, it's in the paddock," she remarked. I hope both Jean and Fabergine (a filly by Beautiful Crown) have speedy recoveries.

MONDAY, OCTOBER 22

It was so pleasant on Sunday to open the stable for owners, as we had been shut down since late August. About 30 attended and everyone was amazed at how well the horses looked.

YIPPEE!!! We're racing on December 1. I was honoured to be invited by Racing NSW's chief executive Peter V'landys to attend the media announcement today.

Important points to come out included: all horses that have had EI will be blood-tested before they can race; this expense will be met by Racing NSW; and all metropolitan race meetings from December 1 will be open to all horses *and* the general public. What a great day it will be.

As Peter said, other than wars and the Depression, the only time racing stopped was in 1814 when Governor Macquarie put a halt to the very popular thoroughbred meetings because people were unfit to work for many days afterwards due to excessive celebrations.

TUESDAY, OCTOBER 23

Emails from satisfied owners and racing fans continue to pour in. We appreciate and thoroughly enjoy reading all your positive and encouraging feedback. Here are a couple of examples:

Hi All,

I'm only a fan of the stable, but what a great job you have all done keeping everyone informed, not just your owners on your website. I visit it every day to check up on the horses. Good to see Bentley Biscuit back home; can't wait to see him race. All of you take care and keep up the good work.

Regards,
Steve Edwards

Hi,

Just a short note to pass on to Gai.

My name is Les Heimann – I am 66 years old and from the time I was about 13 years old my idol was TJ Smith.

I've always loved horses and the thrill of thundering hooves and the satisfaction of "getting it right" has been a lifelong fascination for me, even though I've never been more than a "five-bob punter".

I spent a lot of time sitting on the outside fence at the turn into the straight at Canterbury when I was a kid. My friend and I used to walk down a huge storm-water drain from Ashfield to Canterbury and then climb up on to the fence and watch – and listen – to how races were won and lost on the turn. Boy, did those jockeys con each other.

I was so excited after Sebring galloped brilliantly on Saturday. Wearing blinkers for the first time, Sebring absolutely blasted the track running 34.1 seconds for the 600 metres, with his final 200 in 11.2 seconds. It was the best gallop I have seen by a Tulloch Lodge two-year-old this season. He will trial on Friday at Warwick Farm.

SATURDAY, JANUARY 5

Sebring continued on from his recent impressive trackwork performances with a blistering eight-length win at the Warwick Farm trials yesterday. The time (51 seconds) was almost a second quicker than the fastest of the other two-year-old trials. The son of More Than Ready is more than likely to make his race debut at Rosehill on January 19.

It was interesting to hear Percy Sykes reminiscing about TJ in the early 1950s. When Dad noticed a horse had not urinated, he said to Percy: "He hasn't peed. Give him a diuretic." Percy replied: "Why don't I make up a saline solution mixture to get him to drink more so he can relieve himself." Percy told me: "It was your father's observation that prompted me to think of a way to hydrate horses. The method then was to use a diuretic ball, which really caused the horse to dehydrate."

This breakthrough has seen the introduction of langs and doca. Langs is a hypertonic (high concentration) solution of sodium chloride and sodium citrate that increases blood sodium levels and stimulates the thirst reflex. The doca is a substance that increases sodium absorption. When horses sweat and dehydrate they can lose enough sodium from their body that they do not get thirsty and so don't drink to rehydrate themselves. By replacing the sodium, they feel thirsty and will drink.

When I told Percy and Leanne (Begg, the stable veterinarian) that I wanted to freshen up Certain Magic after his hard run on Tuesday (in a Randwick 1200-metre race) we decided to give him a dose of langs and doca. It was amazing how the gelding rushed to his water trough and drank thirstily, showing that after the race he was dehydrated.

Isn't it a joke that the three girls – Mum, her friend Marge and yours truly – can't work Foxtel. If only Jock was back at home. He was a death-adder on the racing channel. I'll have to move into the 21st century and learn how to use the blasted thing.

TUESDAY, JANUARY 8

Sunday at the stables was followed by lunch at home (supplied by my darling husband) with great mates Sarah and Frank Steen. I have dubbed Frank "Australia's greatest social barometer". This man can size up any situation and has his finger on every pulse. He and a group of friends from Melbourne attended the Jose Carreras concert at the

Opera House, and Rob and I were going to the Sunday evening concert. Luckily Frank warned us that the great tenor does not have quite the punch in his voice he used to, although he still maintains a wonderful presence. Frank also mentioned on the same program was a super female singer. What might have been more correct was that we have a great Australian soprano star in our midst in Emma Matthews. What a glorious, clear and powerful voice! What a vivacious presence and truly enchanting personality. One minute we were crying with the beauty and poignancy of her voice, the next, standing and applauding – similar emotions I have felt on the racetrack.

Beside us that evening sat a most attractive, tall, tanned and exquisitely dressed and bejewelled European lady. Noticing she was alone, as we left, we swept her up with us for pasta and coffee at Carlo La Rosa's Rossini Restaurant at Circular Quay. Naturally the bewitching hour approached only too quickly for *The Lady Trainer* and we wished dear Agnes Waser adieu and agreed to meet for dinner the following night at Watermark, Balmoral Beach, which we enjoyed.

People often ask me, "How did you meet so and so?" I always say, "I said hello" or "I gave a smile". I find it fascinating meeting new people: they always have something new and interesting to say and often have a different slant on life. This lovely lady was no exception.

TUESDAY, JANUARY 22

Sebring won on debut at Rosehill on Saturday. My husband Rob (who combines bookmaking with in-depth form study) said it was the strongest form race this season. Sebring missed the start of the 1100-metre race and had to cope with interference, so Blake Shinn quickly moved him from the back of the field to sit outside the leader with the pace quickening around the turn and he sprinted up the straight to come away from Over The Wicket.

SATURDAY, JANUARY 26

I spent this morning discussing publicity ideas for the AJC autumn carnival. As TJ used to say, "any publicity is good publicity".

My old mate Jock has been struggling over the past week. His doctor gave him 48 hours to live and said we might not see him before we returned from the New Zealand sales. However, this Scotsman is made of sterner stuff. Yesterday when I visited him he had rallied, sitting up in his chair. I must say he was looking the worse for wear but his spirit was fighting on. If only my horses had a heart like Jock's, I'd have a stable full of champions.

THE LADY TRAINER: "Heavens, I do look tense," was Gai's reaction to this photo of her on her morning rounds at Tulloch Lodge. "But doesn't the beloved one look so cute," she added of Bello, her King Charles spaniel and poodle cross.

PHOTOS IN THIS SECTION: JESSICA OWERS (unless otherwise named)

GAI'S GUYS AND GIRLS: (clockwise from top left) 50-year stalwart John Brady ('Crewy'), assistant trainer Tania Rouse, stablehand Bevan Bell and pony rider Alex Vanny on Stormy.

MORNING CHORES: (clockwise from left) physio Tom Simpson, foreman Steve O'Halloran with multiple Group 1 winner Theseo, trackrider Lauren Taskis and veterinarian Leanne Begg.

THE LITTLE GENERAL: Gai's father, the great trainer TJ (Tommy) Smith, is immortalised in bronze in the centre of Randwick racecourse, the track he 'ruled' for more than 30 years.

GAI'S GATES: the Desert War block of the Waterhouse stables has a small set of barrier stalls – the horses walk through the barriers (gates) on their way to trackwork to get used to them.

HERE'S LOOKING AT YOU: inspecting yearlings gives Gai a head start for the sales. Here she looks over a youngster at Yarraman Park in the Hunter Valley.
PHOTO: SLATTERY MEDIA GROUP/LACHLAN CUNNINGHAM.

SPOT ON: Gai and assistant trainer Tania Rouse discuss the team's work from the Randwick trainers' tower, which Gai suggests looks like the Tardis (time machine) from *Doctor Who*, the television series she had a part in as a young actress.

HEAD START: track rider Alex Jenkins adjusts the head collar on Polar Eclipse at Tulloch Lodge; stable goat Thelma keeps an eye on proceedings.

TRIAL TALK: Gai discusses horses' performances at Rosehill trials with jockey
Mark Newnham. PHOTO: SLATTERY MEDIA GROUP/SEAN GARNSWORTHY

ON TRACK: Neil Paine (left) and Nash Rawiller are key jockeys in the success of Gai Waterhouse
Racing on provincial and metropolitan tracks.

MONDAY, MARCH 31

The trainers have requested a meeting with the AJC's Richard Freedman tomorrow before the first race at Randwick to discuss the possibility of carnival horses working on the Kensington track (inside the main grass track) or course proper. Greg Rudolph from Racing NSW has asked that he can attend, as our request for gallops, trials and anything that could benefit the horses is being refused. Weekend Hussler (the Victorian visitor who won the Randwick Guineas) was given free rein to gallop on the course proper on Friday, the day before the Guineas. Everyone's delighted that he was able to have that hit-out. The trainers have no problems with him having use of the facility, it's just that they would like similar treatment for their carnival horses.

TUESDAY, APRIL 1

It was fabulous to see Gary Kretschmer, an American dirt technician brought in to help, taking charge of the dirt track at Randwick this morning, directing the AJC/Turnpoint staff. It took 10-15 minutes longer, going two laps in the grader around the track. The grader must have stopped at least four or five times to adjust the blades so that it could properly harrow the surface. The jockeys reported that the surface was much more consistent. The problem until today was the track was too soft, even to the point of getting heavy. Bravo – a move in the right direction!

Later in the morning several representatives of the trainers met Richard Freedman and David Hodgson from the AJC and Greg Rudolph to discuss the use by carnival horses of the Randwick course proper and/or Kensington tracks. Progress was made and I am sure the AJC committee, in its wisdom, will sort this out.

FRIDAY, APRIL 4

Sebring and She's Meaner worked side-by-side over 800 metres this morning in a leisurely tune up. A trial on Tuesday at Randwick will bring Sebring back to 100 per cent fitness – he had a little blow after this morning's session. She's Meaner is the most competitive creature I have trained in years. Every time Sebring's nostril got in front of hers she didn't like it. Funnily enough, I know a woman with similar traits to this filly.

TUESDAY, APRIL 8

Amelia's Dream continues to do well at the Randwick Equine Centre. The filly's leg is in a support bandage and she is resting comfortably.

When Sebring's owners (members of the Star Thoroughbreds syndicate put together by Denise Martin) met, the Shahem and Mullens families learned that they lived in the same street in Manly. The odds of that happening are certainly longer than that of Sebring winning the Golden Slipper.

The handsome chestnut returned to the track today in heat nine of the Randwick barrier trials, his first appearance since winning the Listed Breeders' Plate (1100 metres) on March 1. This morning, jumping quickly from his outside barrier, he led before settling in fourth position out six and seven horses wide on the track. Given rein by Blake Shinn on straightening, he swept past his opposition to score by almost two lengths.

He did not run last week or this Saturday because he had a slight temperature rise about two weeks ago and was treated with penicillin. This medicine has a three-week withholding period, which means a horse cannot race during that time. Officially, Sebring becomes clear to race from next Monday. This trial was extremely important to me to make sure I have him spot on for Slipper day.

TUESDAY, APRIL 8

Possum magic – Rob and I have a game we play, childlike I agree, when walking each night after dinner with Baci, our blind poodle: spotting a possum, bat or any other marsupial. I'm a weight-for-age performer. Maybe the eyes have been trained after years of early hours spotting the horses – assistant trainer Tania Rouse explained to me that when she is lifesaving at the beach she is able to pick a swimmer in trouble from a long distance. She puts it down to watching the gallops in the wee dawn hours, and I think she's right. Anyway it pays dividends with spotting possums in the night time.

I watched the galloping gourmet TV show called *Ramsay's Kitchen Nightmares*, and could not believe Gordon Ramsay's language. It may have suited the stable yard or abattoir, and I could not help but think that only a handful of years ago such profanities would not be shown on popular television. Haven't our standards slipped when we take this as acceptable?

THURSDAY, APRIL 10

There were hundreds of telephone calls today between Denise, Robyn Hartney, Blake Shinn and, of course, yours truly. The main point was: would Blake, Sebring's regular rider, appeal his suspension for careless riding yesterday so he could ride in the Golden Slipper? He has studied the video carefully this morning and has been advised to appeal. As you can imagine every available jockey from Hong Kong to Melbourne has been on the phone and Robyn has asked them to wait until we know Blake's fate.

I have just been to Valonz in Paddington to have my hair coloured as white hairs were seen to be multiplying at a rapid rate. Luckily it is only white hairs and not heart

CHAPTER 3

The team's heroes and hard workers

FRIDAY, JULY 4

'm often asked which horse has been my best. It's difficult to answer the question when you have trained such wonderful athletes as Desert War, Bentley Biscuit, Grand Armee and Pharaoh, to name just a few, and this season the champion two-year-old Sebring and the beautiful staying mare Tuesday Joy. But Dance Hero possessed unbelievable cruising speed and no matter how hard his opposition tried he almost always beat them. Jockey Lenny Beasley said there were extenuating circumstances at his only loss in seven starts as a two-year-old: "He didn't see the hole at the start of the Breeders' Plate, which caused him to stumble." In 2004, Dance Hero won the Magic Millions race for two-year-olds, then the Group 1 Triple Crown in Sydney (Golden Slipper, Sires' Produce and Champagne Stakes) and as an older horse won the Group 1 Salinger Stakes at Flemington during the Melbourne Cup carnival

MONDAY, JULY 7

Hasn't the NSW Government got the Papal visit horribly wrong? World Youth Day should be a truly joyous affair but, instead, it's a complete debacle causing such animosity where there should be love and goodwill, and all because our Premier (Morris Iemma) couldn't get the venue right.

Today's my first truly full day at Warwick Farm. And I mean full, arriving at 4am and leaving at 4pm. There were 18 trials teaching the horses how to race and many owners made the pilgrimage to the Farm to view their charges. With the trials starting at 10am, we were all pooped by 3pm when proceedings closed.

FRIDAY, JULY 18

I enjoyed an anecdote today from Peter V'landys, Racing NSW's chief executive. He talked about when he was walking at Randwick and there was my dad's statue right next to Holy Jesus! All I hope is that they are rubbing shoulders. Mum nearly joined them on Wednesday afternoon. She went to lunch, had a couple of glasses of bubbly and led the singing – only to come home and collapse! All thanks from the bottom of my heart to Sonia Dejager, who so ably assists me at home. The young lady is trained in case of such an incident and she quickly turned Mum on her side and gave her mouth-to-mouth and called the ambulance. Mum is recovering well.

TUESDAY, JULY 22

Rob and I are very honoured to have been invited to celebrate the coronation of His Majesty King George Tupou V in Tonga next week. It's not every day that one gets invited to a coronation. I must say it's my first and will probably be my last. Rob and I both had a discussion last night about our national dress and we, being Aussies, wondered whether any of our countrymen would be there in stubbies and thongs.

WEDNESDAY, JULY 23

A very important birthday for 'Crewy', also known as John Brady, who turned 73 yesterday. John walked into Tulloch Lodge more than 50 years ago, a young kid with a crew cut. He said, "I want a job, boss." TJ replied, "Go and grab that broom and get started, and your name is Crewy." Crewy is now the No. 1 man at Tulloch Lodge. His wisdom is next to none and his brew – the nutritious feeds he makes up daily for my horses – has contributed for decades to Group 1 successes. This afternoon we joined Crewy to raise our glasses at the Lansdowne Hotel.

Where have all the race meetings gone? Today the races are on at Gosford and it's not even a metro meeting. Why couldn't the tracks we have in Sydney have covered most of the Wednesday metropolitan meetings? People are creatures of habit. Years ago everyone used to take Wednesdays off and go to Canterbury (or Warwick Farm or Randwick or Rosehill) and the course was full of punters and owners and the sport was alive. Then we started to move the fixture from a set Wednesday to a Monday, Tuesday and even a Friday. Regular racegoers stopped going to the races. Now we have one final nail in the coffin of racing ... more than two months of metropolitan meetings have been shelved to the provincials. Come on boys, let's try to get it right.

Isn't it crook – wait for it – that the AJC and STC (Sydney Turf Club) have decided in their wisdom to abandon the $200,000 bonus for the winner of four separate three-year-old fillies' races, appropriately titled the Princess Series. It is not like the bonus has been won every year; in fact, the last filly to win all four races (the Silver Shadow, Furious, Tea Rose and Flight Stakes) was Angst in 1993. Now the bonus has gone and instead the highest point-scorer over the series receives a trophy. Ho he, ho hum.

THURSDAY, JULY 24

Sebring will not race in the spring. Due to some slight bone bruising, as the result of a growth spurt, he will be spelled. He will return to the stables in eight weeks' time. The horse had a scintigraphy (bone scan) at Randwick Equine Centre yesterday that identified an area of stress-related bone bruising in the right fore cannon. We are erring on the cautious side. Fundamentally the colt is being given time to mature for his campaign in the autumn as a three-year-old before retiring to Widden for stud duties next year.

FRIDAY, JULY 25

Blake must not have been thinking clearly when he left home early one day this week – when he arrived he said, "Oh, I don't have my riding boots." Luckily, one of his pals had an extra set in the car. As you can imagine, Blake copped a ribbing for several days.

MONDAY, JULY 28

Amelia's Dream has just finished week 19 of a 40-week rehabilitation programme at Muskoka Farm, on the Hawkesbury River. She is now walking 25 minutes a day and this level of exercise will gradually increase over the next few months.

THURSDAY, JULY 31

Whiz kid Blake Shinn, at the tender age of 20, has became the youngest premiership winner since Malcolm Johnston claimed the title in 1975-76 when he was the stable apprentice for my dad, TJ Smith. Blake rode 79 winners to beat Nash Rawiller (74), making it a Waterhouse quinella. Hugh Bowman was third on 43.

FRIDAY, AUGUST 1

Tonga is abuzz, with people and dignitaries everywhere. There are T-shirts being sold printed with the face of His Royal Highness. The main street is ablaze with colour. In the downtown department store, extra large is the most popular size. We all joined His Majesty on a yacht for several hours and I must say I felt a million miles away from cold, old Sydney.

We attended the investiture of the Order of the Crown and the Illustrious Order of Queen Salote. Representing our family was Rob's father Bill Waterhouse, as the consul-general of Tonga in Australia, and Rob's sister Louise, as the honorary consul.

Queen Salote was the grandmother of the current king. There is a story told that she insisted on having her carriage roof down on the very wet day in 1952 when our present Queen Elizabeth was crowned. She was reported to say, "The people want to see me," and they truly did. It also was reported that one commentator asked the late Noel Coward (the famous English playwright and actor), "Who's the chap beside Queen Salote?" "Oh," said Coward, "It's her lunch."

THURSDAY, AUGUST 14

David Jones doesn't charge you to walk through its doors, nor does Crown Casino, nor any club, pub or TAB. Why should anyone who wants to go to the races have to pay to walk on to the course? The powers that be believe that is their revenue source. Oh do come into reality – what revenue source? There's no bloody person on the track these days except pensioners and licensed people, who include trainers, strappers, bookmakers and clerks.

On August 23 at Warwick Farm entry will be free. The $12, which is the cost of walking through the gates, can no doubt be spent on having a bet, a drink or a sandwich. It also means that the people who live in the west of Sydney will see value for money and take their families. Racing should be about the family. Get rid of the rotten, outdated and completely constipated entry fee. Throw the gates open and make racing a bit exciting.

TUESDAY, AUGUST 19

Foreman David Meijer departed Sydney with the love of his life yesterday morning – he and Tuesday Joy made the first step towards our bid for the Melbourne Cup, travelling in the float with the mare to Melbourne and stopping overnight at Tarcutta. My evergreen and reliable man on the spot in Melbourne, Des Boyle, was waiting at the stable gate to welcome them. Des has been around our Flemington stable for as long as I can remember and he waits patiently from carnival to carnival for the horses and the girls and boys to arrive.

A few words on some key stable staff as we prepare to move back from Warwick Farm to Randwick over the August 30-31 weekend after moving out for World Youth Day celebrations:

Tania Rouse: Tania is an exceptional person. As my assistant trainer she is next to none. Training a team of 140 horses, plus spellers, is like organising a military

Kate Grimwade, Lea, Rob and I are on the yearling inspections around Scone. It is a crucial time of the year for the trainer and owners as the horses you select are the ones that will be your material for the next three to four years. So far the drafts are a little patchy – the pedigree page reads superbly but some people, I believe, underestimate the nutrition of the horses. One stud will have a strong, strapping yearling while another just down the road has a skinny, finer-boned and weaker type. I believe the only reason is because of what they feed them.

WEDNESDAY, MARCH 11

We are having the loveliest time touring the studs; it is one of the great pleasures of being a racehorse trainer, or a mate or an assistant of a racehorse trainer. The three of us – Kate, Lea and I – rock 'n' roll from barn to barn, always viewing the yearlings outside, in rain, hail or gale-force winds. The reason for that is you can see the faults, or positives, more clearly. You also see the horse walking which gives you an idea of its action.

Basically, you have three minutes to make up your mind if that horse is the right one for you to train. I'm looking for the right mental attitude and physical appearance and, at the same time, asking myself if there is room for development. It's no good buying a speedy, tight type as in another 18 months to two years they won't have developed. You want a horse with a big stride. All this has to be picked up in this short space of time. I said to my assistant Kate Grimwade, "It's like taking a mental photograph of each horse and carrying in your mind the attribute that most attracts you." I also say, "It's like sighting a handsome bloke – you know in a quick glance his attributes." When looking at a filly she needs to be pretty, attractive and have a lovely disposition with a good head. At some stage she is going to be a mother, so you don't want her throwing plain-looking foals and you want her to be a good broodmare. I can cope with most faults with horses, except prominent sesamoids or when a horse 'toes out' too dramatically or has closed hocks, although one is very forgiving of the stock of the noble Redoute's Choice as it's very much a trait in his progeny.

What an amazing establishment Paul Messara has in the Hunter. His training facilities at Arrowfield Stud are state of the art. It must be a joy to train horses in this environment. We have certainly been well watered and fed at our stops at the different studs. I think by now they all know that Gai and the girls have a healthy appetite and their sugar levels drop very low after viewing a couple of dozen horses. Biscuits and tea are supplied at regular intervals. Bloodstock manager Duncan Grimley's delightful wife Diane supplied the most delicious coconut slice and chocolate brownies – it's amazing how one's horse improves after a couple of pieces of these beautiful sweets. But the pièce de résistance had to be the pumpkin salad supplied by John Messara's charming wife Kris, who was looking as gorgeous as ever. John is a passionate man who loves his racing dearly, and what he has done for the Australian breeding industry is second to none. Arrowfield have certainly fine-tuned nutrition with their yearlings. They have the size and athleticism and bone for bulk. It is consistent in the whole draft and the same every time I view Arrowfield yearlings.

FRIDAY, MARCH 13

Our most talked about two-year-old, More Joyous, trialled brilliantly at Randwick today. Darren Beadman flew in from Hong Kong to ride her. Tania Rouse was there to saddle the filly, as this is her task on race day. I asked Darren, "Does she feel like a Slipper favourite?" and he said, "Most definitely." He also said of the small filly, "If she is to get back in the stalls she may miss the start by half a length. My job is to have an attendant holding her so she's right up the front and jumps quickly." Darren also used special packing under his race-day saddle. He told me an old towel is much better than a new one, as it does not slip. He also used non-stick padding, which he had purchased in Japan, and said was fantastic. Anyway, his gear and expertise paid dividends this morning and the filly passed the test with flying colours.

Our last day of the yearling tour included a visit to Widden Stud, where we saw almost 40 yearlings – progeny of nearly every leading stallion. We then had the pleasure of seeing two horses I previously trained: Strada has grown into a magnificent type and is an excellent example of a precocious son of Danehill; and, of course, our favourite freshman sire Sebring has settled in nicely. High-quality mares that have been booked to Sebring include Elegant Fashion, Press The Button, Rose Archway, Brief Embrace, Familial and Bacchanal Woman.

SUNDAY, MARCH 15

Manhattan Rain stole the show with a dominant win in the Group 3 Skyline Stakes at Randwick yesterday and has booked a start in the Golden Slipper, along with More Joyous and Horizons.

TUESDAY, MARCH 17

Danny Power, journalist, bloodstock agent and well-rounded racing man – he purchased (on behalf of owners) Doriemus, who spoiled one of my better chances, Nothin' Leica Dane, when winning the 1995 Melbourne Cup – visited the track this morning and was surprised by the brisk pace, a bit similar to George Street on a Friday afternoon. Horses, riders, directions flying and focused attention by the team in the tower. Danny was in Sydney to interview me for his publication, *The Thoroughbred* magazine. "Why don't you have a training farm?" he asked. I told him, "I love training at Randwick, enjoy living in Sydney, I'm accessible to my owners and I think we do a good job where all the horses are under one roof and so one is less distracted."

THURSDAY, MARCH 19

What a cruel thing for any family who planned to go to the races at Newcastle yesterday and had packed their lunch for a lovely day out. On arrival at the course they were met by security guards who asked everyone to leave their food and beverages at the front gate, forcing them to use the on-course caterers. In this period of economic downturn and with everyone talking recession, wouldn't you think the clubs would allow free entry and bring your own food? It's fine if you've got the dollars in your pocket, but the average person is feeling the pinch. They want to come racing and have a couple of dollars to put on a horse but they are forced, if they want to have something to eat, to spend nearly $9 on a sandwich. This is so wrong.

FRIDAY, MARCH 20

Tuesday Joy had her first piece of work on the grass track at Nad Al Sheba in Dubai in preparation for the Group 1 Dubai Duty Free on March 28. The mighty mare had travelled remarkably well with her trusted attendant and my stable foreman Dave Meijer and veterinarian John Peatfield. The trip was a long, gruelling one, going from Sydney to Melbourne to Hong Kong to Dubai. Clocking up numerous frequent-flyer points, she arrived yesterday, doing the trip with her eyes shut, so to speak. Dave told me last night she was ready and waiting for her work this morning.[17]

Sydney Turf Club sent a letter to members regarding the mooted merger with the AJC. I don't feel completely comfortable about the proposal. Competition is a great thing, but a merger seems to be very much a forgone conclusion. It will be interesting to see how it is received when the AJC has its annual general meeting.

SATURDAY, MARCH 21

Theseo passed the $2 million mark at Rosehill today when he had a wonderful all-the-way win in the Ranvet Stakes, chalking up his third Group 1 victory.

---

17 Tuesday Joy finished ninth in a field of 16 on March 28 and returned to Australia to prepare for the spring rather than going on to Europe with the Prix de l'Arc de Triomphe as her target, as owner John Singleton originally intended.

More Joyous was exactly that when she won the Group 2 Reisling Stakes, giving her immediate entry into the Golden Slipper. Owner John Singleton's passion for the sport has never wavered and I had to giggle when he and his partner, Yvette, hoisted Darren Beadman on their shoulders. John is quite keen on getting people off their feet in the mounting enclosure. He once picked me up and twirled me around his head. Another time he tackled his ex-wife, Julie. Heaven knows, if he wins the Slipper on April 4 what he'll be up to – I'm wearing protective gear!

Northern Meteor was sixth in the Group 2 Canterbury Stakes, but his supporters should not give up on him. There was a real track bias at Rosehill – one had to be six-eight away from the fence and as the day progressed the jockeys got even further off the rail ... quite silly, really, to think one has to remind the jocks to keep off the fence, as it is the most direct way to the winning post. But not so on Saturday.

MONDAY, MARCH 23

A new recruit to the jockey ranks at trackwork is Grant Buckley. Boy, has that guy got a great smile! I asked Grant what the difference was between my training and other NSW trainers he would normally ride for. He said: "Where I normally ride trackwork everyone goes 15 seconds to the furlong." My horses go about 14 seconds every furlong, but beforehand they have weeks of trotting and cantering and working on the High Performance Galloping Machine and visiting the pool twice a day.

TUESDAY, MARCH 24

This morning has been a long and hectic affair. Rising at the normal wee hours, applying a bit of make-up so I didn't scare anyone, then arriving at trackwork. Upstairs to meet the David Jones girls, where young Kate was ready and waiting, and 'voilà', we burst on to the Channel 9 *Today Show*. It was full of fun and laughs, then a quick dash down to Nerida Winter's shop in Double Bay to organise my two hats for the races – one a floral piece to go with my David Jones/Paul Smith outfit and the second a cute yellow and black feathered fascinator to go with my (Imelda Marcos) Escada top. You won't miss me. It's bright yellow.

It was then back to Randwick for the launch of the AJC Tooheys New Autumn Carnival. I don't know if so many leggy fillies have surrounded the AJC chairman, Mr Ross Smyth-Kirk, before. Megan Gale looked radiant, Kate was as gorgeous as ever and AJC Ambassador Erika Heynatz is a most attractive blonde. Last, but not least, was your very own stumpy Waterhouse – I've decided I need extensions, not to my hair but to my legs! It was a successful event.

TUESDAY, MARCH 31

Horizons, ridden by Steve O'Halloran and carrying a lot more weight than the other two-year-olds (no offence Steve), glided over 600 metres wearing blinkers and a stiff breeze up her hammer and tack. This was the best piece of work I've seen from this daughter of Choisir for many weeks. She knows where the winning post is, the form around her is excellent and the thing most in her favour is she loves the wet. Needless to say, rain is forecast all week.

Manhattan Rain worked with a partner and strode strongly over 800 metres before finding the line in glowing fashion. He will take a power of beating in the Slipper, and, with Nash riding, will be wearing blinkers in the big race on Saturday.

Neil Paine thought More Joyous did one of the most lyrical pieces of work he's ridden in a long time. This filly is set to pounce and deserves to be Slipper favourite. She has always been the most talented of any of the females going into the race.

WEDNESDAY, APRIL 1

I asked young jockey Kathy O'Hara the other morning when talking about the three-year-old filly Bondi Blonde, "Are you a Bondi blonde?" I'm not sure if Kathy is on my wavelength or, for that matter, understands my sense of humour, but she is a great girl and a terrific jockey.

MONDAY, APRIL 6

What a remarkably talented colt Manhattan Rain has developed in to. He was the only entire to fill a place in Saturday's rain-sodden Golden Slipper, with the winner Phelan Ready a gelding and the second-placed Headway, a filly. Darren Beadman (More Joyous, 15th) is a remarkably observant jockey. He made the comment halfway through the day that he was concerned that the first 600 metres of the Slipper would be run on a good track, as it had not been raced on that day, and then, all of a sudden, they would tumble into a quagmire for the final 600. Darren and Blake Shinn (Horizons, 12th) elected to go forward, trying to get their fillies on the bit and coping with the conditions, but they were at a disadvantage; they didn't handle the wet.

TUESDAY, APRIL 7

Gooree racing manager Andrew Baddock had an entourage this morning at trackwork, including a young trainer from Canberra, Nick Olive, who attended to watch the horses work. Nick commented: "It's amazing how relaxed your horses are. Nothing fires up. They all walk around with their heads down concentrating on the task at hand."

I explained that when they do get a bit fresh I give them double work. Nick looked at me questioningly, so I told him it's like a kid in school – if he's jumping around, being naughty, he distracts the rest of the class. It's no different for horses. I want my lot to return to their box, have a lie down and rest. Dad always told me when you walk in the yard the only way to tell a good trainer was to see horses lying down, as you knew they were contented and doing well.

Northern Meteor will now be set for the Group 1 TJ Smith (1200 metres) on April 18. This son of Encosta De Lago has had the disadvantage of running on two rain-affected tracks, which I believe harmed his winning chances when he was sixth in the Group 2 Canterbury Stakes and seventh in the Group 1 George Ryder Stakes. He has certainly lost no fans. As I reflect on his Group 1 win as a lightly-raced three-year-old in the Coolmore Stud Stakes and his amazing fourth in the Group 1 Newmarket when resuming, I think how tough he is and what a marvellous turn of foot he has. This, of course, cannot be seen on rain-affected going.

The Easter Premier Sale has been wrapped up at Newmarket. Quite a few were passed in, but on the whole it was a very strong sale with excellent yearlings on offer. Amanda Skiffington flew in from England and is a valuable part of a well-oiled Waterhouse team, all determined to find the very best fillies and colts for the stable. A new recruit to the ranks is Hugo Palmer, who is here for a year to improve his skills so that one day he can become a trainer in England. My mate Lea Stracey is in charge of the catalogue. She has a memory like an elephant and the disposition of an angel, which is well and truly tested at moments throughout the sale. Kate Grimwade, my bloodstock assistant, is hot off the Darley Flying Start course. This young Englishwoman has immense talent and when she has been asked to make a comment on a yearling I inspected she would tell me her thoughts. Lea would write in the book my comments and at the end of the day it was quite clear Kate has a very astute eye. Ali was in charge of data entry, which is a job in itself loading every comment from Amanda. Greg Nash is the vet and the unsung hero is Denise Martin, who gave her preferences for purchases. Of course, one never knows how we have fared until the yearlings are tested at the racetrack in the next six to 12 months.

Nash Rawiller and wife Sarah have gone to Phuket for five days. Eating little and drinking little does not sound like a good recipe for a holiday, but Nash understands perfectly and will not overdo things. With both stable jocks on the sidelines (Blake is injured), Chris Munce has secured a couple of choice rides on Saturday. This highly-talented horseman does not get the same exposure as the top jocks. My husband has a theory about why Chris is doing so well since his comeback after spending time in jail over tipping for profit – during his time off Chris had to keep very fit and this extreme fitness has made him a better sportsman.

I sit here darning a serviette, a job my dear mother would kindly do for her darling daughter. I looked at her sewing basket and there are socks and napkins with holes in them and I thought, "Oh Mum, where are you? I could do with your assistance." Then I thought I must get on with the job she would expect me to do. I must book a visit to my optometrist, Michael Angelos, as I'm having great difficulty threading my needle. Many of you know Michael as the part-owner of Dance Hero.

MONDAY, APRIL 13

Northern Meteor's planned retirement to stud at Widden was announced at the William Inglis sales yesterday. It has become the norm recently that when a colt wins a Group 1 he is shuffled off to stud. I think it is a shame, as the potential of these wonderful horses is never fully achieved.

Isn't it amazing that every week in Queensland they seem to run an open company or black-type two-year-old race? In Sydney there are not as many two-year-old options ... Racing NSW and the AJC and STC have to address this situation and change it. Fillies don't have a long lifetime of racing; if they haven't got black type by the time they are three, there is every chance they will never achieve it.

TUESDAY, APRIL 21

Manhattan Rain won the Sires' Produce Stakes on Saturday. When the colt came into my stable for his first race preparation in late October last year, he was not always the most fleet of foot and was quite slow thinking, a little reminiscent of his half-brother Platinum Scissors. But the more I worked with him, the more he responded. It was so satisfying to see him win his first Group 1 race.

A major stud contacted me on Sunday to see if it could secure Manhattan Rain. I spoke to Iris O'Farrell, manager of Mr Yaseen's horses in Australia, and she said simply, "No, not until the colt is finished racing does Mr Yaseen intend to consider any stud offers." May I commend you, Mr Yaseen. From a trainer's point of view so many young horses are retired so early and never get the opportunity of fulfilling their race career. I completely understand why this happens as it is important to secure a stud deal and the dollars earned as a stallion are far greater than what one can earn on the racetrack. But, boy, it's good to know Manhattan Rain will be able to continue to star on the track.[18]

WEDNESDAY, APRIL 22

What a pleasure it was to see Joe Janiak win the prestigious Group 1 TJ Smith at Royal Randwick on Saturday with his amazing sprinter Takeover Target. Officials came to me after the race and said, "They need you on the podium," to which I replied, "I haven't won the race (Northern Meteor was second)." They replied, "No, you've got to present the trophy to Joe." No one likes winning Group 1s more than yours truly, but I must say I was over the moon for Joe and his son Ben and for the racing public in general. Anyone at Randwick would have witnessed the scene of the crowd standing and wildly clapping the old horse. Rob and I have got to know Joe over the past few years on our trips to Royal Ascot. He's a wonderfully unassuming man who loves his horse, enjoys the camaraderie of racing and loves to travel. Why wouldn't you when you've got a horse like Takeover Target?

FRIDAY, APRIL 24

The great debate at present: do we stay with two clubs, the AJC and STC, or fall under the banner of a racing board? My two bob's worth is that the two-club system has great merit. The committee members are there for the right reasons. They are intelligent racing folk who are passionate about the sport of kings; they are unpaid, which is a very admirable thing, and they also have faces – because they can be easily recognised, people feel they are able to speak directly with them. Board members can sometimes be removed from the everyday racegoer and they become a faceless group.

SATURDAY, APRIL 25

There's a new man in Gai's life – don't tell Robbie (ha ha). His name is Trent Langlands and he is a personal trainer to my great mate Lea and yours truly. I now know what my horses feel like when they first come into training. We power up the hill. I'm not bad at that part of the exercise and I've had a bit of practice over the years. Then Lea and I get down on our mats and roll around on the floor – not a pretty sight. I'm dressed in bright orange and Lea is in the black leotard, so you wouldn't miss us in a million years. We have great fun and find this exercise very necessary for one's anaerobic fitness level.

---

18 Muzaffar Yaseen is a Sri Lankan businessman.

I have also arranged for Blake Shinn and Kathy O'Hara to begin working out with elite athletes and now personal trainers, Tani Ruckle and Michael Lynch. Nash keeps himself fit at the gym and does lots of walking and running and is one of the most aggressive and strongest riders in Australia. I just feel that Blake and Kathy really need to work on their fitness and become stronger riders. With the new whip rules coming out, jockeys will have to use all their strength and aggression with their body as they will not be able to hit their horses as many times.

MONDAY, APRIL 27

Downtown Byron Bay is typical of many beach resorts in that it has lots of shops selling junk or items you think you need, then once you purchase you just put it in the back cupboard. Yesterday I lashed out, purchasing a bikini! Was it change of life, or just being determined to lose the flab, or that I left my swimmers back home? All I could think about was the lyrical song, "It was an itsy bitsy, teenie weenie, yellow polka-dot bikini that she wore for the first time today." Lea and I were power-walking along the foreshore yesterday, determined to move the flab, and we bumped into a group of guys – luckily I didn't have the bikini on as one of them is an owner of Curraghmore, a Choisir youngster in the stables.

We enjoyed a fabulous lunch with the beautiful and petite Delvene Delaney and her remarkable husband John Cornell in their pub, the Brunswick. Delvene and John bought land in Byron 20 years ago after making a huge success of their life in the entertainment industry. Talking of moving north, bloodstock agent Steve Brem is relocating to Toronto, Lake Macquarie. He's found a sleepy hollow and all he needs is a wide-awake wife.

THURSDAY, APRIL 30

Saturday was a wonderful day's racing, a grand finale to a mixed Randwick carnival. The revamped committee may have some entrepreneurial ideas to improve the attendance for next year, but one thing they must do is speak to Randwick City Council – the streets have been spewing with rubbish and, as I said to AJC chairman Ron Finemore, it must give such a bad impression to the interstate visitors, especially the Melburnians who present such immaculate streets and a wonderful concourse of promotional photos and banners during their carnival. There is much to do on the AJC committee, but what I like is the roll-up-your sleeves attitude of the chairman and his team ... I fear time is running out for the club unless they can really get their act together, and it would be a crying shame if individuality was lost to a faceless board.

My latest acquisition is a set of heater lamps, which I had the pleasure of using on Tuesday Joy, Theseo and other carnival horses when they were in Melbourne, courtesy of owner Lloyd Williams. Lloyd is one of the most astute racing men in Australia and at his Flemington stables he has every conceivable aid to get his horses fit and ticking over. For 15 minutes a day I have my horses stand under the heat of these lamps. They are extremely popular in England and Ireland, where the weather is cold and damp ... we are experiencing a snap of winter in Sydney at the moment.

I enjoyed a great meeting with Racing NSW CEO Peter V'landys and Ray Thomas from the *Daily Telegraph,* discussing the re-launch of the Punters' Club. It is going to be a most exciting affair and I will make it so. Every Thursday and Sunday a column will appear with my thoughts on the horses and, most importantly, a 'black-book' tip.

My great mate from my Rose Bay convent days, Louise Lloyd, or as I fondly call her 'Snowy', is one of the most artistic and imaginative women I know. She makes the hanging baskets for Tulloch Lodge, Tempest Morn and Bounding Away, which bring a country air to the suburban stables.

MONDAY, MAY 4

When I opened the *Sun-Herald* yesterday I made a bee-line to the S magazine and I must say within seconds of reading daughter Kate's article, I was laughing out loud. Kate has a regular column titled 'Kate Waterhouse – My Week'. It's a must read!

It was also interesting to see on the internet a gorgeous photo of Kate for all to view. A famous overseas photographer took the picture while he was in Sydney for fashion week. I asked Kate how he knew her and she said: "He didn't, he just asked could he take my photo."

WEDNESDAY, MAY 6

Kate and I were sorting through some photographs yesterday and we found an autograph book that Mum would take on her travels and gather famous names from the 1960s and bring them home for her daughter Gai – they included Academy Award-winning actress Greer Garson, actor James Stewart, cowboy Roy Rogers and Trigger, and Australian entertainers and authors Col Joye, Chips Rafferty, John O'Grady and Claire Dunne. Mum sweetly wrote the following inscription for me in the front of the book: *1962 Christmas. To my darling daughter, Love from Mummy*

FRIDAY, MAY 8

Well respected and greatly loved journalist Bill Whittaker wrote his final line today, leaving his beloved wife Alice and children Maree, David and Mark. Bill was sickened by the dreaded melanoma and in only a few short months it sapped the spirit of this great man. Over the years in racing, I've come to know many journalists – some I like and respect, but Bill was a man among men; he was unassuming, neat in his appearance, always polite, never had a barb, wrote a thorough and correct account and was able to entertain the racing public for decades ... we will all live in the knowledge that he is happily describing the great race in the sky with TJ and Val.

THURSDAY, MAY 14

Randwick trainer Grahame Begg was very complimentary of my young apprentice Daniel Ganderton this morning at trackwork, saying for the three rides he had for him yesterday at Randwick he gave him 10 out of 10 in skill, patience and just showing real initiative and horsemanship. In the past 10 days Daniel has had a change in direction. He has changed his focus on his riding and everything is starting to full into place for this young man. It is hard for the apprentices as they are meant to be mature men and women, but really a lot of them are just out of nappies.

MONDAY, MAY 18

Glamour filly Amelia's Dream is back in work after her latest injury and enjoying a couple of weeks pre-training at Muskoka Farms.

TUESDAY, MAY 19

Max Presnell, from the *Sydney Morning Herald,* wrote an interesting piece about endangered jumps racing last Friday. He quoted John Wheeler, a grand trainer of horses both on the flat and over the jumps in New Zealand and Australia. Wheeler said: "They (Victorian racing officials) listened to the animal rights people from day one, and they should never have. They reduced the size of the fences to appease them and that increased the tempo of the races, which became more and more dangerous."

Wheeler has hit the nail on the head. Jumps racing in Australia – now only in Victoria and South Australia – should never be lost. People love to watch it and it is a natural way of a horse racing, but the jumps are too low. If it is to survive after all the debate, the jumps must be made the same as they are in New Zealand. It will slow the tempo down and the number of injuries will disappear.

It was a wild and windy day at Randwick this morning and most of us would have preferred being snuggled up in bed, but there were horses to be exercised. Blake returned to the saddle this morning. He has been down in Melbourne with his mum and step-dad, nursing a sore foot. Amazing how the babes respond with a bit of TLC from parents.

Nash Rawiller was slightly out of humour with *The Lady Trainer,* causing me to raise my voice on one or two occasions. Don't worry, we kissed and made up. It's very much like having a football team and I'm pushing the boys forward to do what I want with the horses and when the conditions are so unsavoury, as this morning, it is hard on everyone.

There is much discussion over the use of the whip. The only time I have ever witnessed excessive use of the whip "Down Under" was when master jockey Lester Piggott rode a horse I owned, called Noble Player. Jockeys are constantly being conditioned to be competitive to the finishing line and a suspension can be incurred if they dare drop their hands and don't ride their horses out. Consequently, the Australian punter is assured of getting a fair go when he backs a horse. Limited use of the whip makes the rider less competitive and in harness racing in France, where it is now banned, I am told leaders win the majority of races. Isn't that absurd?

TUESDAY, MAY 26

I didn't realise Daniel Ganderton enjoyed lollies until I went into his house on Friday to inspect a hole in the ceiling and there on the kitchen bench was not one, but many bags of jelly babies and snakes. I've explained to Dan since then that this is not the correct diet for the aspiring apprentice. Hopefully, after he was cautioned last Saturday following Joku's race at Randwick, where he came back in over his allotted weight, the jelly babies might be thrown in the bin.

Quite an amusing time this morning in Queensland. Jockey Mark Newnham flew to Brisbane to ride the gallops on the Eagle Farm course proper. I messaged him as I was approaching his hotel in the early hours of the morning, so he'd be downstairs to go to the track. There was no reply. I messaged again, and still no reply. He was there waiting and off we drove to trackwork.

When I landed in Sydney later in the day, another Mark Newnham, who I had inadvertently messaged, sent a text back saying, "Sorry Gai, but I unfortunately couldn't make the weight."

A lovely couple visited my yard yesterday. They had purchased Theseo's full brother at the Magic Millions sale last year and were interested to know why Denise (Martin of Star Thoroughbreds) had not purchased him. As I keep a note on every yearling I inspect, Kate Grimwade was able to go back and look up my comments, which read, "Big, plain type. Off hind hock – old injury? OK."

They wanted to see what happens in Tulloch Lodge and what is different from the other stables. They were greeted by Kate who took them on a tour of the yard then they came back to the main stable where I was with Percy and Leanne, Drs Sykes and Begg, checking and rechecking horses. Ranjeet (Singh) was busy putting horses on the High Performance Galloping Machine, Johnny (Livingstone) had Dreamscape under the heater lamps and (Sabbir) Alam, 'Dema' (Dymtro Ivanov) and Scotty (Henley) were busily grooming, cleaning and swapping horses from box to sand roll. 'Crewy' (John Brady) was very busy going about his task as he has for over half a century. 'Lofty' (Brett Killion) supervised proceedings and Nicky (Matura) assisted in the many chores that have to be done before we say night-night to our four-legged friends.

I left the couple to make their decision, but I explained that if their horse was to come to me he had to spell at a property that understood exactly how I like the horses condition-wise, then they, as I say, slot into the system. Jane (Abercrombie) is advised if their condition is right for them to commence pre-training; most horses do about three weeks of trot and canter work before entering the yard to begin their preparation.

This morning I was pumping iron – not really; I was doing a light training session with Trent. I know the hard work now means that when I join my children and husband on the ski slopes in December I won't be making excuses after every third run to go for a cup of hot chocolate. Trent mentioned that on occasions he has trained jockey Hugh Bowman and said, "He's the most professional athlete I've come across. No one pushes themselves harder and is more focused in getting fit." Doesn't it show with the way Hughie has been riding?

Blake has started a similar program and Nash also. Young Daniel kicks off his new training regime next Monday. Australia is not like in England where the jockeys are riding over arduous courses. Our jocks ride on well-manicured, even tracks and their level of fitness is far below that of the English jockey.

Several of my jockeys have been visiting sports psychologist Grant Brecht. He said they all had one thing in common – their hunger to be highly successful. Each has different issues to address with Grant: Nash and Blake, their high suspension rate; and Daniel, just dealing with living in a big city away from his family. The jocks have a lot to deal with and are constantly under pressure performing at the highest level and keeping their weight down; and now, with the new whip rule, riding competitively without incurring suspension. I would hate to think of the number of times I would be outed if this applied to my driving.

TUESDAY, JUNE 9

What a sad indictment with only eight Randwick-trained horses represented on the eight-race program on Monday. Why? They are programming all the wrong class of races. The Monday meeting should have had more thought and consultation with the trainers. What a travesty!

FRIDAY, JUNE 12

For more than 50 years 'Crewy' has astutely fed many great horses in Tulloch Lodge. He is a most unassuming gentleman who goes about his business quietly. He doesn't say much, our 'Crewy', but if ever I need help he is wonderfully observant and always spot on with his comments.

The other evergreen is Robert Paris. I've known Robert since I was a child when he worked with his father Charles doing odd jobs as the handyman at the stables. When Charles passed away Robert took over the job and not a day passes without this quietly spoken person coming in and out of the different stables. What you don't realise is the horses we love so much are objects of destruction – no woodworm could work better and no demolition squad could work quicker than a horse when he has his mind set on doing something.

TUESDAY, JUNE 16

Herculian Prince, which is quite amusingly mis-spelt, arrives at Tulloch Lodge next week. The three-year-old gelding has three wins and two seconds from his six starts in New Zealand. Rob suggested I change his name to the correct spelling (Herculean), to which I replied, "I've only done that once and it was a disaster. He's won his races with this spelling error, so we'll let it be."

WEDNESDAY, JUNE 17

What's going on with the modern trainers? Are they complete wimps? We get a bit of rain and a wet track and all they want to do is pull the plug and scratch their horses.

I've never seen anything like it – 22 scratchings today at Warwick Farm and there were 22 at Canterbury yesterday. Horses in the wild live in conditions far inferior to the wet tracks of Canterbury, Warwick Farm, Randwick and Rosehill.

THURSDAY, JUNE 18

I loved Dave Meijer's comments on the grand mare Tuesday Joy. He said her condition was so huge he thought she might have swallowed one of John Singleton's other horses.

FRIDAY, JUNE 19

Seems to be great nervousness and apprehension over the forthcoming announcement (about restructuring racing administration) by the NSW Racing Minister, Kevin Greene, next Tuesday. What a cruel blow if the two clubs, the STC and AJC, are made one and Racing NSW becomes the governing body.

It is wrong to think that the administrative board of Racing NSW and the two clubs could not sit down and have a sensible talk about their favourite subject instead of being called in like naughty boys and girls to hear the decision, which has been made with little or no consultation between the major players. I, for one, have never been asked my opinion, even though I've voiced it regularly in my blog.

Racing is something I feel passionately about and I care about the future of our industry. I'm sure there would be many others like myself who would like to be consulted before the announcement next week.

The best result would be, rather than amalgamate the two clubs, to demerge the AJC's Randwick and Warwick Farm and the STC's Rosehill and Canterbury and have one secretariat for the four. Four honorary committees working for their course would get people racing.

TUESDAY, JUNE 23

I'm leaving on a jet plane but, unlike the song, I promise I'll be back again! I must say I'm really looking forward to this European trip. Don't ask me why; I'm not working any harder than usual, as my hours are always long, but I enjoy what I do. For the first time in 20 years we don't go to Royal Ascot and are taking a more leisurely approach. We will still visit studs and racecourses and will attend the races at both Newmarket and Longchamp in Paris. Every day I still do the work list; silly fool, I'm sure my husband thinks. I speak with my assistant Tania (Rouse) every night because it keeps my mind on what is happening and makes it easier when I return as the horses aren't too foreign to me. You see, the horses change so quickly. My foremen do a daily report which means I'm able to read at my leisure and then when I speak with them that night I make adjustments if it is necessary.

Young Blake and his jockey girlfriend Kathy O'Hara depart for their overseas holiday next week and will be in Newmarket at the same time as Rob and me. I think it's very important for the jocks to travel as they learn so much and it opens their eyes to different styles and conditions and makes them more tolerant and accepting.

I read an article recently in which Malcolm Johnston (TJ Smith's stable jockey in the 1970s-80s) commented on how he visited a sports psychologist on Dad's advice in the 1970s. Isn't it amazing that all this time has passed and I still think exactly the same as my Dad? Unlike Malcolm, Nash, Blake, Kathy and Dan have all learned enormously from their regular visits to Grant Brecht. You might say, 'How can that be when Daniel only recently fell out of favour with the stewards over his behaviour?' But the incident illustrated how Dan can correct these issues. If he did not have Grant he would have no one to discuss his feelings and emotions with. Racing NSW should seriously think about having a permanent sports psychologist working with young jockeys.

WEDNESDAY, JUNE 24

Young Daniel is carrying all before him, winning the Listed June Stakes on the Bart Cummings-trained Kroner just over two weeks ago, then, at Gosford today, winning the Listed Takeover Target Stakes on the Allan Denham-trained 40/1 chance Strat's Flyer. It was Dan's 50th metropolitan success, which means he will claim 1.5kg in the city from now on. Well done, Dan!

FRIDAY, JUNE 26

Each day while I'm away the jocks text me their best of the morning, many of which Tania or Robyn (Hartney, racing manager) have discussed with me earlier, but it's a good exercise for the boys and also keeps my finger on the pulse.

Have arrived to a very wintery reception at Mazzaro Bay in Taormina, Sicily, not what one was expecting this time of year. Our great friends, the Stanleys (Peter and Frances), were already in the swing of things, with 16-year-old son Hugh ready and waiting to get up to all sorts of capers. Gai and Rob are particularly looking forward to the arrival of our son, Tom. The jet-ski is one of the great passions for the boys, similar to a motorbike but on water. Rob and I take a much more sedate approach for our time at the beach.

This is the worst decision ever made in racing! The Ernst & Young Report to Racing NSW recommending club (AJC and STC) mergers is a most improbable document full of "blue sky" assumptions, such as suppliers will give 10-15 per cent discounts for the increased volume of purchases from a combined club and sponsors will flock to the combined club. But I suspect the NSW Government is determined to force the mergers, so the report is only cover for a decision already made.

The AJC and STC understand perfectly how their clubs function. The AJC is suffering the effects of mismanagement over a long time, but chairman Ron Finemore and vice-chairman John Cornish are two exceptional businessman who have the expertise and passion to bring the club right into the 21st century. Bill Picken and his team at the STC are working steadily to make changes that will generate the necessary dollars that the club needs. To think the Minister, Kevin Greene, has given them just two weeks to show cause why we may need a second level of bureaucracy, one that the Minister and the report so strongly advocate.

Racing NSW is centred in the city. How will it make itself available to be at the racetracks for the everyday running of racing? Who will be on this new board? Do we have any candidates in mind? I would imagine certain people are well and truly in place to take over the various roles. What will they be paid? Already Racing NSW has to pay director fees to board members. The AJC and STC committee are unpaid and do the job for the love of the game. You can't buy commitment and passion in the way these people are prepared to work; it's not nine to five for the AJC and STC board members. Also what is going to happen in the next few years when the likes of Newcastle and Hawkesbury have to be renovated? If one of the metro tracks is sold, the wear and tear on the others will be huge.

I love racing and my whole life has been in and about the sport. It can so easily be fixed if the Minister, Racing NSW CEO Peter V'landys, the current Racing NSW board members – Alan Brown, Alan Bell, Ken Brown, Kim Harding and Arthur Inglis – and the chairman and vice-chairman of both clubs sit down and discuss it with a view to keeping respective boards in control of their race-clubs.

Tomorrow the STC and AJC meet to discuss their future. What the clubs should be made to do is be more accountable to Racing NSW, so everyone can see where the dollars and cents are being spent. A radical change is not necessary and the Minister should be mindful of this.

Trainer John Hawkes raised an interesting point at trackwork the other day when he said that when the clubs merged in Adelaide, racing "went backwards" over there.

I spoke to the two people compiling the (Ernst & Young) report at Randwick one morning and neither had walked on a racetrack until then. They had no idea about Flemington, or even where it was. The report should be taken very lightly.

THURSDAY, JULY 2

Yesterday a meeting was held which was meant to represent the interests of racing, with a view to the supposed merger of the two clubs. What surprised the AJC and STC, and other racehorse owners and punters, was that the clubs' board members were not asked to attend. Where were the bookmakers and the punters? Are they completely forgotten? One man (leading breeder John Messara) seems to have taken the reins of racing well and truly into his grasp and seems to be telling everyone from the Minister down what is going to take place ...

Dear Mr Greene, listen to your participants, not just one person. We are your nuts and bolts, and we are being throttled and tossed aside and treated like incompetent fools. This is not the way to run racing.

FRIDAY, JULY 3

The Ernst & Young report says fewer people go to the races every year. Will any more attend the races under Racing NSW? The answer will be no. What will happen to the major sponsors? I'm a David Jones ambassador and I know that David Jones is certainly not keen to be sharing the same pitch with Myer, the main competitor. How would it be if Emirates had to share sponsorship with Virgin? Sponsorship will not double, it will decrease. Blind Freddy would be able to see that. They talk about saving costs. I bet their costs will escalate unbelievably in two years.

The newly-formed Brisbane Racing Club took two years to be born, following many meetings and discussions by both clubs and Queensland Racing. Yet here we have the "Hurry Up Stakes". Why the rush gentleman? With Racing NSW and the clubs all fighting for survival and power, I think racing in NSW will be the poorer. We look fools to the outside world when most of the other states get it so right.

MONDAY, JULY 6

Rob and I are in England and are heading to Newmarket today. I'm excited about the prospect of witnessing some really marvellous English racing at the July meeting. I had the pleasure of having dinner with Kathy and Blake in London last night – they remind me of two babes in the woods. They are enjoying a new experience and what a great opportunity for them both. They will join us over the next few days and hopefully ride out on one or two mornings.

Rob, Lea (Stracey), Bruce (her husband) and I enjoyed a day steeped in racing history and interesting characters, starting with our visit to Sandringham, the Queen's stud and winter residence, which is run by Joe Grimwade and his wife Lindsay. If the surname sounds familiar, they are the parents of Kate, my racing and bloodstock manager.

We visited paddock after paddock full of beautiful mares and their attractive, well-grown foals and yearlings. Two stallions stand at present, Royal Applause, a sprinter of enormous appeal, and the more recent acquisition Motivator, the 2005 English Derby winner. They are completely different types with Royal Applause a long, lengthy type with rather poorish feet and Motivator a more compact and very alert type.

We then visited the church where the parents of our great friend Frances Stanley, with whom we are staying in Newmarket, are buried. The small cemetery is only for parishioners. Trying to find the two graves, we asked a rather elderly parishioner, who immediately pointed to the far right corner. I would say he has known most of the inhabitants.

On to Sandringham, and what an amazing home with some of the great treasures the Queen and her family have collected. Joe told us Her Majesty comes to Sandringham every December, staying through to February, and the business of the monarchy is run from her country residence.

We had a hearty lunch with the Queen's racing manager Sir Michael Oswald and his wife, Lady Angela. Michael came into my life when I had the pleasure to train for Her Majesty the Queen Mother. Michael managed all her horses and she was a member of a Star Thoroughbreds' syndicate and was given a share by the publican who owned the Mackay Hotel. She gratefully accepted it and Michael, of course, corresponded with us regularly. In the early days the filly was known as "Fluffy the Wonder Horse", but Denise Martin in her wisdom thought Clarence House was a more fitting title. (It was the Queen Mother's residence.) When Fluffy, or Clarence House, departed our stables, I suggested to Michael that the Queen Mother might care to race a rather nice mare called Life Is Beautiful with long-time owners George and Kay Cloros. The Queen Mother accepted the offer kindly and her racing colours were flown to Australia.

After farewelling Kate's parents, who were a pleasure to meet, we went back to the yard to meet trainer Sir Mark Prescott and were also joined by bloodstock agent Amanda Skiffington. Mark is quite famous for his punctuality and has been known to turn his most important owners away if they are even a few minutes late. Yours truly, being a bit slow from the barrier and one who is usually running a little behind the clock, made sure we were sitting outside the yard before the appointed time. Mark basically has four yards, but I have never been in any stable that works better.

We were privileged to see his collection of gaming sports and beautiful paintings of cock fighting. He even has the original spurs the fighting cocks wore from the voyage of Captain Cook. Then to the boxing; there were some of the most marvellous photographs. Finally, the bullfights; Mark loves his bullfights and has some of the most detailed photographs.

THURSDAY, JULY 9

Yesterday's Group 1 Falmouth Stakes at Newmarket was won by the French horse Goldikova, trained by champion French trainer Freddie Head. When Freddie was a teenager of 16 he was apprenticed to my late father. Freddie was a hell of a rascal and Mum many-a-time would pull us apart as he was always trying to drown me in the swimming pool.

Thank goodness Freddie has grown up; he was champion jockey before he retired to the training ranks and his father, sister and grandfather are all champion trainers. We will have the pleasure of their company next Tuesday at the Juddmonte-sponsored meeting at Longchamp.

This morning we were up early and off to the stables of globe-trotting trainer John Gosden. Blake and Kathy were there waiting with Amanda. She found me a very good style of stayer and Blake was to ride him over 1400 metres on the Al Bahathri, built by Sheikh Mohammed so the horses at Newmarket would have an even surface to work on all year. It is a straight 1800-metre gallop, a Polytrack that has a steady but steep incline.

Blake was instructed by John to travel just behind the lead horse and John said, "If you want to give him a pipe-opener over the last furlong feel free". Blake did exactly that, giving him a swift tap on the shoulder and the colt powered up the rise.

Rob has replied to this Australian Racing Board press release dated July 8, 2009, that contained a comment about me by ARB chairman Bob Bentley:

> The racing industry is unquestionably at the cross roads on a wide range of issues, with the quality of our decisions likely to have a lasting impact on the livelihoods of more than 50,000 Australians.
>
> By way of demonstration, the comments that have been attributed to Gai Waterhouse were less than helpful. Bluntly put, Gai's future is not at risk here. Even in the wasteland that is the UK racing industry, where bookmakers and betting exchanges paying a pittance to racing dominate, there are a handful of big-name trainers like Luca Cumani who continue to do well, but for the rank and file of the industry things are extremely grim. I don't want to see that happen here.
>
> The ARB is not concerned whatsoever about who punters choose to have a bet with. Our sole concern is the erosion of revenue from wagering operators not paying adequate returns to fund prizemoney, infrastructure and country racing.
>
> Prizemoney is not by any means the only thing that is important to the success of racing, but it would be denying reality to ignore its profound impact on all aspects of the industry, from returns to owners, incomes for trainers and jockeys and other industry participants, field sizes and wagering turnover, to name but a few. Prizemoney levels can only be maintained at necessary standards with all wagering operators paying adequate returns, not a "pay what we like" system. Sponsoring races with nickels and dimes is no substitute for the current system of funding that has built the Australian racing industry to its present world prominence. Sponsorship is the model of the UK industry; it is selective and cannot possibly sustain a structured racing program.
>
> I have no comment to make about the merits of specific proposals to merge race clubs. It made sense to do this in Brisbane, but other mergers need to be examined on a case-by-case basis. However, what I will say is that our future industry structures must be on the agenda for review. We need to be on the front foot and making positive and mature decisions as an industry to place ourselves in the best position to survive and prosper. In doing this there are no "holy cows" that cannot be discussed.

The Australian Racing Board has recently taken the opportunity of the Productivity Commission inquiry into gambling in Australia to call for much-needed action on some fundamental wagering issues, including totalisator-odds bookmaking. The ARB is not going to throw in the towel and allow corporate bookmakers to line their pockets at the expense of industry participants, which would be the ultimate result of doing what Gai Waterhouse has suggested.

We need to be able to demonstrate that the industry itself is doing everything it can to operate in an efficient and business-like manner. Governments can be persuaded to take action, but only where the industry itself is dynamic and doing everything it can to help itself. Modern society is in a constant state of change, and racing cannot be cocooned away from this.

Among Rob's comments were:

I am surprised that the board should say prizemoney reductions don't put Gai's future at risk. Clearly this is incorrect. Gai's business is fine-tuned and prizemoney reductions make it unsustainable in its present form. The board is very welcome to see Gai's books, which would give the board an appropriate understanding.

It saddens me that Gai's comments are seen by the board as being "unhelpful". I note the board doesn't say her views are wrong. No doubt, the board sees her views as observations on the undiscussable "holy cows", to which your press release refers.

The comments of which your board complains could be encapsulated by saying Gai prefers the policy of Racing Victoria, which is able to maintain the program and increase prizemoney distributions, to that of Racing NSW, which is requiring prizemoney reductions and contemplating program curtailments.

Racing NSW is involved in a series of cases and arbitrations which have, at best, frozen cash flow. Bismarck once remarked that the art of taxation is to take the most goose feathers with the least hissing. The overriding and real fear is that bookmakers and the (betting) exchange will take the websites out of the jurisdiction and pay no tax at all.

We are now in Paris, one of the truly glorious cities of the world. Rob, Jenny McAlpine (who ably assists trainer David Hayes in Australia) and I climbed to the top of Montmartre visiting Sacre Coeur, the exquisite church with the golden altar and gold-tiled figurines behind it. We wandered through the streets, which was a bit like being up Kings Cross in Sydney, went to a great little restaurant to have a well-earned steak – I haven't had one since I left Sydney – then walked back to our charming hotel, Relais Christine, on the Left Bank.

Paris is really a city of love; everywhere we went we saw couples walking hand in hand, kissing and cuddling along the foreshores of fame. I must say it's quite infectious, unlike Australia where one so often might see young people out drunk at night. Somehow it is different in Italy and France. All the times I've visited Italy I've never seen anyone drunk. No groups of guys or girls out boozing. They have a different attitude to drinking and, as Jenny said, "They are constantly putting ice in their wine, one to cool and two to dilute."

WEDNESDAY, JULY 15

The dawn broke in Paris on Bastille Day yesterday as Rob, Jenny, our new friend Nicholas and yours truly were driving to Chantilly, the famous training centre, an hour from the city, to see Criquette Head-Maarek – she is my equivalent in France, except she has been training for three decades. Nicholas, who so kindly took us for dinner last night and drove us to Chantilly, also has a prestigious pedigree. He is from their stud and is currently concentrating on syndication, which he tells me is very new in France.

Criquette had two jockeys riding out for her this morning – Dominique Boeuf and Stephane Pasquier. They come two mornings a week to partner the horses. We were there for the first lot, commencing at 5.45am. The jocks rode two horses each, then returned to the yard where the horses had a roll and a pick. The jocks had a cigarette and a coffee – smoking is prevalent.

We had a quick cup of coffee at the local and Criquette and I recounted some old stories. I've known this remarkable woman for more 30 years, having the pleasure of living with the family at their Deauville stud.

No peace for the wicked, and back to Paris we travelled to celebrate Bastille Day by joining the march. Rob and Jen and I walked beside a line of the most magnificent bay cavalry horses.

Today, we enjoyed the view from Longchamp racecourse where the Group 1 Juddmonte Grand Prix de Paris (2400 metres), worth $A1.2 million, was won by the Sheikh Mohammed-owned and Andre Fabre-trained Cavalryman. The son of Halling was ridden by a boy-like jockey called Maxime Guyon.

Lord Teddy Grimthorpe, Prince Khalid Abdullah's racing manager and a mate of mine from years gone by, very kindly invited us to be the guests of the Prince's Juddmonte Farms, who were the main sponsors of the day. I was particularly chuffed when he asked me to choose the best turned-out horse in the Grand Prix de Paris.

Eight beautiful equine specimens paraded around the pre-parade ring. (*The Lady Trainer* selected one of Aidan O'Brien's four runners, Age Of Aquarius, a colt by Galileo, who finished second.)

FRIDAY, JULY 17

I called home from Jersey where Rob and I are spending the last few days of a holiday that has evaporated away. I have found out from Robyn (Hartney, my racing manager) that the Randwick trials are off until Monday so we re-group and alter plans for different horses that are heading towards the spring carnival.

To Grouville we trotted, the tiny Jersey town famous for its pottery. Fruit de Mer is one of the beautiful and individual works that is produced from the foundry that started about 1949. We have a set of the Fruit de Mer range, one of which I broke just recently, so the job was to replace it. Grouville also has a great castle amongst many other fortresses along the long, white, sandy beach. I mention the word white because most mainland English beaches lack sand and have pebbles that are a definite 'no no' for the bottom.

TUESDAY, JULY 21

Sark (a 5.5-square kilometre island east of Guernsey) is unusual as it has no cars, only tractors pulling long trailers that your bags get thrown on to. You can take a little bus or do as we did and walk. The islanders get about by bicycle or on foot and if they are going somewhere special in the night time they may book a horse-drawn cart.

We couldn't have timed it better, as lo and behold there was a race meeting; no, not the ponies or horses, but sheep racing. So off we went and bought our ticket. I chose No. 6, which was called Boiling Water (out of The Kettle, which is by Tea In The Pot). The jocks are little teddy bears dressed in different colours and matching hats and they are strapped on by their trainer. They're in a pen and Rover, the trusty sheep dog, waits for the starting gates to open. Several bales of straw are put in their path and Rover has to chase the poor bewildered creatures over the bales. Well, my sheep won and when Rob asked me why I backed him I told him because he was lighter than the rest and I didn't think he'd have to carry as much weight!

WEDNESDAY, JULY 22

I enjoyed a great night in London with Royal Ascot's head of communications and international racing, Nick Smith. Those who have had the pleasure of travelling a horse to this famous course would have met Nick. He's a globe-trotter bringing together the best sprinters in the world to compete in the English sprints. When I asked him what race he would most like to win, without the slightest hesitation he said, "The Melbourne Cup." I asked why and he replied, "Because it's the whole living experience, Gai. It's what Melbourne racing gives the owners and connections, and no one does it better."

FRIDAY, JULY 24

International bloodstock agent Rob McAnulty sent this email regarding next Friday's breeders' meeting to discuss the state of racing:

Hi Gai,

On the issue of this breeder-led splinter group I am firmly in your corner ... You are doing a lot of good work for the NSW racing industry by challenging this group.

No one knows the industry better than you, as an owner, syndicator, leading trainer, and mother and wife of two of the most successful bookmakers in Australia.

Fight the good fight and be successful.

Kind regards
Rob

MONDAY, JULY 27

I had an interesting discussion with owner-breeder Nathan Tinkler (of Patinack Farm) today regarding the elitist group of breeders meeting at the Inglis complex on Friday. He said to me, "I told John Messara I'm not attending." He also said he was surprised no press were invited to the meeting and asked, how could they have the best interest of the industry at heart when there is not a bookmaker among the invitees?

WEDNESDAY, JULY 29

Time is a great healer and I believe it has done an excellent job with the robust mare Amelia's Dream. She will work with Stakes-winner Common Objective on Saturday and many people will make the trip to Rosehill Gardens to see her go stride for stride with him over 1000 metres.

THURSDAY, JULY 30

Yesterday the AJC and STC met Kevin Greene, the Minister for Racing, and presented him with a report, dismissing many of the allegations that the Ernst & Young report had made. One of the most important aspects of the meeting was that the Minister, in his wisdom, had realised it would take time if change were to take place in Racing NSW and he asked for a working committee to be formed.

This morning I had the pleasure of entertaining six executives from Mr Katsumi Yoshida's Northern farm in Japan. With my stable foreman Motohiro Hosoya acting as an interpreter, the group was extremely interested and took notes on my comments. Their quest is to copy the best in Australia and to examine the merits of the High Performance Galloping Machine, which I and others, including Mike de Kock from South Africa, use to increase the fitness level of our horses. They viewed several of the gallopers performing on the machine, visited the pool, saw Frank Fitchett lunging the babies, then went over to the barriers before adjourning to the TJ Smith Room, where we had a further discussion.

I am a great advocate of the swimming pool/beach, for horses can increase their fitness level without pounding on uneven or hard surfaces. The veterinarian who headed the delegation said they had come to Australia to look at the merits of the HPGM and also find out why they should use the swimming pool. Their concern in Japan is the temperatures are below freezing in winter. I explained the pool could be heated and under cover, and told them I had no doubt that, of the two devices, it is the better.[19]

---

[19] Mr Yoshida, one of Japan's biggest breeders and owners, had the 2006 Melbourne Cup quinella with Delta Blues and Pop Rock.

CHAPTER 5

A proud mum, and the whipping boys

I am in Darwin, spending a wonderful 48 hours in Feathers, a bird and wildlife paradise minutes from Darwin airport. There are only four bungalows where Robbie and I, Tom and the clerks are enjoying this unusual experience. There are many varieties of birds, including the rajah shellback, black-necked stork, magpie goose, plumed whistling-duck, comb-crested jacana, little egret, wetlands brolga, gouldian finch and blue-faced honeyeater.

Nash Rawiller is riding at today's Darwin Cup meeting. He had a great day fishing yesterday and I'm sure we will hear about his exploits tonight over dinner. Darwin is an amazing blend of cultures with a large Aboriginal population as well as Europeans and Asians. Everyone seems to wear a set dress code of shorts, T-shirts and thongs. Oops, Kate tells me I must call them flip-flops.

There are more people from Sydney, Melbourne and Adelaide than locals at the cup. The 'Baroness of Bombala', trainer Barbara Joseph, is having a day out. She and her husband drove from Canberra, taking four days to do the 4000-kilometre trip. She strongly recommended the drive to me if, and when, I had the time.[20]

What a shame the AJC did not take advantage of the nail-biting finale in the battle of the premiership between (Darley trainer) Peter Snowden and me at Warwick Farm last Friday. Very seldom do you see such a close finish, and to think Peter got in front by a

---

20 A former Lloyd Williams galloper, Activation, trained by Michael Hickmott and ridden by Stephen Ridler, won the cup. Rawiller was unplaced on Nozi. The crowd was estimated at almost 20,000.

half-point after an early double ... I was able to fight back with Boca Chita (ironically, owned by Darley) and the gallant Moti sealed the win 74.5-73 in the second last race. I am told they had a Saturday crowd at this midweek meeting and ran out of books and didn't have enough tote windows open. Sounds like they were completely unprepared for the numbers that rolled up to see the battle of the two stables. It could have been promoted better than it was, especially after results at the Wednesday Canterbury meeting closed the gap. That's what marketing is all about: many think we have a dud product, but I can tell you it's a fantastic product that is not being fully utilised.

TUESDAY, AUGUST 4

Yesterday at the Darwin Cup the stand reminded me of 'Glorious Goodwood' in England, of course on a smaller scale. The first person I bumped into was Bruce, a man dressed in a coconut bark suit and a wonderful creation on his head – Nerida Winter eat your heart out! (Nerida, the leading Sydney milliner, makes many of *The Lady Trainer's* hats.) I was so taken by Bruce's unusual dress that I asked him if he'd pose with me, which he was delighted to do. Then he proceeded to be my mascot.

I was impressed with the dirt track, which was rolled after every race with a tractor and a grader behind it. Several track maintenance men manicured the surface for the next race and there was little kickback. Horses raced on speed and all the events were fast and furious. The atmosphere was upbeat and definitely a must for anyone who enjoys country racing.

WEDNESDAY, AUGUST 5

I was at Randwick today and I wish I could tell the tale of why Tell Tale, Sheikh Mohammed's three-year-old Redoute's Choice filly, ran so poorly (when last of 12). Our most successful outcomes happen when nominating horses after they have had two trials (she had one). There will be exceptions to the rule, but every so often I get a little too keen and think, "This one's going great. I might just nominate it for a race." But fool I am – talk about egg on my face.

For all the *Daily Telegraph* Punters' Club members, your horse Geffen will be on show at Wyong on Friday August 14. He will be our mascot for the morning, when I'll trial other horses. There'll be a barbecue and I'll be giving away two prizes: a Sunday morning at the stables with Gai; and a day at the races with Gai. I can tell you Geffen loves going to the races and I'll let you in on a little secret: I call him my boyfriend – and everyone at the track laughs – because he tries hard and is so cute.

MONDAY, AUGUST 10

A real star, Kontiki Park, is emerging in the staying ranks. The gelding won impressively on debut, then did the same at Kembla Grange on Saturday, scoring by a runaway three lengths. It is fascinating to see the metamorphosis of this slow-maturing stayer. Eight weeks ago Kontiki Park had trouble putting one foot in front of the other, but as the days and weeks progressed he has just kept improving.

The stable has been missing a depth of stayers for quite some time, but when I first made my name as a trainer they said, "She can train a stayer, but not sprinters or two-year-olds." My husband was able to find some excellent stayers in New Zealand and many Group 1 winners followed.

Kontiki Park, a son of Thorn Park, was purchased for $150,000 at the 2007 Magic Millions sale on the Gold Coast. The owners have shown great patience because the penny did not drop for some time – now that it has, Kontiki Park has notched up two impressive wins from just as many starts.

On Sunday after stables, Rob and I usually go for a walk and take in a sandwich and a coffee at one of the local eateries. Yesterday we wandered down to Balmoral and, lo and behold, the Mudgee food and wine festival was in full swing. I bumped into Johnny Furlong, whose winery is called Two Furlongs. He was my first beau and cousin of my very best friend, Ann Dalton. Ann and her relatives and I spent fun-filled days in the winter holidays at her beautiful home in Bowral. I learned to play golf by crawling under the fence with a golf club and hitting balls. We spent our afternoons in front of the fire roasting marshmallows and boy did we love going out horse riding. We enjoyed a blissful teenage life.

Many thousands of folk were wandering around the Balmoral esplanade, dogs were a dime a dozen and Baci, our blind poodle, was in his element playing with all the puppies. It was a lovely way to unwind after a busy week. The best thing was the wood-fired pizza "WOW", which you can hire out for parties. I'm always thinking of new ideas for our stable get-togethers and I thought this was really novel. The owner who was making the pizza recognised me and said that a jockey called in regularly to have a pizza. I don't know why, but I mentioned the name Neil Paine and with that he said, "Yes that's him. He's a terrific bloke." I somehow can't imagine Neil, light of frame, being a frequent visitor to this pizza shop.

THURSDAY, AUGUST 13

"Who's been sleeping in my bed?" is what young Tom said to reception at Crown in Melbourne yesterday when he went to book in. Tom is one of two people who live almost permanently at Crown Towers, the hotel section of the casino. They informed him that Miranda Kerr had booked in and taken his room – he was impressed. Rob and I once asked Tom, "Why do you stay there? How come you don't have a flat?".

"Mum", he said, "Why would you stay anywhere else? I get my laundry done, my bed made every day, whatever I want to eat and where else can you get up and bump into Katie Holmes, Tom Cruise, Lleyton Hewitt and everyone else I read about in the papers?" I think if we were Tom's age we'd be doing the same.

FRIDAY, AUGUST 14

Last night at Rosehill Gardens was a great awards party for Star Thoroughbreds, with Theseo taking out middle-distance honours and also being crowned NSW Horse of the Year. Part-owner Phil Evans, from Tasmania, informed the audience in great detail about the fun and excitement of the Theseo ride, from the beginnings at Emirates Park to the heady times of Group 1 success. Manhattan Rain (Encosta De Lago-Shantha's Choice), the half-brother to Redoute's Choice, is the most sought-after colt in Australasia by any stud, taking out the Champion Two-Year-Old award.

Daniel Ganderton was named Apprentice of the Year. I felt very proud for young Dan, who has achieved so much in such a short time. It is not an easy thing coming from a small town to the big smoke and he has made the grade in great form and continues to do so.

I felt honoured to be named NSW Trainer of the Year. It was the hardest fought battle and Peter Snowden has done a remarkable job as Darley's trainer in the space of one season and will continue to do so. Belong To Many and the grand mare Hot Danish tied for Champion Mare. All credit for Belong To Many winning that title should go to Barbara Joseph. She has developed this mare into one of the very few topline sprinters in Australia, and I look forward to continuing that success into the new season now that the mare has joined our stable.[21]

This morning at the Wyong trials was marvellous. The CEO of the Wyong club, Tony Drew, and his team should be commended. I took a big team of runners and the hospitality that was shown to us was absolutely amazing. Damien and I drove up just before the trials began and, while not doing a head count, I think there could have been 600 people in attendance. Everyone wanted to say "g'day", shake my hand or grab an autograph. The track looked marvellous and you could smell the sausages sizzling.

---

21 Belong To Many (Belong To Me-Foil, by Snippets) came to Gai after being sold at the 2009 Inglis Easter Broodmare Sale for $525,000 to the Clancy family of Watagan Park, Jilliby, north of Wyong. After two unplaced runs in October the mare was mated to More Than Ready.

The jockeys were fantastic and were interviewed on dismounting. In typical fashion, I intervened with a question or remark.

It was fun, informative and exactly what the people were after. Many were retirees and, at the barbecue at the end of the trials, Michael Beattie from Racing NSW had a draw for a "Sunday at the stables with Gai". Second prize was two tickets for a Saturday at Randwick, joining my owners and me in the Champagne Bar. Mrs Cynthia Cameron won the Sunday at the stables (after the first ticket drawn was a no-show) and Mrs Doris Mitchell won the race tickets. There were photographs with Nash Rawiller and the Wyong Cup. As I am a little superstitious, I refused to be pictured with the 2009 cup, so the club kindly borrowed the 2006 trophy, turning it around so no one could see the inscription. Anything to get people to the races – that's what it's all about.

MONDAY, AUGUST 17

Yesterday, with great pride, I opened the *Herald* to read daughter Kate's column. It was her first as fashion editor with the paper, a position she had dreamt about filling. Following the retirement of the former editor, Kate was given the guernsey. I enjoyed reading her interview with Delta Goodrem – I've always been a fan of this wonderful lady's music. The title of the interview was "I Never Have a Bad Hair Day", and I must say I've never thought about not having hair. Of course, Delta has gone through chemotherapy and, as she stated in the interview, you don't worry what it looks like, you are just pleased to have it. Well said.

I always text Kate on a Sunday – I'm never too sure of my daughter's waking hour on that day – and I commented on all the words I liked in her new column. It particularly tickled my fancy when she talked about "fashion soldiers", and she had a fabulous photo of a Chanel ring. I also like the use of her "stable". I'm not scared to give my editorial comments, but she knows that, like all mothers, I just want her to do well.

I got a real kick this morning when John Thompson, Bart Cummings' foreman, complimented me on one of the methods I use to freshen up my horses. (Next Monday John will take up the reins as Patinack Farm's second trainer at Warwick Farm. Jason Coyle is Patinack's No. 1 conditioner, but John will take on 60 of their horses.) Kroner, trained by Bart, dead-heated in the Premiere Stakes at Rosehill on Saturday – John said the gelding had become very sour, but he had noted that many of my horses, after working, go back over the hill at the back of the course to give them a change of environment and longer cool-down. He elected to use the same method on Kroner.

I thought it was very nice that he would say to me that this was what he'd done. Very few people give you a compliment in this game. I wish him every success in his new position.

John's shoes will be filled by Bart's grandson, James, who is working very hard on learning the ropes from John before he departs. James' brother Edward has taken on James' old role of assistant to his father Anthony. It's nice to see the family involved; if only one of mine were interested!

Daintree Road continues to improve. This is the gelding that was running off the track in his work, but the one-eyed blinker has been applied and, phew, what did he do? He took on the likes of Turf Express (a multiple winner as a two-year-old), jumped and led all the way at Wyong to win his trial on Friday. I could see he was grinning from ear to ear.

Theseo has been moved to my Desert War stable. He has had some wear and tear of his pedal bone (in the hoof) and had three weeks' spell while I was overseas. When he came back in I was still not happy with his action: it had shortened. He appears to be on the road to recovery, swimming multiple laps of the pool. Although he is only in light work I have every confidence he will return and be ready for his major goal, the Cox Plate. Dr Greg Nash explained to Denise (Martin) that if you were to X-ray all the pedal bones of the horses in the stable you would find changes. Concussion over and over for many years means something has to give; luckily they remodel themselves and are able to race on, as Theseo will do.

It's all coming together for my birthday party on September 2. Normally I would dig a hole and hide, but as I saw it was a race day I thought, 'Let's see if we can bring it to life.' So, in conjunction with the AJC, the *Daily Telegraph*, Racing NSW and David Jones we are throwing a Mad Hatters' race day. So have a look in your cupboard for a 'mad hat' and come along. It will be a ball. This day will be especially geared to the young – I want to see the kids having fun, so there will be a cake in the shape of a horse, and everyone will get a free showbag. It will be such fun. It is also whispered that the great Michael O'Loughlin of Sydney Swans fame and the evergreen Craig Fitzgibbon of the Roosters are having races named after them.

'Singo' (John Singleton) called me this morning. He has been in hospital for a hip operation – he's climbed too many mountains and, I'd say, been in too many brawls (only joking, John) and the wear and tear has caught up. All he wanted to know was how Zabeel mare Deedra would run in race four at Randwick today. I told him she had a terrific chance and Nash was looking forward to riding her, and I suspected the distance was perfect. "Are you racing Saturday when More Joyous resumes?" I asked. "Nah, I can't get under the fence," he replied. Not sure what he means by that, but he's laid up for two weeks, so Yvette has her hands full.[22]

Belong To Many is on the comeback trail. She is so relaxed after spelling, and glided over 1400 metres this morning. She still has a long way to go to regain her girlish figure, but I could not be happier with the way she's progressing. King's Admiral has "devil's horns" just above his eyes. Kate Grimwade, my racing manager, informed me that many Cape Cross horses have this unusual bone growth. I always knew he was a little devil, even if he is over 16 hands high.

Grant Buckley certainly looked refreshed this morning – he has had a break from trackwork and taken himself and family to Bali for a week. He's a champion chap, always very agreeable to work with and a very accomplished jockey.

Blake Shinn declared that his mount in Saturday's Listed Show County (1200 metres), Swift Alliance, "will win!" I have to agree with him.[23]

THURSDAY, AUGUST 20

Today has been a series of unusual experiences as the AJC, David Jones and the *Daily Telegraph* have asked me to be involved in photo shoots to promote our forthcoming spring carnival. Anything that helps promote racing and gets the front page and not the back, well I'm all for it.

The first is an article on prominent women in racing and my photograph was taken with a delightful young bookmaker, Brooke Pendlebury, daughter of leading rails bookie Jeff and sister to three other young ladies, all of whom are bookmakers' clerks. Brooke works as a lawyer throughout the week but her passion is for the odds and she cannot wait to take off her high heels and put on a pair of flatties, throw the satchel over her shoulder and head to the track. When I arrived at Randwick, Brooke was dressed so prettily that I thought she was one of the DJ models.

Afterwards I drove back to Randwick for sandwiches by the pool, where I was interviewed by *Financial Review* reporter Fiona Carruthers. Fiona was well informed on her topic of Gai and racing and asked some rather pertinent and interesting questions. We enjoyed watching the horses exercise in the glorious Sydney sunshine before travelling to the Randwick mounting enclosure for the final photographs for

---

22 Deedra, the $2.20 favourite, finished sixth and was retired to the breeding barn.
23 The four-year-old won as the $2.20 favourite.

the Mad Hatters' race day party. There was Sarah (Alice in Wonderland), mother of one small babe and involved with Luna Park in her real life, Lyndsay (Mad Hatter), who works with children in creative workshops, and Romeo, who is involved with the Starlight Foundation. Together we danced and played up for all of 10 minutes, me wearing my Missoni dress and fabulous teal blue hat, which I had asked Nerida Winter to create for last year's Royal Ascot meeting. To make it truly mad and fun I turned the hat back to front; Nerida would kill me.

Our Mad Hatters' day will be on September 2. It's all about having fun – not about big bands and everyone getting drunk, but about families coming to the races and having good wholesome entertainment.

FRIDAY, AUGUST 21

Theseo looks fabulous. He's quite big in the girth and he has put on lots of pudding as he has only been swimming. I feel he is definitely back on track; his action is perfect and I can't thank (podiatrist) Michael Kitchington enough for giving me the necessary information when I visited him. I was looking to get my sore toe fixed and instead he was able to put me on the right track with Theseo.

Bhutane Dane has just completed his laps at the pool. Every afternoon most horses go to the pool, as it keeps them fit and is a nice break from their normal routine. We are so lucky to have the weather in Australia that allows us to swim the horses outside. The perfect example is Theseo, who has just about lived in the pool.

This morning, at the trainers' tower at Randwick, there appeared to be more owners than horses – a group of NAB bankers came out to view trackwork and they had a ball, so much so they even drove to Rosehill to watch Manhattan Rain and Rock Kingdom trial. That's dedication for you! They then said goodbye and drove straight to work. In parting I said, "I hope you don't start to fade mid-afternoon."

Bill Wendt and wife Geraldine were at Randwick to watch their two-year-old Anniversary. They also have a share in Judicial who races at Randwick tomorrow in the Group 3 Up And Coming Stakes over 1200 metres.[24] Bill was saying this morning's training session reminded him of when he was a boy and how his father, who was in the navy, would take him from time to time on the bridge of his ship. Bill couldn't get over how much Tania (Rouse), Damien (Gaffney), Dave (Meijer) and I, standing outside the clocking tower, reminded him of those early days.

Sean Clancy and his son came out to see their bonny mare Belong To Many, who has done a treat since spelling. I love it when the owners get involved with their horses.

---

24 Judicial ran last of eight.

"Outstanding," said Blake of Manhattan Rain's win in his 1030-metre Rosehill trial. "He's so relaxed, if you drop your hands on him he just goes to sleep." The colt never looked in doubt this morning. I had instructed Blake to ride him aggressively, as he is so lovely and relaxed, and I wanted him to derive maximum benefit from this hit-out. He has pulled up well and will travel to Melbourne in the next week in preparation for the Danehill Stakes at Flemington on September 5.

However, Nash said of Rock Kingdom, fourth in his 1000-metre trial: "I thought he was disappointing this morning." Blinkers might put his mind on the job as Nash doesn't feel like he's putting in, but he may not be fully fit yet.

There has been much discussion about the Randwick and Kensington tracks, and rightly so as both are racing in sub-standard fashion. Full credit to the AJC's Darren Pearce and his team for addressing this serious situation by moving next Tuesday's meeting to the Kensington track. It is much better to sacrifice the better track and get the course proper right for the spring carnival. By all means, hold the black-type races on the course proper but the midweeks and lesser-type meetings should be run on the Kensington track.

MONDAY, AUGUST 24

BC3 Thoroughbreds held a 'breeze up' sale of two-year-olds at their Future Stars Day at Sutton Grange in central Victoria. The standout colt was a striking chestnut by Jet Spur out of Fientina (by King Of Kings). A big, strong, relaxed individual, he has a very attractive head and he has great presence. He reminds me of Sebring as a type. He worked well over 200 metres, showing a lovely fluid action and came past the post with his ears pricked ... There were more than 100 people within 20 metres of this colt when he breezed. This did not faze him as he took it all in his stride. He obviously enjoyed his work. He put his head down in a professional manner and did everything we like to see in a young horse's work. From the family of Elvstroem and Haradasun, he certainly has a stallion's page, and, with a duplication of the great Biscay, is bred to go early. We were delighted to secure him for just $110,000.

TUESDAY, AUGUST 25

Horrendous weather at Randwick this morning with gale-force conditions. We who dared to stand on the outside deck of the trainers' hut were nearly blown over. I even had trouble holding my binoculars in position as my arms were being blown about. Mark (Newnham) said that when galloping down the back straight the jocks couldn't work out what speed they were going as the wind was so strong in their face.

It's amazing how a couple of times every year it is so windy at Randwick. I think it blows straight off Botany Bay.

If there were any doubts about putting your money on More Joyous this Saturday at Rosehill they would have been well and truly quashed after watching her work brilliantly this morning. The filly recorded 34.3 seconds for the 600 metres and 10.8 seconds for her final 200 metres.

WEDNESDAY, AUGUST 26

Every afternoon when I was a kid I would ride my pony in Centennial Park. I had the great joy of dressing him – Wilkie and Trigger were two of my favourites – and we would ride up Doncaster Avenue. This is now a thing of the past and I don't think I've seen a kid on a pony for nearly 10 years. The best fun happened when the ranger wasn't looking and a couple of mates and I would gallop through the area opposite the AJC front gates and jump the fallen logs and weave between the trees – heaven help us if the ranger turned up, as he was a mean man.

THURSDAY, AUGUST 27

More Joyous is absolutely electrifying to watch, is so well-named and with every gallop keeps improving. 'Singo' will be very proud of the filly when she races in the Listed Sheraco Stakes (1100 metres) on Saturday.[25]

FRIDAY, AUGUST 28

The trials this morning were a debacle. They were originally put down for Randwick, but a section of the steeple-grass caved in and at the last minute on Thursday afternoon trainers were notified the trials would be held at Warwick Farm. As if that wasn't enough, two of my best horses, Tuesday Joy and Common Objective, were involved in an incident when the starting gates malfunctioned before heat one. Common Objective tore around the course proper with his gear flapping wildly and it was truly amazing that he didn't break a leg or run into a fence. He certainly had a good hit-out. Unfortunately Blake came a tumble, bruising both wrists and his ribs.

Nash on Tuesday Joy, who lunged forward thinking the trial had commenced, broke his nose, which is all a jockey needs going into a major carnival. Full credit to Nash that he rode her with tissues stuffed up his nose and then rode Seventh Reason (third) before he pulled the plug and went to the doctor. Nash's doctor asked him had

---

25 More Joyous finished third as $2.45 favourite. The race was won by Madame Pedrille.

he put his nose back into place. When Nash said he had, the doctor told him he had done a better job than he could have. Nash was quite happy with himself and told Robyn (Hartney) he thought his nose looked better than it ever had. Great to see he was able to retain his sense of humour!

SATURDAY, AUGUST 29

Robbie has given me a beautiful little puppy for my birthday. His name is Bello, meaning beautiful in Italian, and he's a King Charles spaniel and poodle cross. Baci, our blind poodle, has a new lease of life, as he can play and jump around with his new mate. It's so sweet to see and I can assure you it has caused quite a distraction at the Waterhouse home.

MONDAY, AUGUST 31

A busy morning was had by all at the track. There were a dozen of the Darley Flying Start students in attendance, a lovely group of young men and women chosen to come and study for two years with Sheikh Mohammed's Darley Stud. They asked many interesting questions, which is something I love to see, and of course I gave them as much information as I could.

After the track I hurried off to visit my hairdresser Valonz in preparation for the David Jones Spring Collections launch in Victoria. Afterwards, we had a brief lunch with our friend Naomi Robson, whose birthday we celebrated, then on to Melbourne's Crown to catch up on some work and prepare for the long awaited Racehorse of the Year Awards – this is the racing industry's Logie night and as you can imagine the Star Thoroughbreds team is holding its breath for Theseo, the NSW champion this season.[26]

TUESDAY, SEPTEMBER 1

The managing director of Inglis Bloodstock, Arthur Inglis, phoned to inform me that the company was moving to Warwick Farm. What a master-stroke. When we were growing up Randwick was a user-friendly area for horses where everyone had a stable in their backyard or close by. Things have changed, so Inglis is on the move. People in racing forget the centre of Sydney is now Parramatta and so much of the new money is around this area. I congratulate Inglis on its far-sightedness and congratulate the AJC for being so forward-thinking.

---

26 The West Australian sprinter Scenic Blast, a Group 1 winner in Melbourne and at Royal Ascot, was judged Australian Horse of the Year.

Many people have asked me for my thoughts on the new padded whip. A gentleman called Brad, a keen racing man from Melbourne, spoke to me last night at the Australian Horse of the Year awards and summed it up perfectly. He asked: "If they say the padded whip doesn't hurt, why do the stewards have to restrain it?"

Master of ceremonies at the Coolmore Stud open day last Sunday was bloodstock consultant James Bester, who excelled when he said of the stallion Tale Of The Cat: "Every muscle is in his testicles. He does for me more than a double dose of Viagra and at $38,500 this remarkably sexy horse is terrific value for money."

I find these days very beneficial: I get to see the stallions whose progeny I'm training; they are a great help for Kate Grimwade and me when we are recommending horses to our clients; and they are a great way of catching up and networking with one's owners. The problem for most trainers is finding the time to see one's clients. You get up early and you're with your horses all morning and then again in the afternoon. Long lunches or dinners really just don't work.

WEDNESDAY, SEPTEMBER 2

At the racing awards night in Sydney on August 13, Neil (Paine), Mark (Newnham) and Blake (Shinn) bought a book of raffle tickets. They thought nothing more about it until two weeks later when Neil was contacted and informed that Gai's jockeys, as they called themselves on the butt, had won a trip to Hayman Island. So the three, plus their wives/partners, are planning a little trip away in November after the carnival. Being mindful of their work commitments the boys are taking only three days off. What a hoot and won't they have fun!

Speaking of fun, our Mad Hatters' race day at Randwick today has been just that, with so many joining in by wearing weird and wonderful caps and hats.

SATURDAY, SEPTEMBER 5

I have noticed real improvement from Herculian Prince. It is often hard for Kiwi imports to settle into our mode of training – most New Zealand horses are trained from paddocks, whereas in Australia most are trained from boxes on racetracks. Herculian Prince had developed a little habit of playing up when the jockey was legged on. So Dave Meijer and I devised a plan, with the assistance of 'Pony Tim' (O'Riordan, who is in charge of the stable ponies), to move to the back of the clocking tower and put Tim and his pony on one side and have Neil Paine legged on from the other.

Blake has stayed in Melbourne since Saturday to partner Swift Alliance and Manhattan Rain in their trackwork. I love to keep the stable jocks on my horses as they know their idiosyncrasies and how their action usually is. It's quite alarming when a jockey isn't as familiar and says, "Oh, he's got a scratchy action." I rely heavily on those few words from the jockeys to put the picture together for me on how my horses are travelling.

There were probably about 20 people who enjoyed the intimacy of a quiet Sunday at Tulloch Lodge. I do a lot of charity functions where people bid for a Sunday at the stables with Gai. If it raises money for a good cause, it's certainly worthwhile. People are so interested and delightful company and many end up becoming owners when they see the fun and enjoyment to be had on a Sunday. It's a bit like a bowling club or social club – everyone has a name tag and, as you can imagine, it's easy to recognise *The Lady Trainer*. The regular visitors also know everyone and become interested in each other's horses, and great friendships have evolved. We trotted the horses up, then I did my rounds of checking and looking at each stable and how the horses were doing. I see more in two hours on a Sunday than I do all week.

I have liked the Secret Savings two-year-old Laduni since the moment I saw him at the Magic Millions sales. He reminded me enormously of Bank Robber as a young horse. When he arrived in the yard he had a crabby type of action so I checked out his shoes and they were great big heavy things often used by pre-trainers thinking they'll last longer. We quickly disposed of them and replaced them with a light pair of aluminium plates, and straight away he was lighter on his feet and moving more freely. To help his balance and co-ordination I asked Mel Morton to put him on the High Performance Galloping Machine, not to gallop but to walk and trot; once again working on his balance. This morning I put him in blinkers, and saw yet another improvement. I really get a kick out of trying to work out these four-legged creatures.

I was so delighted when Swift Alliance greeted the judge in the Hong Kong Jockey Club Stakes at Flemington on Saturday. The win was most convincing and not dissimilar to stablemate Northern Meteor, who won over 1200 metres on the straight course at Flemington last November. I had a chinwag with Blake the day before; I am constantly reminding my jocks about their strike rates and I felt Blake was not utilising the best part of the track in each of his rides. I instructed him to walk the course before Swifty's race. When he came back he said, "I want to be on the grandstand side." No horse had run on the stand side so this was a bold move by the jockey, but Andrew (Baddock, Gooree's racing manager) and I agreed that if he was going to the part of the track he believed was the fastest then we would go along with the decision. It sure worked out beautifully and who would believe a son of Don Eduardo, himself a son of Zabeel, would be such a brilliant sprinter. Swift Alliance is an extremely compact and neat colt with a lovely manner and a very attractive head. One wouldn't pick he had so much brilliance, but when he is under pressure he produces the most amazing turn of foot.

Full credit to the AJC's Darren Pearce, Mick Stanley, Dave Hodgson and the two grader drivers who must have worked very hard over the weekend to get the dirt track back to normal. I tend to really make a noise if things aren't right, but they have taken my comments on board and graded the track much more effectively, and the penetrometer readings were back to normal. I was starting to get hot under the collar, but one can't win Group 1 races working at three-quarter pace, which is all we did last week.

My barrier manager, Scott Martin, flew to Melbourne on Saturday afternoon to work with our magnificent colt Manhattan Rain. The son of Encosta De Lago had jumped out at Flemington on Tuesday and Nash commented to me that he was quite fractious in the barriers, wanting to put his leg up; a bit like a dog cocking his leg. Scott took the barrier pads sent to us by American master horseman Bob Duncan; these are used all the time in America for horses like Manhattan Rain. Scott and Steve (Dennett) worked with the colt very quietly on Sunday morning, without too many onlookers, and the three-year-old responded beautifully and in a most relaxed manner.

I am just about to get on a plane bound for Melbourne with Tom, of whom I see so little these days. We are having dinner tonight and he asked me, "Is it just the two of us, Mum?" I said, "Of course," and he responded with a disbelieving, "Are you sure, Mum?" What Tom and Kate don't realise is I enjoy their company so much I don't want to be distracted by anyone else. Kids are funny, aren't they?

THURSDAY, SEPTEMBER 10

Yesterday was a busy day, starting with my morning at the track; back to talk with owners; nominations; blog; then off to Valonz for my haircut with Kieran, who was going overseas to do a fashion show in New York.

I then went to the Canterbury races where Danehill Dancer filly Dance Idol, who has been very tardy jumping from the barriers, flew the gates (in a 1250-metre Maiden for three-year-olds) to eventually cross and lead. Scott and Heath (Farish) have worked tirelessly with this filly. She was taken on quiet visits daily until she learned the art of jumping from the gates. That time and patience certainly paid dividends yesterday. Unfortunately, having to work hard early in the race, combined with the wind, did not help her winning chances and she finished in seventh spot, beaten by 4.5 lengths.

in work in Sydney will not be racing over the carnival but are being set to race after it. Blink and it's all over and soon enough the next brigade needs to be ready to fire at the provincials, midweek metro and Saturday races.

THURSDAY, SEPTEMBER 17

Talk about working blind! This morning at Randwick a thick fog made it impossible to see much at all. One could hear the foghorns all the way from Circular Quay beeping out their messages of pending danger.

George Mooratoff and his wife Jill enjoyed a leisurely lunch by the equine pool at Randwick yesterday. With Mum's card table and my newly acquired fold-up picnic chairs, Damien popped a bottle of "champers". We walked and talked and watched the horses exercising and swimming in the pool, doing an Ian Thorpe; it keeps their limbs supple and takes the gas out of them so they rest well.

MONDAY, SEPTEMBER 21

Early morning kicked off at Flemington with me watching Manhattan Rain trot and canter with Blake in the saddle. He has come through his race well and it was a good solid effort by this colt, who was only beaten a short half-head and a neck when third in the Guineas Prelude (1400 metres) at Caulfield. He was very fresh this morning so Blake wanted to give him an extra lap of the dirt. But I said, "No we'll let him be a bit fresh as he had a hard run on Saturday."

Limousine driver Jim whizzed us to the taxi terminal where all the drivers have their breakfast. A hot chocolate hit the spot in no uncertain terms. Then it was off to Moonee Valley to see Swift Alliance put in an outstanding gallop. It truly was an exceptional piece of work, galloping over 1200 metres with the blinkers on so he could focus and he found the line with such vengeance.

Yesterday Fleur Blanch, foreman at Bounding Away, had a giggle when the owners of Danewin three-year-old War Relic came and did a measurement on their horse in the box. They were measuring him for what she thinks must be a new rug; a bit like the emperor's new clothes!

TUESDAY, SEPTEMBER 22

Poor Daniel Ganderton has been in hospital with a broken shinbone following a horrible fall at Newcastle races last Thursday. Thanks to the help of 'Singo', who knows everyone in the medical profession, including Dr Nathan Gibbs (the Sydney Swans' medical officer), we decided to try to move him back to Sydney from Newcastle to have his operation. On Sunday, after many calls between John, myself, Nathan and Dan, we tried to organise the best possible surgeon. I'm happy to say last night Dan was moved to St George Private Hospital in Kogarah by his mother Sheree and girlfriend Kelly. Dan is booked in to have his operation tomorrow morning.

Three barrier gates arrived at my Desert War stables on Friday. Two are the normal type – the same as those used at the races – but the third has no running rail and is slightly wider to accommodate an unsettled horse. Now all my babies walk through these gates upon departing the stables each morning and others, such as Encosta De Lago mare Above Perfection, whom Heath Farish was finding a little hot and bothered over at the mile barriers, was taken quietly for a maintenance session at the end of trackwork this morning. Heath said of the mare: "She was led into a closed barrier. Stood nice and relaxed, backed out, then led back in and locked in and once again stood nice and relaxed before being sent on her way." No jumping out; just quietly, quietly as they do in America.

WEDNESDAY, SEPTEMBER 23

We had a very welcome guest at Randwick the other morning in the form of Peter Garrett, ex-Midnight Oil singer and federal Labor politician. He arrived at the track at 5am with his assistant Jenny and camera in hand to take photos of the horses. He tells me he's going in a photographic competition for politicians. Peter was great; it was the AJC "morning of the stars" and he mingled with everyone. He is the most gregarious person.

I can't believe the bosses allow cartoon racing in our TABs. Do they really want to stop people following the races all together? Racing is still very strong in Australia, but is not being aided by the powers-that-be and by allowing this computer-animated racing game. It just takes more and more people away from racing.

THURSDAY, SEPTEMBER 24

Young Daniel had his tibia operated on yesterday and is recovering in hospital. Robyn just spoke to him and he is expected to come home to Tulloch Lodge this afternoon, which will make it easy for the staff and his friends to pop in for a visit. At this stage Dan looks like he will be sidelined for the eight weeks, but knowing his determination I'm sure he will be back in the saddle as soon as he possibly can.

Bank Robber a little wake-up at the top of the straight and the gelding stretched out beautifully. All is on target for his first run back from a spell in the Group 2 Schweppes Stakes on Cox Plate day at Moonee Valley.

This morning at Flemington Tindal pulled his front shoe off, so I adjourned to the limousine driver's coffee shop with Jim (the driver) and the young Frenchman Geoffrey Pontall, whose father trains in France. Jim very sweetly bought some muffins and cheese on toast and a cup of coffee to keep me going. When we asked young Geoffrey, who is learning the ropes with me, what would he like to pick for breakfast, he said, "Nothing." I then gave him instructions on how important breakfast was and told him it was fuel for his brain and he would never break down if he ate well. I think he was wishing he hadn't come for coffee with *The Lady Trainer*.

Shoe back on, Craig Williams trotted Tindal up and the colt was sound and good so he went off to do his work. He galloped on the grass over 800 metres wearing blinkers because I want to inject speed into the colt and make him concentrate on the task at hand. He showed quite a lot of ability in his second preparation for John Sadler, Lloyd Williams' trainer, winning a 1400-metre Listed race at Flemington, but has not regained that form in his most recent runs.

We then went to Caulfield where Manhattan Rain awaited. Rain had fallen, so by the time I arrived at 7am the track was cut up. I therefore instructed Blake to hold him together over the final 100 metres in a 1400-metre gallop. He had a good blow and definitely needed the hit-out, but the style and strength of his work was excellent. I trotted him up at the stalls, as is my custom, and he looked free in his action and was bright as a button.

I was impressed when Brenton Avdulla advised me daylight-saving started on Sunday morning, but I was even more impressed when my iPhone automatically adjusted the time it displays to the correct time. In order of love, the iPhone rates right up there. Young Brenton rode 17 pieces of work for me this morning, between his gallops and trot and canters, and the youngster finished about 8.15am.

WEDNESDAY, OCTOBER 7

What a great start to Brenton's time here at Tulloch Lodge. At his first ride for the stable, aboard Dance Idol, he was able to salute the judge at Canterbury today. Dance Idol was left in front from the barriers and Brenton kept his composure, letting her stride along, playing her like a big fish. She had the opposition chasing and off the bit a long way from home and strode clear late to score by two-and-a-half lengths. The young man spoke well to the owners and I'm sure he will have many more successes.

In Monday's *Daily Telegraph,* columnist Ken Callander made a comment about Rock Kingdom's improved form. Now, anyone who understands weights will realise that when Rock Kingdom was sixth of 10 runners in the George Main Stakes (1600 metres), his first attempt at weight for age, he was totally unsuited, whereas on Saturday when he won the Epsom, also 1600 metres, he went back to a handicap. It was hard to get the perfect lead-up to the Epsom and I was not sure – nor were the owners – if he could make the weight-for-age rise. It is now history he failed. The blinkers, in my opinion, had not a great deal to do with it. I thought long and hard after his George Main failure whether I would accept for the Epsom and how could I beat the others at such compressed weights. I made a decision early in the week to run and I put him in blinkers as I wanted him ridden positively.

As I mentioned yesterday, the biggest question last Saturday was why the track was so heavy from the start of the day, considering we had only 11mm of rain leading into the meeting. The truth is that one of the sprinklers had malfunctioned and stayed on all night a couple of days before the meeting. Because none of the Turnpoint or AJC employees lives on course, no one knew. The sooner the AJC committee takes on board this major issue the better standard of racing we will have.

THURSDAY, OCTOBER 8

Manhattan Rain had Blake Shinn grinning from ear-to-ear at Flemington. He had not been 100 per cent happy with the colt on Tuesday at Caulfield as he thought he still had a bit of conditioning to do, so I asked him to stay in Melbourne and accompany the colt daily in his work. Yesterday he did two laps of the Flemington dirt and this morning, with Tindal as his partner, the pair bowled over 1400 metres coming home their final two furlongs. The most important thing is the colt recovered quickly after his gallop and, unlike Tuesday, his respiratory rate was back to normal in a twinkle. I didn't want either colt to be beaten so I told Blake to make sure Manhattan's nose was just in front. I really believe I have the horse to win my first Caulfield Guineas on Saturday.[29]

I visited David Jones this afternoon for a very important cause, with every DJ store in Australia donating today's profits to breast cancer. I spent one-and-a-half hours talking with customers, greeting them and pointing to my breast cancer badge, explaining I was here to make them aware of the disease. Most of the customers did not need to be told as they were in the store spending their hard-earned knowing the proceeds were going to such a worthy cause. Cancer killed five of my six aunts.

---

29 Manhattan Rain ($9) finished third to Starspangledbanner and Carrara in the Guineas.

Over the past week I have had pressure placed upon me by the stewards to let my on-loan apprentice Brenton Avdulla ride horses that will start long odds. I have had a policy for a long time in not letting my apprentices ride long-shots, as I like to try to keep their strike rate strong. These boys have such a tiny window to make an impression on the public, trainers and owners before they lose their valuable claim – they are very sexy with a 3kg claim, less with 2kg, and as the claim diminishes they cease being the flavour of the month. It's quite sad to see many of them start having weight problems.

I asked young Brenton did he object to what I was doing? His reply: "Gai, I left my last manager because he put me on anything and everything, and that is not what I want." What a smart young man. Most of my apprentices have been reluctant to follow this rule and have allowed their manager to take rides even though I have advised them not to. The other day a Sydney trainer was quite aggressive and rude while questioning my racing manager Robyn Hartney on why Brenton was not available to ride his horse on Saturday.

What the stewards should be doing is asking why these long-shots aren't racing in their right races. They should also be schooling the boys and girls who ride in races to keep their weight down. The other morning I saw Brenton walk out of the house where he is living and I said to him, "What are you eating?" "A chocolate biscuit, Gai." I told him he should be ashamed of himself and said, "You don't see me eating like that. The only way to keep your weight down is not to eat rubbish. Have a banana instead." Brenton will feel more like a monkey by the time he leaves Sydney, but he certainly won't be riding like one.

I think a few comments are required following Gerry Harvey's comments on television on the issue of betting agencies, bookmakers and the tote, and licence fees. The owner of Harvey Norman, the Magic Millions sales company, a stud and hundreds of horses said:

> "Gai's a really nice girl and she's a horse trainer. But she's got a son that's a bookmaker and she's got a husband that's a bookmaker. So she goes to bed at night and they say, 'Ay, Mum, ay Wife.' You know ..."

Well, it is patronising, isn't it? I wonder if 'boy' Gerry's good wife Katie Page would take kindly to similar pejorative terms about her. I'd back Katie to be able to think for herself, as I do. I'm pleased I won that case back in 1992 (to get a trainer's licence although my husband was a disqualified person), and pleased Gerry wasn't a judge. And Gerry said:

"Of course it (Betfair operating in Australia from a Tasmanian base) is a concern. Tasmania is a little island in Australia that didn't have much going for it in this area. So, you know, they are just – the Tasmanian Government – they are taking advantage just like the corporate bookies are. They think, 'Oh, there's a loophole, we'll take advantage of it, we'll rip the rest of the states in Australia off.' That's all they're doing. They know they are doing it, they are getting away with it."

Gerry doesn't understand the issue. Under the legislation, all operators pay the same, wherever they are based. The question is: will the Federal Court say the law is invalid? Gerry again:

"The silly buggers like Tabcorp or me or whoever else is in the racing industry all putting our bit in, and they just say, 'Mate, I'm taking advantage of you, I know that, but that's how the system is, what do you want me to do?' Put your bloody share in, mate, put your share in like the rest of us, and stop the bullshit."

But, of course, it is not true. We are not "all putting our bit in". Gerry, as a breeder, vendor, sales company owner and horse owner, is taking his bit out as I do as an owner and trainer. It is racing customers, the punters, who are "putting on the party". Shame they are ignored. And Gerry said:

"If they are successful, there's no racing, it's as simple as that, and they know that. It will all go back to picnic races. So it's just total destruction of the racing industry as we know it. They know it; we know it."

What Gerry says here is right. If racing loses the court cases, it is a huge problem. Sadly, outside of Racing NSW and the breeders, no one thinks we can win them. If we win, much of the betting industry will go offshore, out of Racing NSW's grasp. If we lose, Racing NSW will negotiate with the betting industry. Good luck! We'll need it.

If the vast majority is right about our court prospects, now is the time to negotiate, as Victoria has done. Don't get me started on the differences in approach between Victoria and NSW.

TUESDAY, OCTOBER 13

I put blinkers on Tindal and instructed Nash to give him a searching gallop over 800 metres. I told him to yell in his ear and make sure I could hear the noise in the clocking tower. He tends to be a bit of a timid colt. I'm trying to make him into a man so when he retires he may be attractive to a stud.

A letter from Aunty Shirley, wife of my father's brother Pat, of Chancellor Park on the Sunshine Coast in Queensland:

Dear Gai,

We were reading the *Telegraph* today and it brought back memories from many years ago. Your father was with us in Griffith once, and he said, "Gai wants to be a trainer! She says she could be as good as Betty Lane." He didn't seem to think that would be sensational and was laughing about it.

However, the next time he was up he said, "You can't teach anyone to train, it just has to be born in them and I've tried her out. I've taken her to look at the horses and given her a catalogue and told her to go around and mark the horses that she thinks would be worth buying, and she has come back with six of the eight that I was interested in, so I think she's got a good eye.

He also said that on a Sunday morning he would sneak around so as not to wake you, but when he would come downstairs you would be there waiting for him to go to the track. He said a lot of the know-alls in the racing game used to say, 'Isn't it a shame that you didn't have a son to carry on from you?' He said, "I could have had a son who wanted to be a window dresser, but I've got a daughter who is as keen as me."

I can assure you he was very proud of you and had a lot of confidence in your ability.

All the best with the big races coming up.

Love,
Aunty Shirley & Uncle Pat.

THURSDAY, OCTOBER 15

At Flemington, Manhattan Rain (Craig Williams) worked with Tindal (Blake Shinn). I wanted Tindal to grow up and be a competitive racehorse, so I had him work on the inside of the three-year-old colt. They bowled over 1200 metres, but on Saturday I'll give them much shorter and sharper work.

At Randwick, the horse that most delighted me was Seventh Reason, who has returned bigger and stronger. Mark Newnham said when he saw a horse in front of him at the top of the straight he focussed and chased it. Maybe I need a pacemaker for Seventh Reason when he races in the 2000-metre handicap at Hawkesbury next Thursday. (Just joking! Pacemakers aren't allowed in Australia – I've written before how I don't agree with England, which allows them.)

I thought I had fractured my hip about a week ago, as it was that sore. So I took myself to the Bridgepoint physio and sports injury centre where a young man named Campbell cured me in three sessions. He gave me some exercises, which I've been doing at home, and used his elbow to knead the sore points. Physio is an essential part of life for both horse and human, and stable physio Tom Simpson does as good a job as young Campbell. I must say he has slightly bigger patients to work on, but it is amazing the relief he gives four-legged creatures.

The committee at Randwick is doing a grand job and, even though an election is pending, I would not be putting any new faces on the board. Ron Finemore and John Cornish have a great working relationship with the other board members and they have turned Randwick around and are about to do the same with Warwick Farm. They had the smell of an oily rag to work on and the most important thing is they are listening to their participants and doing a grand job.

FRIDAY, OCTOBER 16

I have a lot of time for Star Thoroughbreds' filly Dream 'n' Believe (by Shamardal). These horses are like my children and I think about them seven days a week, 365 days a year. I'm a great believer in patience and it's amazing what time can do with a horse's development. Steve (Dennett) partnered her and she went around with her head beautifully down and composed and found the line in 11 seconds dead. She will trial in about two weeks.

You might think I'm barking mad, but my treasure Bello has his say in the blog:

> I've met a girl. She's white and wears a red collar with big studs in it. I saw her at Mum's stable yesterday and she belongs to the farrier, Wally. First, I was a bit nervous about saying hello, but she came straight up and put her paw on my shoulder. Then the next minute she had me on the ground and then before I knew it she was on top of me. I had never experienced anything like this before.
>
> At home, Baci and I play all day – he jumps on top of me and pushes me out of my bed and I hear Gai say how Baci reminds her of old Jock. I wonder if I remind her of young Tom, as Baci and I have a great relationship. He's like my grandfather and is good to be around and is always caring for me. But the other day I was really able to help him. He fell in the pool and Gai didn't realise so I started to bark loudly, making the biggest noise I've ever made. She ran out and pulled Baci out of the water and although he was very shaken for quite some time he was okay.

With Wally's dog, I don't know her name but, boy, do I like her. We must've wrestled for a good 15 or 20 minutes as Gai was busy looking at all the horses. I fell in lots of puddles and all the stable boys and girls came out to watch us. Hopefully I'll see her again soon.

MONDAY, OCTOBER 19

On Saturday in Melbourne I thought our best chance was Gold Water (ninth in the Tristarc Stakes), as she had run so well first up two weeks before, beating the mares that finished in front of her on Saturday. But the tables were very much reversed and Typhoon Tracy, who was beautifully positioned throughout, travelled in second spot and produced too good a turn of foot for the others in the final furlong.

Steve Dennett, who is a great thinker (Rodin sculptured a statue in his honour), said to me today, "We may have done too much with Gold Water leading up to the race." In Melbourne the jocks ride trot and canters; that never happens back in Sydney as they (the jockeys) are basically kept exclusively for gallops. "Maybe they have done a little too much on their quiet days," concluded Steve. Our physio (Tom Simpson) visited two days before and we both wondered whether this could have affected the mare in an adverse way. After a sluggish performance, it's important to look at carefully what has taken place and question why.

I read an interesting article on Friday in Melbourne's *Herald Sun* newspaper about a lady, Ruth Frith, who is no less than 100 years old. Not only did she compete in the World Masters Games, but she had some very interesting comments, such as "to succeed you have to be true to yourself and have to believe in yourself and believe in what you do". She puts it down to attitude and being happy with what you've got. I must say they are very sensible and true words. It is probably the motivation that drives me forward, which I'm sure is the same for dear Ruth. I can only hope I'm training winners north and south of the border when I'm 100 years old!

TUESDAY, OCTOBER 20

I've been particularly pleased with the progress of Tindal. He is a very timid colt and I was worried about him going to the trials yesterday at Cranbourne. Last year he was scratched at the barriers and I wondered whether he might have had a bad experience and would remember it, as this could colour his racing future. I had Scott Martin, my barrier expert, fly down to Melbourne on the weekend and he accompanied him on a quiet visit to the barriers on Saturday and Sunday. Tindal loved all the attention – they're just like kids or husbands and need lots of TLC with a firm hand but a loving one. My husband, with very big ears, is sitting in the room whilst I'm dictating this blog.

I'm making my annual pilgrimage to the Victoria Racing Club. I feel very blessed for I have been lucky enough to rent boxes on Flemington racetrack, as only recently a leading Victorian trainer's application was knocked back.

Victoria does a superb job and this morning at Moonee Valley's Breakfast with the Stars it was like a raceday. The horses paraded before each gallop and the course TV coverage was excellent, as was the commentator, who filled in the history of the horses as they went through their paces. Racing is a public sport and a spectacle people love to come and watch.

WEDNESDAY, OCTOBER 21

I attended a luncheon at the Royal Automobile Club in Melbourne where racecaller Bryan Martin interviewed me on all different aspects of racing and my life growing up in the Sport of Kings. Question time arrived and one of the first was: "What is your daily exercise regime?" I answered: "Every day, I do the wiggly woo." I then proceeded to show the people attending by kneeling on the podium and wiggling my hips from left to right. By this time they were certain *The Lady Trainer* was quite mad. Well my demonstration, how silly it may have looked, certainly got a roar of applause. I do these functions while in Melbourne because I like to carry the message of racing to the everyday person. I want people when they turn their tellies on or pick up the paper to look for the racing section. With so many other sports to compete with, we must do our best to obtain the major share of the sporting dollar.

THURSDAY, OCTOBER 22

Glorious morning at headquarters (Flemington) where I was out early as always to catch the worm, which well and truly eluded our stable last Saturday. Unlike Randwick, there are three clocking towers at Flemington. I go to the little one used by Mark Kavanagh, Danny O'Brien and Mat Ellerton, as it has a good balcony and I prefer training outside because there is too much noise and too many distractions inside.

I instructed Blake that he was to work Tindal over a comfortable six (furlongs). I told him to keep alert and yell in his ear. He went on at the mile-and-a-quarter, then did one almighty shy, moving quickly to the right, then to the left. Blake nearly came off him, but a few corrective slaps to the shoulder straightened him out and he produced the best work I've seen from him so far. He was focused and did not try to jump shadows. He is not only improving fitness-wise, but mentally too.

Melbourne and the carnival is an endurance test for even the best of them. This morning is no different from home except there are only a handful of horses to train. I am constantly on the phone to Tania (Rouse), Lofty (Brett Killion), Dave (Meijer) and my office, keeping abreast of how the horses are going at Randwick.

Today was the launch of my father-in-law Bill Waterhouse's book *What are the Odds? The Bill Waterhouse Story.* Bill did a marvellous job; people often forget his great age (88). It was lovely to see young Tom bounce off his grandfather and recount stories, including how he was quite shocked when he first came into the business by the cavalier fashion in which his grandfather took on all who ventured to bet with him. Tom said learning to become a bookmaker with his father and grandfather was the most compelling and exciting thing he had ever done and he made his mind up early that this would be his chosen career. Tom has gone from strength to strength, and the knowledge of both father and grandfather has given him an old head on young shoulders, a valuable asset for anyone in any business.

FRIDAY, OCTOBER 23

I was at a VRC function last night singing for my supper and was interviewed by the delightful Simon O'Donnell. It was a fun evening with about 500 people in attendance. I fielded many questions including what I ate and drank – hot lemon and orange with lots of honey and fruit and yoghurt in the morning. I told of how I make a 'smiley' face with the fruit for my beloved one, or with a down-turned banana when he is out of sorts, which may I say is very seldom. A couple of my boys and girls were there and had a real giggle seeing the other side of their boss.

Another win with Tindal: I love to have a challenge and it was a pleasant one this morning. With the pony on his right and Viking Legend on his left, Tindal went straight on the track without a hiccup. Hopefully all the hard work will pay dividends when he races on Melbourne Cup day.[30]

SATURDAY, OCTOBER 24

Today was a particularly long day, rising at 3am to be at Flemington by 4.30am. Only two horses galloped because the rest were racing at Moonee Valley. Then, back for a quick sleep, brekky, hair done, form completed and then off to the races. It's always an emotional rollercoaster and I'm often asked if I am nervous on these big days. I'm never nervous, but I must say I'm very much on the toe. I know how important these days

---

[30] *The Lady Trainer* changed her mind and did not run Tindal at Flemington.

are and I want everything to go right. The expectations of all our owners are high and sometimes I can be dealing with close to 100 people in the space of a couple of hours.

It was a disappointing day; not that the horses did not race well, just that our expectations were so high with two really good chances in the Cox Plate – Rock Kingdom finished eighth and won $100,000 in prizemoney and, of course, Manhattan Rain finished second to So You Think, pocketing $440,000 in prizemoney. The hardest thing for all concerned is that you're not in the winner's circle.

After the races we caught the 6pm flight back to Sydney, then went straight from the airport to the wedding of Madeleine, daughter of my best friend, Lea (Stracey). The wedding was at Palm Beach, Sydney, where Kate and Luke flew the flag until the rest of the family arrived. I met Lea at a birthing clinic some 28 years ago and we have been firm friends ever since. Not to be at her darling daughter Madeleine's wedding was sad, but at least we made it for the speeches. She is a Grecian princess and the groom and his attendants looked smart. Eventually, at 1.30am, a very tired *Lady Trainer* fell into bed.

TUESDAY, OCTOBER 27

Today darling Rob, Lea and Bruce (Stracey) and racing manager Kate Grimwade all made the trek with me to Makybe Stud, the picturesque property near Geelong owned by Tony Santic, where the great mare Makybe Diva now resides. We enjoyed a quick cuppa and a yummy chicken sandwich before we inspected all the yearlings for next year's Magic Millions, Easter and Melbourne Premier sales. After two hours taking in the equine beauty we viewed the 200,000 young trees that Tony and his wife Deslee had planted. Today was a glorious sunny jewel of a day and the grass swayed under a gentle breeze as the yearlings slept in their paddocks. It was bliss. We enjoyed a delicious lunch presented by the local caterers and we all ate far too many sandwiches with yours truly feeling like Porky Pig!

WEDNESDAY, OCTOBER 28

My team and I saw two Purrealist foals yesterday at Makybe and they were both dead ringers for their dad, with great muscle definition and powerful hindquarter. They looked strong and precocious types. Everyone is always looking for the more precocious get-up-and-run yearlings and most people love the progeny of this first-season sire.

Nash Rawiller is working hard at winning this year's Sydney jockeys' premiership. I see great determination from this jockey in difficult times, as he has been bouncing the ball over the past few weeks, travelling from Melbourne to Sydney and back, yet he is always at the track to ride work. No doubt this type of regime helps keep his weight down and has him at the top of his game. There isn't a jockey in Sydney who has a better strike rate and I'm hoping Nash can put this into play over the next four days at Flemington.

On Saturday at Flemington the stable will have two Group 1 representatives, Gold Water in the Myer Classic and Viking Legend in the Victoria Derby. No horse goes into the Derby with better credentials than the son of Elvstroem – he has finished in the first three at his past four starts. There is much debate whether the Derby should be reduced from 2500 metres to a more fashionable 2000 metres, as has happened in France, and in some cases back to 1800 metres in America. I'm probably one of the few who think it should stay at the distance. It's a great spectacle and, interestingly, is invariably won by a precocious three-year-old that has the ability to stay.

THURSDAY, OCTOBER 29

Mark Newnham was impressed with the unraced Redoute's Choice filly Cubism at Randwick, saying it was his best of the morning and he liked her very much. This remark was quite coincidental, as last night we dined at the renowned Vue De Monde in Little Collins Street in Melbourne. We always find time to have one meal a year in this fine restaurant and last night we had the pleasure of having a private room with a table big enough to be a dance floor. The seats were covered in numbers taken from the back of the seats at the MCG, a novel idea I must say. One had to be a little more robust in one's conversation because of the distance from one side of the table to the other. We were visited by chef Shannon Bennett, who informed me he owned a share in the above-mentioned Cubism. Shannon proceeded to ask me how the filly was going and whether she could win a race. It was like exchanging recipes, with me telling him about all the different things his filly had been doing. I was admiring the rather arty wall in the restaurant when the maitre d' explained that when Shannon was having lunch with his family, eating chops and barbecue sauce (doesn't sound too extravagant, but very tasty), he made a design with the barbecue sauce on his plate and took a photograph, and there was his new design for his original tableware.

Viking Legend has come through his grades and has raced against most of the Derby field beating many of them on his way to Flemington. Tom Simpson, our physio, found a little tightness over the back of the colt and worked on it, saying by Saturday he will be jumping out of his skin. So will the owners if we can win the coveted Group 1 prize!

Brightexpectations goes straight into a Group 3 race at his very first start. Very rarely do I do this and it is only if I have a good two-year-old. Nash and Blake are as keen as mustard to ride him, but as we all know only one jockey can be there on race day. Steve (Dennett) suggested I flip a coin, as that way neither would feel as though he had been hard done by.

Philip and Patty Campbell run a very hands-on organisation at Blue Gum Farm, at Euroa, with three very active stallions. Elvstroem, at $27,500, is the standout boy. He is a magnificent horse with tremendous size, great shoulder and hindquarter with a deep girth and wonderful presence. Already admiring of him, I was absolutely bowled over after seeing him in the flesh. Around the paddocks we drove and Tahni had gathered all the yearlings into yards, so we were literally face-to-face with 30 youngsters. Sarah shut the gates and kept us well informed. The weather has been glorious and perfect for looking at yearlings.

FRIDAY, OCTOBER 30

I had a nice conversation with Flemington track manager Mick Goodie today. He told me he walked the track at 7am, 9.30am, 1pm and finally with us at 4pm. Four times would he walk the circumference of this mighty racetrack. I asked Mick where he lived and he told me he lived on course. What a great shame the AJC track manager cannot be as accessible by living on course.

Last night I attended two very glamorous events in Melbourne. The first was the Louis Vuitton spring racing cocktail party, where everyone looked gorgeous, including Megan Gale and Lara Bingle, who wore the cutest space odyssey outfit. Michael Clarke, her beau, showed off his cute hairstyle and the pair made a super couple. I gave a quick talk about how great the quality of fashion is, plus a few valued tips before being whisked off to Flemington to the Chairman's Dinner. The VRC does a fabulous job. The dinner was held in a smaller auditorium than normal, but that was because of economic pressures when they were originally planning the event – next year, with the 150th running of the Melbourne Cup, all extra dollars will be aimed at making it the best carnival ever.

Olivia Newton-John was the star attraction and what a beautiful woman she is, having fought the dreaded cancer. She looked pretty in a divine outfit and spoke of how important it was to have funding and how they are trying to raise $150 million to build a new state-of-the-art hospital in Melbourne. She then came out in a cheeky black sequin outfit with the star auction item a serenade from Olivia to a special person. One man bid $33,000 and generously gave the prize to the 'Cups King', Bart Cummings. I left early at 10.15pm, but trainer Mark Kavanagh told me this morning at the track that it was so touching to see Olivia sing to Bart and his darling wife Val.

Why was there such a difference from today at Rosehill to when Chinkara Dancer trialled a week ago at Randwick and ran wide on the home turn (when last of six runners)? Well, I had her ridden by the same person each day and had a bubble-cheeker applied to the left hand side of her bridle (a small piece of rubber that presses into the side of the horse's cheek when she wants to lay out). We do not need to use it very often, and the desired effect was achieved today – Chinkara Dancer won the six-horse trial by a length and a half.

MONDAY, NOVEMBER 2

After the third race at Flemington on Saturday, Mick Goodie walked the track so I asked Blake and Nash to accompany him. Nash's jockey brother Brad joined in. Only one took a going stick, and that was Nash, who never left Mick's side – I happened to watch them from the stand through my binoculars. Nash is so keen to acquire knowledge but, then again, he has maturity on his side being a decade older than young Blake.

The best racing in the world is the four-day carnival at Flemington. The VRC does a remarkable job in beautifying its racecourse, with facilities second to none. The flowers and marquees are magnificent, and the beautifully dressed men and women are enough to take one's breath away. I have been coming here for many years and I could only admire the spectacle and grandeur of the day on Saturday, Victoria Derby day. Viking Legend was third in the Derby, won by Monaco Consul from Extra Zero, and Gold Water finished well back in the Myer Classic after racing at the front of the field. The brilliant mare Typhoon Tracy won it.

WEDNESDAY, NOVEMBER 4

I made a decision yesterday after watching the Melbourne Cup without having a runner in it to have Robbie work harder on finding us some lovely stayers. He's already put his running shoes on this year and found Herculian Prince, who will have his first Australian start this Saturday with Kathy O'Hara in the saddle. He's now found and purchased an exciting three-year-old, Descarado, who will be set for the AJC Derby. Descarado is by the hot-pot staying sire High Chaparral, sire of Monaco Consul and the Cox Plate winner So You Think. It's interesting that the spelling of both horses' names is not quite correct. Could this be a New Zealand trait? It is quite amusing. Robyn (Hartney, racing manager) tells me that when she asked for a rating on Herculian Prince, Racing NSW took an age to come back with the answer. Robyn called to ask what the problem was and was told Racing NSW couldn't find the horse anywhere. Robyn explained the unique spelling of the horse and the problem was solved immediately.

I can't wait to get back to my beloved Randwick after the Flemington carnival. Not because I don't like being in Melbourne and training at Flemington, but I much prefer the challenge of a big team. Getting them in my mind, interacting with the riders, the fast tempo ... all of that gets me going. The stable has had a very quiet carnival and it's frustrating.

Despite that, I must ask, "How special is the VRC?" My girlfriend Lea enjoyed her birthday at the Cup on Tuesday. To celebrate, Susie Loewy in my office had asked Kelly at the Chairman's Club to organise flowers and balloons. The flowers consisted of the most beautiful yellow roses with two golden horseshoes and balloons spraying out of the middle. Placed at the centre of our table it was just superb. After our main meal we enjoyed a little chocolate cake with happy birthday and a couple of candles – not too many!

Everywhere you go in Melbourne you see famous faces. I met up with Kate and Luke and Tom and his girlfriend Hoda (Vakili) for dinner. Kate had been covering fashions in the birdcage for *The Sun-Herald*. She looked more like a model than a fashion writer, wearing an off-the-shoulder peach-coloured satin top partnered by a cream full-fitting skirt. Add to that a matching coloured straw hat, courtesy of the genius Nerida Winter, with the most amazing shoes. She must have had them off under the table when having dinner, as when we departed the restaurant her little feet were crammed back into them. I pointed to my sensible, boring footwear and she said, "Beauty is pain, Mum." I had to tell her that when she is 50 or older she might not think quite the same.

Continuing our round of yearling inspections took us to Eliza Park, where the yearling manager Frank Oliver informed us there were three farms and he managed the one that catered for the babies. They have a lovely compact parade ring and the babies walked out as though they had done it all their life. On to Erinvale Thoroughbreds, where five yearlings paraded in an outstanding barn environment that has a high ceiling, which is lovely and cool for the young horses to rest and grow.

FRIDAY, NOVEMBER 6

Jill Mooratof, wife of George, owner of the retired Group 1 winner Bentley Biscuit, wrote to Jane Abercrombie in my office:

> Just for anyone interested, Bentley Biscuit is now living in Terrey Hills (a northern suburb of Sydney some 25km from the GPO) and is being re-trained as an eventer with James Meurer (an expert on natural horsemanship), whom I believe has done quite a bit of work with Gai's horses in the past and Biscuit was well known to him.

It is quite fascinating watching James work so calmly teaching the horse to just relax and enjoy life without any pressure. Biscuit has a few issues, but James is quietly and confidently working him through all the scary things out there in the bush. Biscuit loves his walks.

There was no grass available for gallops at Randwick this morning and the dirt track has not completely settled since renovation, so the whole team trotted, cantered and visited the pool. I have engaged Queenslander Alan Davies, who is the expert on the High Performance Galloping Machine, and he is working with several of my boys and girls training them in the technique of this remarkable fitness enhancer. Thank goodness there are two machines in our stable, otherwise I would not be able to keep the horses at their peak condition. The dirt should be back to normal by early next week and I would rather err on the side of caution and not gallop on it until then. American dirt specialist Steve Wood said to me a few months ago that it takes about 10 days to settle after a renovation.

I was not aware of any of the AJC or STC committee members being present at Flemington this week when Shocking won the Melbourne Cup. But if they were there, I hope they took copious notes on the professionalism of the committee and the staff. I found myself writing down all the things I saw and that I would like to see at Randwick or Rosehill. It's the little touches that make visiting Flemington so special and why sponsors love being part of the carnival. With tough economic times, race clubs have to bend over backwards to make their carnivals something to die for.

CHAPTER 7

The road well-travelled to the yearling sales

MONDAY, NOVEMBER 9

Jumped on a plane yesterday morning for Queensland with Lea Stracey, Kate Grimwade and young Englishman Hugo Palmer, who is learning the ropes with me. Jon Haseler, was waiting for us and whisked us off to his marvellous stud, Glenlogan Park, in beautiful Beaudesert. The new colt on the scene is Real Saga. Manager Steve Morley asked me if I had seen much of the colt when he was racing and I said, "Only his tail." Steve explained to all of us he has been unbelievably popular and his book could have been filled three times over. We viewed the elder statesman Show A Heart. What a remarkably consistent stallion. He's a magnificent horse who really stamps his progeny: massive bone, big strong chests and powerful rumps.

Steve, acting as our tour guide, has wasted no time in programming 11 studs today. My only request is that *The Lady Trainer* and team are watered and fed as many times as we stop. By the end of the day we end up being like stuffed piggies. Not only did we see two glorious fillies at Murray and Sue Murdoch's farm, but the sandwiches and pineapple juice were to die for. Murray and Sue are perfectionists and it shows in every blade of grass and the meticulous way they look after their horses.

Driving over the gap towards Warwick is like a scene out of *Lord of the Rings;* the mist, the trees and thick forest, and the mountains are almost volcanic in shape. The hospitality has been second to none. Each stud has very much its own flavour, but one thing the team agrees on is the great bone and substance of the young horses.

A new day has dawned and Hugo and Kate are busily entering data from yesterday's stud visits. Each horse seen has a notation made on it, then we confer with vet Greg Nash as he starts his rounds at the Magic Millions. He already has viewed many of the yearlings while X-raying. Denise Martin could not syndicate a horse without having an X-ray result. All I'm looking for is a horse that can stand up to training. I don't mind if it's slightly over at the knee, as long as it moves fluidly and hits the ground correctly. No horse is perfect.

One of the true highlights was our last farm, where John Bottrell had one yearling to show us. His wife had just that day returned from open-heart surgery, so he had two major events happening (wife coming home and *The Lady Trainer* arriving), but John was there to bring out a Red Dazzler colt. I asked him if he had any others. He proceeded, with his breaker Jay, to show us his other yearlings. They were all marvellous at figure eights. Jay has done a grand job, as they could all turn on a sixpence.

One of my favourite places to visit is Raheen Stud, where Basil Nolan snr, wife Di and Basil jnr) give us a grand display of their well-bred and well-grown yearlings. You do have to be a bit of a mountain goat, but maybe that's why their horses have such good bone. They are bred in elevated conditions and they all looked healthy and athletic.

We went to lunch at Eureka Stud with Colin McAlpine, "King of the Darling Downs", and his son Scott and wife Grania. The McAlpines stand Red Dazzler, a Red Ransom horse who has stamped his first crop of youngsters remarkably well. After viewing yearlings, the stallion was led down by young Dale. Not a whinny or a scream. He just showed himself off.

The stud tour is in the final stages. Last night we stayed at Ron and Debbie Gilbert's Highgrove Stud and a foal was born (by Redoute's Choice out of Angelic Smile, making him a half-brother to the Group winner Fravashi). I had asked whether there would be any chance that Lea, Kate and I could have our nails done at the local beauty parlour at day's end. Debbie organised for the beauty parlour to come to Highgrove and Nicki, the most capable of manicurists, told me my skin was terribly dry and I would have to exfoliate. She didn't stop at me – she moved on to Lea and Kate – rubbing this substance into our hands then wrapping us in Gladwrap so we looked like Daleks. I felt like I was back on the *Doctor Who* set. Then she filed and pared our cuticles and nails and we all felt downright gorgeous. In the midst of this, Colin, Highgrove's stud manager ran in to say the foal was being born. We all rushed into the front paddock where the bonny colt popped out with Colin and Steve's assistance. Most of the party of 15 had not witnessed a birth before, so it was so exciting for them and a highlight of the trip.

THURSDAY, NOVEMBER 12

Back at Randwick today after inspecting the yearlings at studs, and I felt like a pig in mud. With Tania (Rouse, assistant trainer) by my side, we inspected every horse as they came out as I need to readjust them in my mind.

Common Objective will be back wearing blinkers in the Gosford Gold Cup next Wednesday. I took them off several months ago, planning to extend him and get him to relax in his races, but it has had the reverse effect. He has been out of the winners' circle for some time. Mark Kavanagh made the comment that Melbourne Cup winner Shocking could not win a race if he was not in blinkers.

MONDAY, NOVEMBER 16

Many wonder why I chose to start off such a talented three-year-old in Hidden Gem in a Maiden at the provincials, after his devastating four-length victory under Mark Newnham as $1.60 favourite at Kembla Grange on Saturday. I have enjoyed great success over the years sending these types of horses to the provincials. Next step is the non-metro age races, which are a great idea and give the owner and trainer and horse time to have two bites of the cherry, meaning you can win your maiden like Hidden Gem did and then come to town, as he will do on December 3.[31]

WEDNESDAY, NOVEMBER 18

Gulliver's Travels have nothing on jockey Neil Paine, who recently visited the biggest city in central China, Wuhan, which is in the process of becoming the country's racing capital – it has about 10 million people and is developing a complex similar to Sha Tin in Hong Kong. I asked Neil what it's like to ride there and he said it was hysterical, as the fastest time they run is one minute 35 seconds for the 1200 metres! They run about 15 seconds to the furlong, which is so slow, because of the incredibly heavy sand.

It's great fun visiting the studs around Scone. The one thing that stands out is the professionalism of the studmasters and their assistants and handlers – some of whom are only in their late teens yet lead these strong colts and often wayward fillies.

---

31 Hidden Gem went on to race on the Kensington track on December 11, not December 3 – Nash Rawiller rode him into fifth place as the $1.90 favourite.

At Arrowfield today one young lass was trodden on and Steve Irwin quickly stepped in to take over the parade of the colt. Sam Fairgray scooped up the young lass in an example of chivalry personified and when we were leaving she had her foot in a bucket of ice. I remember falling off a pony, which shows my capability as a rider, and was trodden on when he landed on my leg. The leg blew up like a balloon and the doctor said RICE – rest, ice, compression and elevation. Hopefully the lass will be back at work, as I was, in a very short time.

Gerry Harvey's Baramul Stud was next cab off the rank and manager Paul Thompson is always marvellous, informative and wonderfully obliging. His team is extremely good at preparing the yearlings, and one that took my eye was a lovely filly by General Nediym from the Danehill mare Wandane. This youngster is a half-sister to a smart filly I train, April In Venice (by More Than Ready). 'The General' was used to the hilt during EI, so it's no wonder the poor old fella fell off his perch – he must have had every second mare available visiting him. (General Nediym died of colic in January 2009.)

Gerry's stud houses 800 horses, all owned by him; his partners in Magic Millions, Rob Ferguson and John Singleton, prefer to concentrate on the boutique type of stud.

The next stop was Widden, where the freshman sires are considered to be among the breeding forces of the southern hemisphere. Champion two-year-old Sebring, the fastest three-year-old in Australia, Northern Meteor, and, of course, Strada, Stratum and Snippetson, all reside here. It would have to be one of the most picturesque and truly beautiful grazing areas in Australia, with the rugged cliff echoing gunshots of Captain Thunderbolt in my imagination. Amazing blue skies sweep the valley that rolls before us.

Our final port of call was Patinack Farm at Sandy Hollow, where we viewed one of the surprise yearling drafts of the Magic Millions sale. All were beautifully presented and looked terrific.

THURSDAY, NOVEMBER 19

We are on the road back from the stud tour of Scone where Kate, Lea, Hugo and I have inspected more than 600 yearlings. From my point of view, the visits give me a great opportunity to catch up and hear what the breeders have to say. Discussions range from views on racing, programming and stallions, and those running the studs are also extremely interested to hear what my team and I have been up to, which is part and parcel of learning and building relationships, which both parties clearly enjoy.

At this morning's gallops we were all under a little pressure because four of our jocks have gone to Hayman Island: Kathy O'Hara, Blake Shinn, Neil Paine and Mark Newnham won the trip in a raffle, as I mentioned a couple of months back. They asked some time ago if they could be missing in action in November for four days and I told them to go ahead. It seemed a million miles away then but, of course, time flies. Nash (Rawiller) just got on with the job, as did Steve (O'Halloran), Scott (Henley), Brenton (Avdulla), Johnny (Livingstone), Ranjeet (Singh) and our new French rider Nacim (Dilmi). When 'Damo' (Damien Gaffney) saw the list he said, "No way will we get through all these before the dirt closes at 6.15am." Well, thanks to brilliant organisation by Lofty (Brett Killion), the smooth flow of horses and everyone in the middle, we did.

I cannot understand the big hoo-ha about the heat at Rosehill on Saturday, and the more the press wrote about it the fewer people showed up to the races. The Sydney Turf Club must have been rather disappointed with the lacklustre crowd, with people dissuaded from stepping out in the horror weather conditions. They didn't label us a sunburnt country for nothing. People make such a thing about the horses getting too hot.

There was a statement made just recently that there are too many racecourses in NSW and that they are like post offices – everywhere. I must say I thought it an overstatement. One of the great tragedies of modern-day racing is that the authorities are so keen to reduce the number of racecourses. It's sad for country followers of racing, as the racecourse has always been a great meeting place. All rationalisation does is stop people going to the races.

I had a good chat to boutique Queensland breeder Ron Gilbert, who was talking about the nursery habits of newly born foals. Whatever Ron and Debbie do at their Highgrove property, all I can say is they do a top rate job, having only been in the breeding business a short while. Ron made a statement when we were visiting recently that the foals that jump up quickly, immediately after being born, are invariably their best. This has been on my mind ever since and I couldn't stop myself from asking which foal was the quickest to get off the ground. As the yearling he named had looked particularly precocious, I put it in my little black book and committed it to memory.

I've not been happy with the way the team has been going, so I made an executive decision on my return from Melbourne to sharpen the horses' training. Years ago Lloyd Williams rang my Dad and said, "Tommy, my trainer is in a drought and can't win a race. What would you do?" TJ said, "Sprinting, Lloyd, sprinting." Well that's exactly what I'm doing with my team, as most are carrying too much condition with that sharp turn of foot missing. Instead of going back to the mile and a quarter the horses are going straight on at the mile, enjoying short and sharp tone-up work without going over the long distances pounding the ground. It's amazing how after a few gallops horses such as Princess Quality, who reminds me rather of the "magic pudding", is coming to hand superbly. Another is Rockwood, who really put in one of the nicest pieces of work I've seen for some time. Nash let him slip over 600 metres this morning and the master horseman was extremely happy.[32]

WEDNESDAY, NOVEMBER 25

Mr Trinidad wearing blinkers, and with Ranjeet Singh riding, slipped up 600 metres. I told him I wanted to hear an Indian war cry and young Ranjeet, who hails from Rajasthan in the north-west of India, obliged. This big lanky son of Encosta De Lago showed me some signs of being a racehorse.

Schneider can be a bit of a worm as he wiggles around the track and has a tendency not to gallop straight. He was greatly improved this morning, wearing blinkers and with a stronger rider on his back. The most important thing in training horses is to get them to concentrate on the task at hand: being a racehorse. They also need to be in possession of speed because if they don't have a cruising speed and a turn of foot it is impossible for them to win races. Not all are naturally endowed with these attributes and there are many times when a trainer has to teach them to pick up and travel on the bit so they can cruise through their work. Schneider and Mr Trinidad are the types of horses that need that bit of assistance, but when the penny drops it can give the trainer and owners the greatest pleasure.[33]

I loved Seventh Reason from the moment I saw him at the farm and then at the Magic Millions sale. He knows he's had a kill (winning a 1600-metre Maiden at Kembla on Saturday). It's funny when horses win how they distinctively take a step up and have an air about them – a confidence like Seventh Reason had this morning.[34]

Antiguan has had a turn-around since last Sunday. When my horses parade for their owners at open day each Sunday I look very carefully at them and I thought this gelding's coat did not look quite right. I must say he has done an absolute treat and I expect him to run a really good race on Saturday at Newcastle.[35]

---

32 Princess Quality had two trials before finishing fourth in a Randwick 1100-metre race on December 26; Rockwood won a Kensington 1400-metre race on November 28, lumping 62.5kg.
33 Unfortunately, Mr Trinidad and Schneider were not up to it and were despatched from the stable.
34 After fourths at his next two starts, Seventh Reason won again at Canterbury on December 23.
35 Antiguan, the $1.90 favourite, won over 1200 metres, ridden by Mark Newnham.

More Strawberries, the half-sister to All American, is a particularly beautiful filly. 'Singo' specialises in beautiful females and in this case she's four-legged, big, black and bold and Strawberry Hills bred. For a boutique establishment, Strawberry Hills has one of the best strike rates (runners to winners), especially Group 1 winners. I love doing business with John. He's straight down the line and is passionate about racing (my sort of man). The filly jarred up slightly after her work this morning, so she is off to the paddock and won't be seen on the racetrack until February next year.

MONDAY, NOVEMBER 30

I love the new benchmark system (where horses' ratings can go down as well as up) because it gives horses like Rockwood, who has been out of form, a chance to get back into the winners' circle. He and Joku (who deadheated for second) were the best horses in Saturday's race and that's why they were weighted with 62.5kg. Punters ran a mile from them fearing they are carrying too much pudding and even the owners are worried when they see the huge impost. The owners of Rockwood, however, were laughing all the way to the bank with the gelding showing his superiority to score by a half-length, starting at $8, aided by a brilliant ride by Blake. He had the horse carrying the weight while he moved his arms and legs in unison as he rode the horse out. After the race I pulled Brenton (who rode Joku) aside to watch Blake in action and told him he has to do the same in order to make the weight move with the horse.

Rob and I departed Sydney yesterday morning and we are both suffering from traveller's derrière – too long sitting in planes. We landed in Miami (I can see where the Gold Coast got its inspiration from). We are staying on the waterfront close to the racetrack and the person we've come to visit, trainer Wesley Ward, lives in a condominium next to our hotel. We rang him tonight and he came over straight away to share his thoughts and a meal. He is an interesting person and a great mate and admirer of the American Hall of Fame trainer Bobby Frankel, who died earlier this month. Wesley breaks in all his own yearlings. He had success at Royal Ascot this year and is planning his assault on the Hong Kong and Australian legs of the Global Sprint Challenge with five-year-old Cannonball, who was second in the Golden Jubilee Stakes (1200 metres) at Ascot.

TUESDAY, DECEMBER 1

We are learning much from the wonder man Wesley Ward. What a remarkable trainer we met this morning at the track, which is only up the road from our hotel. His barn is one of the older types where everything works amazingly efficiently. The horses are walked for 10-15 minutes before they step out on to the sand-type track. The horses are far bigger in condition than what we see in Australia but, as many of you know, the trainers are allowed to use steroids, the diuretic Lasix, the anti-inflammatory Bute and many other drugs, all of which are banned substances in Australian racing and have a withholding period of around three weeks, whereas in America it is approximately four days.

I think we have a far better system for the care and maintenance of our horses, but one thing the Americans do well is teach their horses gate speed. I asked Wesley how many times his youngsters visit the barriers and he said he could not count, telling me they go again and again and again, becoming so familiar with the structure that even if another horse plays up they don't blink an eye. All his two-year-olds work over a furlong (200 metres) in the early part of the season and progress to two furlongs by the end of the season. No one in America is more prolific with two-year-old winners than Wesley and he trains them to be two-furlong specialists. He told me quite clearly they are so brilliant and fast over two furlongs that by the time the others have caught up they are well past the winning post.

"Gai, you train them to run 1000 metres, whereas I train mine to run two furlongs and they still beat them at the 1000 metres," Wesley said. Six two-year-old races have been run at Gulfstream Park, Florida, this season and his 11 starters have produced six winners and five seconds and, therefore, five quinellas. What a remarkable effort, as is his 62 two-year-old winners overall this season.

The American horse is so well educated and there rarely is a hiccup at the barriers. Oh, if this could only happen in Australia – not that we are the poorer horsemen, but having an experienced breaker like Matty Bathis out in the middle at Randwick educating the young horses is a thing of the past. Very few go to the little barriers, and I believe every two-year-old entering the system should have a barrier certificate from the stewards at the small barriers. Only when ticked off as passing all the criteria (Are they relaxed? Do they load quickly? Have they jumped well?) would they go on to Friday jump-outs. But most go straight to the big barriers and are poorly handled, hit with whips, bustled along … that's what we call horsemanship.

After the track we travelled to the farm Wesley rents. It was a most fascinating part of the day. The boys and girls who worked at the track met us there. The young horses cantered two laps of the sand and one bucked off one of the kids. Wesley quickly took control and, despite wearing only a pair of loafers with jeans and having no helmet or vest, he displayed great horsemanship to jump aboard and the colt behaved himself perfectly. Then an amazing long trailer rolled up with half a dozen yearlings that hadn't been ridden yet arrived. They weren't in stalls, but in the one area on the float. Getting them off was a masterstroke. I imagine they were terrified, but after much prodding and pushing they were eased down the ramp, saddles put on, and on the kids jumped. They rolled out on to the track, displaying how well the Americans educate their horses. This is the daily trackwork regime for Wesley and his team and I felt privileged Rob and I were able to see such a masterful horseman. I can't wait to get home and implement some of what I've seen today.

WEDNESDAY, DECEMBER 2

Another day at the track in Florida presented a slow morning as everything galloped or pace-worked the day before. Most of the horses walked, which is something I would never do back home – I trot and canter them, or they go off the pony the day after a race or, on occasions, if they were going to provincial tracks and it had been hot.

A pool for the horses is something one never sees over here, but it would be of great assistance to their training as the horses are much bigger in condition than what we see at home and their breakdown rate is very high.

After our visit to the track and a long chat with Wesley we headed off to have lunch with Brian Lynch, an Aussie now training in Canada and the US. Brian, from Wagga in NSW, has promised Wesley a trip to his home town when they come 'Down Under' for the Lightning Stakes at Flemington early next year. Wesley is confident the Group 1 Lightning is a race his horse Cannonball can win and I have little doubt he can give it one hell of a shake. Over lunch we discussed different training techniques and it was a great privilege to chew the cud with like-minded intelligent people from different countries. It's the only way to progress and learn.

Back to the farm and the babies (brumbies) had been herded off the truck with all bar one being clipped head to toe. They were hit with tranquillisers and their winter coats were removed because it is very warm in Florida. After being shampooed and hosed they were attached to a lead on the walking machine. Several got away, but they had a pony or two in attendance to round them up. It's amazing how accepting these youngsters are.

I saw my first in-your-face mountain lion in a cage on the farm. I'm not sure if I agree with this policy (of confinement), but gosh they are magnificent.

We enjoyed a most interesting time visiting the training track on which Brian prepares his horses for Frank Stronach, owner of Gulfstream Park racecourse. What a truly magnificent complex. Wesley says nothing gets a cold for the weather is always warm; if they do get a sniffle it only lasts a day. Up north, they can be sick for weeks and have to be given penicillin.

Rob and I are off to visit the Fort Lauderdale Art Museum – a little culture for *The Lady Trainer* – to see the work of the famous American artist/caricaturist Norman Rockwell. Fort Lauderdale is quite glorious with waterways on either side and oversized yachts. The depth of wealth in America is mindboggling. One thing I found interesting is that all the cars have number plates behind and not in front. I find it an eye-opening experience travelling overseas, as everything is so different from home.

All the carnival horses are back in work at Randwick, including Rock Kingdom, Manhattan Rain, Viking Legend and Swift Alliance, who braved the wet conditions and strode over 1200 metres in steady fashion. Swift Alliance has bulked up and looks a treat and I'm looking forward to him contesting some of the major sprints this autumn.

THURSDAY, DECEMBER 3

We enjoyed an easy day viewing seals and alligators on a tour of a wilderness park in the Everglades. The alligators were huge – they say they do not eat people, but I wouldn't trust them as far as I could throw them. We zapped through the waterways with water lilies flying everywhere. All went without a hitch, then we mounted a huge military-style land cruiser, which was elevated so we could see all the wildlife, including buffaloes, wild horses and emus. By this time I was starting to doze – it doesn't take much to put *The Lady Trainer* to sleep. On to lunch and there was much yankee-doodle-dandy, with the portion sizes enormous. No wonder there are so many overweight people. The amount of food, on the whole, is excessive, although the figures we saw in Miami are comparatively neat.

I was delighted with the win of Essence Of Success at Hawkesbury yesterday because it brought together again a very successful partnership with Josh Parr. I was his boss when he was apprenticed to me, and he has made the graduation from apprentice to jock very well, something few apprentices manage. He is able to ride aggressively, which suited this daughter of Encosta De Lago. Weighing in at just 462kg, there is not much of her, but she showed enormous courage to work hard early from her wide gate and still have enough left to score by one-and-a-half lengths. She may not be ready for the city tracks this preparation – I like to give most Gooree horses a light first prep, winning a couple at provincial level then moving them on to bigger things at their second and third preparations.

Steve (O'Halloran) is adamant the Punters' Club pal Brightexpectations will win on Sunday, following his final gallop this morning. I immediately rang part-owners Lea and Bruce Stracey and told them to get to Wyong as he'll be the horse to beat.

Shadow Assassin was a complete nightmare when he ran last on the Kensington track on Saturday, after playing up behind the barrier and missing the start hopelessly. The stewards asked Tania (Rouse, my assistant trainer) why he did not lead. Tania explained he had a mind of his own and had a rather fragile and delicate disposition if he was upset. This morning, with head bowed and striding strongly, he found the line in 11.3 seconds in his final piece of work before Sunday. I asked Frank (Fitchett, foreman at Desert War stable) to lunge him as I thought he was far too fresh on Saturday, prancing around with his tail raised. I didn't think he had his mind firmly on the job and ran accordingly.

FRIDAY, DECEMBER 4

After a long day travelling, Rob and I arrived in Aspen. Many of the great sports people of the world have homes in this glorious town and they enjoy the wonderful skiing conditions, just as Rob and I do.

MONDAY, DECEMBER 7

Two very important events occurred on the weekend. Firstly, Jane Abercrombie married Danny Cully and was given away by her father *and* by workmates Alison Schofield, Robyn Hartney, Steve Dennett, Kathy Williams, Tania Rouse and Louise O'Halloran. I was thinking of Jane and wishing I could have been there to throw some rice and shed tears of joy. Any of you who have had the pleasure of dealing with Jane would know the amazing person she is; she treats everyone as though they are the most important owners in the stable and no matter how difficult the situation might be she rides through it and helps the owners accordingly. She is always pleasant, has a great sense of humour and has been the backbone of my stable for the past 17 years. When Jane returns to work you will be able to call her Mrs Cully.

Then, at Wyong, Brightexpectations won the $200,000 Magic Millions. Part-owners Joe Manning – the master of Littledale Lodge where many of our horses have agisted over the years – and his wife Lou were at Jane's wedding. Robyn told me they were able to drop in to watch the race on the way to the reception. Other owners include my best mate Lea and her husband Bruce. They were on hand at Wyong and Lea said, "It was unbelievable. I can't tell you how excited we were." All the other owners, including my dear friend Arthur Menzies, were jumping for joy, as were all the *Telegraph* readers who backed Brightexpectations – he is the paper's Punters' Club horse. What a lovely two-year-old to be involved in. This colt is by the leading sire in Australia, More Than Ready, and there are exciting times ahead.

I've come to the conclusion that, in America, TV has done to death the story on Tiger Woods and his poor wife. We now know every gruesome detail of Tiger's sex life – what hope does this couple have?

If I watch another gridiron show I'll scream, but the worst aspect of watching TV in America is the amount of violence that is recaptured during the night. An endless amount of muggings and stabbings is shown. No wonder there is so much violence in the modern day when it is broadcast 24 hours.

The thing I liked best was the weather man putting his umbrella up in the studio, with fake snow falling, while he was giving his weather forecast for the day. Such a cute idea.

Rob and I are sitting in front of an open fire in Aspen in a restaurant called Little Mel. There is great value in the restaurants as the Aussie dollar is strong and the recession in America is keeping the prices down. We're just waiting for Tom and Kate and their partners Hoda and Luke to arrive to enjoy the next 10 days skiing.

THURSDAY, DECEMBER 10

To say the weather in Aspen is cold is the understatement of the year. Today was truly the most freezing day on the slopes. I had so much gear on I felt like the Michelin man. Tom is an awesome skier; he doesn't have much time for it now with his bookmaking business, but he does go hard and fast, up and down the slopes. Kate is super at the sport and she looks a picture and will slot in with any group. Rob's been skiing for years and takes it all in his stride, while I'm a "Kembla Maiden" wallowing in the shadows of the A-graders. I get up and down most mountains, but the better-groomed and kinder slopes show me up to advantage.

The cold weather plays havoc with everything. School starts late as it's too cold for the kids to start at the normal time. All night long the machine works the roads, shovelling snow. One dares not take off one's gloves to adjust goggles when they are frozen over. How lucky we are in Australia with the sunny weather, as the people here shovel the snow away from their doorsteps every morning and it is part and parcel of their lives. There are so many different snowfields and different runs and then, of course, there is the absolute beauty of the Colorado mountains and the coastal clear air. Talk about rejuvenating days.

Back at Randwick, Captain Marvel just keeps improving. Mark Newnham put this gelding in his own black book and has been texting me from Sydney, telling me he's the most improved three-year-old in the stables. This lovely son of Catbird will trial at Rosehill on December 22.[36] Extreme Mover will be ridden by Nash Rawiller at Rosehill on Saturday. Dividing the rides between both my stable jocks (Blake Shinn is the other) is the main objective, as I like to give each of them every opportunity of winning prizemoney.[37]

I will continue to battle the elements before heading home next week. I can't wait to see the horses, my loyal staff and all my owners. I never stop thinking about the horses while I'm away, but it is nice to spend quality time with my family, as all are busy with their respective jobs.

SATURDAY, DECEMBER 12

It was great to see that the big guns Manhattan Rain, Viking Legend and Rock Kingdom enjoyed their first session of three-quarter pace. Three-year-old filly More Joyous is due to start pacework next week.

MONDAY, DECEMBER 14

While all my boys and girls are enjoying the warmth of Sydney, the Waterhouse family battles the elements at Highlands, one of the resorts close to Aspen Mountain. Today saw poor visibility and heavy snow storms with blustery winds. *The Lady Trainer* wished she was in other places. On the run, Kate said to me, "Mum, keep your legs together, you're not astride a horse." It was the best tip my darling had given me all day. Once the legs were together I powered through the powdered snow. But I can't wait to get back to Randwick to attend trackwork and the races on Saturday.

TUESDAY, DECEMBER 15

Best of the morning by far was Brightexpectations, who I firmly believe is most capable of winning the Magic Millions two-year-old race in January. He keeps improving, which is what I look for in any horse, but especially the two-year-olds. This son of More Than Ready is so unassuming; he has a stack of growing to do and you won't know him when he has a decent break after the Golden Slipper.

Stablemate Extreme Mover will more than likely head to Brisbane for his lead-up to the Magic Millions and take his place in a race named after Bruce McLachlan, an event that had been named after my dad, TJ Smith. The Queensland Turf Club informed me last year they would need to drop one of the black-type two-year-old races named after my famous father. I told them my preference was to keep the

---

36 Captain Marvel ran second in his 1030-metre trial.
37 At Rosehill, Extreme Mover won over 1100 metres, starting $1.90 favourite.

TJ Smith run over the winter carnival, as I felt it was more prestigious and, as a Group 1 race, I knew Dad would have liked that.

The More Than Ready-Multicultural filly has been sidelined for yonks – not through injury, but because the owners were not able to get a name acceptable to all parties. They put forward one slightly risque name that was tossed out and, finally, her name has arrived. It is Rardame. The two-year-old will make her debut at Rosehill trials next Tuesday.[38]

Theseo's action has been great since he returned from the property of Kim and Ryan Faulkner. Time is a great healer and the pedal bone which had given him problems last preparation is "so far, so good". The Star Thoroughbreds champ is happy to be back with the many people who love him. He won't be seen at the trials until late January.

Today was most testing, as we spent many hours on the snow. At 8am sharp at the base of Aspen Mountain the Waterhouse entourage met a group of people, got into the 'snow cat' and went off over the other side of the mountain where white powder greeted us. Quite incredibly, on my first run, I fell at every turn, prompting the guide to say, "Don't look at the trees. Go where you want to go and keep your legs together and enjoy yourself." With these tips for the second run, I felt more like poetry in motion. The snow was so soft all the way down the slope – it's moments like this you feel like you're a downhill racer.

We had lunch in a tiny hut with a dunny out the back, which reminded me very much of when I was a young girl and used to go every Christmas to Griffith. I loved working in the Griffith bookshop, where Aunt Shirley and Uncle Pat did a grand job teaching me the ropes and how to look after the customers. I remember one day, when Mum came to stay, we could hear a noise from the outside loo and we found that Mum had seen a snake. I was always wary after that about visiting the loo there.

THURSDAY, DECEMBER 17

Apprentice Ben Looker has come to the stable on loan from his master John Shelton at Grafton. Ben appears a nice, bright and willing, young man. Let's hope he can make an impression in the next few weeks when he starts to ride for the stable and other trainers in Sydney. Ben has ridden more than 170 winners around the Northern Rivers and is great value, considering his extensive experience, claiming 3kg in the city and 2kg at the provincials. Star Thoroughbreds' impressive last-start Kembla Grange winner, Kinnersley, will be Ben's first ride for the stable on December 26 at Randwick.[39]

---

38 Rardame ran second over 900 metres in her trial.
39 Kinnersley was fifth at Randwick for Nash Rawiller. Blake Shinn won on him next start, also at Randwick, on January 1.

We also have a touch of Panama with the young Spanish speaking Geovani Castillo, who is knee-high to a grasshopper. He has a lovely seat on a horse, but we might have to work a bit on his upper-body strength. From what I've seen, these boys are really superb horsemen.[40]

Viking Legend has found a girlfriend, but I wish he could leave that type of business until he goes to stud. The girl in question is Cap Dancer and she is a real stunner. Robyn (Hartney) thinks it's her four white socks that have set her apart from all the other girls. We will have to make sure the pair are kept well apart. Aren't I a spoilsport?

Joku is everyone's favourite, none more so than young Monica Barrera, the grand-daughter of Edward Cojuangco (Gooree's owner) who celebrated her birthday yesterday. Monica rides out for me each morning and in her younger years was a keen equestrian. You may have heard her dulcet tones when she answers the phone in the office a couple of mornings a week.

Rabbuka came out with two pink flowers, one on either side of his bridle, this morning. Heaven knows what the crew was up to! Nash jumped aboard the mighty gelding and said, "Hello what's going on here?" Robyn, as quick a flash, said, "He looks a pretty boy in pink, doesn't he?" Everyone enjoyed a great laugh and were even more impressed when both flowers stayed firmly intact during the gallop. This leads me to the Pink Stiletto race day, which will be held in conjunction with the Mardi Gras next year. This innovative idea by the AJC will try to capture a sizeable crowd from the people who flock to Sydney to celebrate this great party. The Mardi Gras is held only a few kilometres from the track and the Pink Stiletto concept is a sensational way to bring new blood to the races. I've heard a whisper that Clare Balding, the BBC racing commentator, may be making an appearance.

Only three weeks until the Magic Millions. This year's sale is an interesting affair, with most southern studs not wanting to be at the Gold Coast over the New Year period as the costs are astronomical – many are not showing their yearlings until January 2. With more than 1000 to view I don't know how the average trainer or agent gets to see them all. My team and I have viewed at least two-thirds of the catalogue, but we still have plenty to do before Christmas.

I live in wonderment how such a simple concept has had the greatest influence on Australian breeding. Often the best two-year-olds that come out of this sale don't have the best pedigree, but they are precocious, fast, tough, good-boned horses and, in most cases, the early foals can be your early runners. We look to have two runners

---

40 Geovani stayed only a month because of a problem with his visa.

on the Magic Millions race day on January 9 – Brightexpectations, winner of the MM Slipper at Wyong, and Extreme Mover, who won impressively by three lengths at Rosehill last Saturday.

I heard a whisper that Nicole Kidman is going to join us on a flight back to Sydney. She is not the only famous one on board, as we bumped into cricketer Shane Warne. He really does look terrific. He told me he had been to Vegas competing in a poker competition, but he was knocked out early. The rest of the time he enjoyed some shopping and relaxing. You never know who you might meet on a flight back to Sydney in the new Qantas Airbus.

When we arrived at LA airport we were greeted by a young woman working for Qantas, Megan McGreavy, who informed us that she was the great granddaughter of well-known bookmaker Arthur Singh. Rob told a funny story about how Arthur always wore an expensive Morrie Benjamin suit with the cheapest of ties. "Why?" young Megan asked. Rob replied, "He always enjoyed having soup at the races, which he would regularly spill on his tie." Megan had a giggle. It's wonderful how in this small world of the Sport of Kings you can never be far from someone who knows you.

FRIDAY, DECEMBER 18

Home, sweet home. Oh how I love the sunburnt country and glorious Sydney. The rain was pelting down when we arrived on our Airbus, which I must say is well worth travelling on with its spacious four classes and bar and celebrities galore. Nicole looked beautiful in her pyjamas and her day wear. Shane evaporated once on the plane, but he could've been partying at the bar above. Yes, there were two levels with the toilets double the size.

Preparations are under way for Christmas at Tulloch Lodge this Sunday. A letter has been received from the North Pole confirming Santa will be coming at 11am sharp. I wonder if he's coming on the Airbus? Also confirmed are a number of his helpers. Santa will deliver presents to all his dear children and Christmas carols will be sung by the choir from the St George Coptic Orthodox Church. A beautiful cake has been made by Joanne from the Cupcake Room. It will just melt in your mouth.

I read in the *Telegraph* today that the Wesley Ward-trained Cannonball jets into Flemington on the 29th. I've sent Wesley an email telling him not to forget my Flemington stables are available. It was really worth the time and distance we travelled to meet and look at his training methods and, although they are different from mine, it made me think long and hard on what I do with the two-year-olds because they are his specialty. Wesley will be the first American trainer to race a horse on Australian turf.

Sunday was a very special day – just like every year at Tulloch Lodge, we celebrated Christmas (five days early) with Santa, cowgirls, cowboys and stable pony, who I must say was a very popular attraction for the children. The choir from the church in Bowral Street was wonderful and sounded even better with yours truly encouraging jockeys Mark, Blake, Kathy, Neil and Nash to join in with the mothers and children as we sang the Christmas carols. I had to giggle when I saw Blake with his hand over his face, embarrassed, as I sang my way through *Hark The Herald Angels Sing*.

Viking Legend, as Tania said, "has come in from the paddock very horny." "You mean coltish," I replied. Whatever you would like to call it, he is thinking seriously about other things. The colt looks marvellous. He is big and strong and focussed when he is on the track, but has a wandering eye off the track.

In exciting news, Rob has found another stayer from New Zealand – Just A Blaze (The Gladiator-Schwepps A'blaze), a four-year-old with one win and two placings from just the four race starts, whom I purchased last week.

My driver Damien Gaffney cracked the whip as we tumbled into the car after trackwork. It was on to the helipad at Rosehill and on to the Upper Hunter Valley and George Altomonte's Corumbene Stud, the breeder of Sebring, Wager and Eagle Falls. George has been a great supporter of my stable and presents a particularly well-balanced, good-boned and athletic group of yearlings. Toby Frazer does a grand job getting the yearlings to peak at the right time.

Lea (Stracey), Hugo (Palmer) and I spilled in and out of George's four-wheel drive, going from paddock to paddock inspecting the Magic Millions and Easter draft. Then it was back into the chopper and off to David Jones.

What a master stroke from the Magic Millions to get David Jones on board as a sponsor for their race. 'Singo' felt it was time to up the ante and he certainly did that by bringing in this great retail store. I love the MM advertising campaign and the way they have made a small, one-off event into a world-class sale.

Some very important news – Damien and I have a new car. Damien got chatting to people from BMW, who said they were looking for an ambassador for their 740-series BMW. So for a month Damien and I are delighted to have the opportunity to renew our association with BMW. The colour? I thought it was champagne, but have since been told it is cashmere. BMW also sponsors the Magic Millions, so there are three prestigious brands in one fabulous event!

Montana Flyer had a stint at stud, but it wasn't to be for this mare and she is back at my Tempest Morn stable. She is still fat, but going well. Talking of fat, I'm sure Obama, the horse not the president, has been eating cupcakes or even some of that delicious Christmas decorated cake provided on Sunday at the stable. Theseo is going super and is on target to have his first trial in three weeks' time at Warwick Farm. All going well he will return to Melbourne for another Australian Cup bid and go one better, in fact a nose better! (Niconero beat Theseo by that margin in the cup last March.)

WEDNESDAY, DECEMBER 23

I had to laugh at Ben Looker at the trials yesterday. He rode Classic Intentions, who finished a long last, and I asked what he thought of the run. He said, "He might need longer and a bit more time, Gai." I said, "Ben tell me the truth. Can this horse ever win a race?" Ben replied, "Gai, I don't think so. I don't think he's any good." I had to laugh at the young man who thought I wanted to hear a positive report. Of course the truth is always the best recipe.[41]

Dan (Ganderton) gave the thumbs up to Lorne Dancer and told me he would fight out the finish on Saturday, even with the heavy impost of 64kg. One owner rang yesterday demanding why I would run his gelding with such a big weight and I told him to relax, hop on a plane, bring enough to have a bet and enjoy the day. It's funny how punters shy away from highly-weighted horses in these races.[42]

More Joyous is so well-named. She was in cruise control this morning, gliding around like only a Group 1 horse can do. It was poetry in motion.

I told young Ben I knew he didn't own a Rolls-Royce and said hopefully one day he would. I put him on Manhattan Rain and said, "This will give you a feel of what it will be like to ride in one." He came back grinning from ear to ear and said he had never ridden a more beautiful horse.

Artist Vivian Falk came with a photographer to study *The Lady Trainer*. Vivian was a finalist in the 2007 Archibald Prize with her portrait of Liberal Minister Malcolm Turnbull. She wanted to paint me at home, but I said, "No, I would rather you see me doing the thing I love the most, which is training horses." So with the wind blowing a gale, the team was snapping frantically.

Lea arrived at Randwick to meet Damien and me, and off we travelled to Reavill Farm at Freeman's Reach, about an hour from Sydney, but not before Lea looked at

---

41 Classic Intentions left the stable, unraced.
42 Lorne Dancer, ridden by Nash Rawiller and starting at $6.50, was second to Mr Unforgettable, who carried 55kg on a 53kg limit.

her Magic Millions charge Brightexpectations, who will carry our hopes on January 9. At the stud we inspected the yearlings with Danny Swain, the studmaster, who turned them out in regal form. John and Sheenah Rippon are very pleased with their draft and I was happy to give them the thumbs up as all horses were well-grown, good-boned and attractive types for all tastes.

The hottest racecourse whisper has it that a leading NSW stud has put it on Racing NSW that if it merges the two race clubs – the STC and AJC – and then sells Canterbury and Warwick Farm, it would put on a $15 million race day. I hear the Minister was very impressed and that it could become a fait accompli unless we in racing who really care about the industry do something about it. How will Sydney cope with just two tracks, Randwick and Rosehill? What a joke! The STC and AJC are doing a marvellous job and how would, or how could, the merged club do any better? I bet it couldn't.

I did two interviews for the Pink Stiletto day, which will be held at Randwick racecourse on February 26. One interviewer asked me how many pink stilettos I owned and I said, "None at the moment, but I'm sure I'll have a pair by race day!"

The two-year-old races are on everyone's mind this time of year, with the Magic Millions just around the corner and then the richest juvenile race, the Golden Slipper, being only a few months away. Racing NSW does not take the programming for two-year-olds seriously enough. We have four races programmed from December 26 to January 2 and then NOTHING until Saturday January 9 and then NOTHING until the next Saturday. How the devil do they think we can qualify for the better races? Come on ladies and gentlemen, please program us some two-year-old races midweek and at the provincials every Saturday!

TUESDAY, DECEMBER 29

Back on Christmas Eve our neighbouring streets were a hive of activity. Rob and I walked to the street famous for Christmas bling, where all the homes try to outdo each other with tinsel, glitter, flashing lights, Santas and reindeers. We decided to rate the homes on all their different kinds of bling, which was great fun. All of a sudden at the end of the street out popped Santa – a roly-poly number scampering along before he stopped to give me a lolly. Mum always taught me not to take sweets from strangers, so I was a bit apprehensive. Surprise, surprise – off came the wig and beard and standing there in front of me was a woman. She has been doing a wonderful job as Santa for the past 15 years. It was so funny chatting away with her and with the children walking past thinking 'where has all Santa's gear gone?'.

Christmas cards are wonderful to receive, but a laborious job to send out. A couple I received really stood out: Frances and Peter Stanley from New England Stud in Newmarket had a wonderful photo of them standing in the rain with their three children and their talented race filly Moneycantbuymelove; Joe and Lou Manning had a wonderful shot of them proudly holding the 2009 Darley Cootamundra Cup won by Stratofortress. Joe has been in the business all his life and the win was near and dear to his heart. Cathy Hains, Scott Whybin and their two beautiful children send family shots every year – hard to beat and it's great to see the children as they are growing up. Arthur and Charlotte Inglis, of William Inglis & Sons, sent the loveliest animated shot of their god-daughter Elizabeth Campbell, who lives in France. There was a collage of photos and a lovely letter inside. I have a great idea for next year, but you will all have to hold your breath and wait until then!

Most people know they can ring at any time via my pager service and it is answered and passed on to me. Everyone uses it – I don't have a direct line so I don't get distracted. The other day my print-out gave me a message from a John Cincotti to ring him. I didn't recognise the name and thought I would leave it as I was quite busy. Later on I decided to ring the number and when I began phoning it Damien said, "That's Singo's number." He is so on the ball. I asked for John Cincotti and 'Singo' started to laugh. He told me whenever he rings "that stupid pager service" they always get his name wrong, so he told them to spell it any way they like.

My adorable 'Bello Blog' has another tale:

> I'm in the bad books again. 'She who must be obeyed' came home from the movies and flew off the handle at me. Her girlfriend, Snowy, had put some plants at the front door with little balls on them so I thought, "Great, I'll kick them around the yard." In doing so, and without real intention, I completely undid the two little Christmas trees. I got a severe reprimand from my cranky mistress. I don't know if other dogs have the same problems with their master/mistress, but she is very hard to handle.
>
> On Christmas Day I was given a red bib by Dan, the apprentice farrier, and my mistress had some reindeer antlers, courtesy of Sonia (Dejager). When I didn't wear them, my mistress put them on her head instead and wore them all morning at trackwork, which looked very funny.

English bloodstock agent Amanda Skiffington arrives tomorrow to assist Denise Martin and me in inspecting the yearlings. She will go straight to Coolmore Stud in the Hunter with Kate Grimwade. I saw the yearlings quite some time ago and it's great to get a second opinion and bounce off each other so we can present to the owners a well-selected yearling.

Captain Marvel was very impressive, recording 34.6 seconds over 600 metres and 11 seconds flat for his final 200 metres. The gelding is on target to debut next Thursday at Wyong, but his owners are in a quandary as to whether they should sell him or race him. I advised them the amount offered from overseas interests would not buy too many horses, but then again it's nice to have the cash in the hand.[43]

Randwick races on Friday and the AJC has kindly given me permission to gallop five of my carnival horses between races. It will be great to see the champ Theseo back in action.

I'm preparing for the Magic Millions sale on the Gold Coast and packing the suitcase, ably assisted by Sonia, who will travel north with me and my entourage. It's a major job up there, where for 10 days a team of five will have Sonia playing house-mother, preparing our breakfast, getting the washing, shopping and ironing done. The hours are long as we look at numerous yearlings with my backup group next to none.

I have just flown into the Gold Coast and the Jetstar plane was more like a cattle truck. Michael Keegan was on the plane, on his way to visit his wife, friends and family. Michael and Helen were watching the TV one day a few years ago and saw an advertisement for the Magic Millions. Interested to know more, they took themselves off to the sale and bought a horse that took their eye, by Zabeel. Since then Michael has become a keen racing fan and will no doubt be cheering when his last-start winner Seventh Reason lines up on Saturday at Rosehill. Why is Kathy O'Hara not partnering this colt? Well, she was given the ride but elected to ride one for trainer Guy Walter that she had ridden at its last start. She certainly did an excellent job in the win at Canterbury and she gave a glowing report on the boy this morning after partnering him over 1400 metres. Hugh Bowman will take the ride.[44]

Group 2 winner Montana Flyer made an impressive return with an easy win in the quick time of 42.8 seconds for a trial over 740 metres at Randwick today. The mare was retired and sent to the breeding barn in June, but was unable to become a mummy so returned to the stable for another race preparation.

---

43 Captain Marvel was sold to Hong Kong after winning at Wyong.
44 At Rosehill, Seventh Reason was ninth. Kathy was second on Daad's Overtime.

The Magic Millions sale commenced today with 1000 yearlings on offer, all of whom we have viewed – starting in October and continuing right up to this week. We like to take our time inspecting them as this way I can get the horses in my mind. I also love to see how they have changed and developed – some go ahead in leaps and bounds and others fall backwards and struggle. I can tell you they are the ones you don't want to buy.

We have two great chances in the Magic Millions races on Saturday: the son of Falvelon, Extreme Mover, to be ridden by Blake Shinn; and the son of More Than Ready, Brightexpectations, to be ridden by Nash Rawiller. Hugo Palmer was left in charge of the barrier draw and unfortunately the news was not so good with the stable runners drawing 15 and 16. We gave Hugo terrible lip last night, but he copped it on the chin.

We have a young man we call 'Swop', Swaroop Tulsidas, a business student from France, who is travelling around with us, trying to learn about the selection process in buying racehorses. We also have Naomi O'Sullivan, whose uncle, Ray, is a fellow trainer at Randwick – Ray O'Sullivan and I have known each other all our lives and young Naomi has been assisting with data entry. Then there is the vet Greg Nash, trainer Gai, racing manager Kate Grimwade, bloodstock agent Amanda Skiffington and Lea.

I had to laugh. I have great admiration for breeder Judy Marheine of Stratheden Stud and when I saw her yearlings a week ago they were like small whales and too fat. I told Judy they weren't showing themselves off. Judy and her father and mother bred Assertive Lad and these excellent breeders have flown the flag successfully for the past decade. They are no different today as their draft is excellent. Yvonne Smith, the owner of Assertive Lad, has reminded me on many occasions why she bought him, saying, "He was poetry in motion."

Yesterday was a long one with Mark Newnham and his dear father picking us up at 3.30am for trackwork. Not that I'm not used to getting up early – I enjoy it, but this time of year the days are long as we are out with owners every night.

Last night we enjoyed a delightful meal at an excellent restaurant with young Tom Magnier (of Coolmore), who told a fascinating story of how Aidan O'Brien had been chosen as successor to Vincent O'Brien (no relation) to train for Coolmore in Ireland. Paul Shadden, who assisted Tom, saw this young man at a meeting and took notice of his great attention to detail and then went back and explained to the boss (Tom's father John) he was the man to engage. Aidan met John Magnier, who arrived, as Tom explained, with a list of questions a mile long. John told him to train for his clients for a year, "after which we'll know if you are able and ready" to take on the training of the Coolmore horses. It's been several years since he took over and Aidan has become the most successful trainer in Europe.

Daniel (Ganderton, whose indentures have been transferred to Paul Messara, who has stables at Randwick and Scone) was in terrible strife yesterday when, through no fault of his own, the plane he was booked on to attend a stewards' inquiry in Queensland broke down and could not leave the tarmac. Unfortunately he was not believed when he told the stewards of his predicament – Dan is a very capable young man, but I think tampering with a plane would be far beyond him. He lives to see another day and is going north tomorrow for the inquiry before riding Deer Valley, the second favourite in the 1200-metre Magic Millions three-year-old race on Saturday.[45]

FRIDAY, JANUARY 8

A great second day at the sales yesterday when I bought the Encosta De Lago-Ha Ha filly for $700,000 on behalf of Craig Thompson from Hallowell Stud in Western Australia. Craig has been an owner in my stable and was keen to secure the best-bred and best-type yearling to race and then breed from. It was a fierce bidding duel, with Debbie Ingham also determined to secure this glorious filly. When Debbie noticed that *The Lady Trainer* and Craig were fierce competition, she threw in a couple of bids. Her family's trainer, Chris Waller, was surprised to say the least, but I'm sure he would have been delighted at Deb's determination. However, Craig was resolute that the Ha Ha filly would be bought by his trainer and at $700,000 the filly was ours. Why was she so expensive? Firstly, she is by Australia's leading sire Encosta De Lago; and secondly she was the best-bred female in the sale. Ha Ha had been one of the top Danehill fillies to go through the ring almost a decade ago and I was given her to train by John Singleton and Rob Ferguson. The filly went on to win the 2001 Golden Slipper, the year I trifectaed the race, with Excellerator second and Red Hannigan third. She also won the Tea Rose, Silver Shadow and Flight Stakes, the Magic Millions for three-year-olds and the Apollo Stakes. She was crowned Australian and New Zealand champion two-year-old and three-year-old – hard to get better than that! Her filly was a lovely type with heaps of improvement, and that's what I like to see.

The owners of the Magic Millions – 'Singo', Gerry Harvey and Rob Ferguson – with the grand assistance of Gerry's wife Katie, have done a remarkable job promoting

---

45 At the reconvened hearing, stewards found Ganderton guilty under AR135b for not taking all reasonable and permissible measures the previous Saturday to give Deer Valley every opportunity to win a three-year-old handicap. They suspended him for two months, a decision later reversed on appeal.

this seaside racing carnival. My darling husband and I cannot keep pace with the extra-curricular activities, but I have been told by many owners that the cocktail parties, barrier draw, high teas and dinners have been nothing short of fabulous. Today, across the road from the sales complex, is a high tea which David Jones' ambassadors yours truly and the delightful young Emma Freedman, daughter of trainer Lee, will host. Darling daughter Kate – whom I have heard is rumoured to be on the Gold Coast but have yet to see her – has had many commitments to attend courtesy of her role as the face of the Magic Millions carnival. She assured me she will be my side today, entertaining mostly women but with a nice sprinkling of the males.

Sky's Andrew Bensley and the media have been swarming like flies on buyers after each important purchase. To secure your dream lot has not been easy, but I do believe my team and I have chosen remarkably well and am confident that the rewards will be seen this time next year.

MONDAY, JANUARY 11

The past 10 days have been very long and intense trying to secure the best yearlings on offer. I believe my team and I have done this and I have the strongest belief that next year's Golden Slipper winner is among those I've purchased.

I returned to Sydney yesterday, but it took forever following a breakdown on the main highway to Coolangatta airport and I missed my flight, so I had to dash to Virgin where, it seemed, nearly everyone in racing in Australia was waiting. Trainer Pat Webster and grandson Jack bounded over to me for Jack to offer me his seat on the flight – he is such a charming young gentleman.

Waiting in Sydney to pick me up was Damien to take me to my first appointment with Roy Williamson, the head starter from New York. I discussed my frustrations with a couple of my horses being slow out of the barriers and he made a few pertinent comments. In the meantime, Ken Retzel, the assistant starter from Saratoga, flew in, and today it was amazing to watch these men work with the horses. Dancing Flame appeared spooky in the barriers, nostrils flared, and breathing short and sharp. "If I jump up she'll spook," Roy said. He got down quietly and waved his hands in quiet fashion next to her and after a few minutes the filly stopped reacting. After about half-a-dozen times with the attendants climbing around the barriers, Dancing Flame was relaxed. In America, a record is kept on all horses, detailing what they do at the barriers and how they react. There is a database that all the American starters and attendants have to research. Why don't we have such a sensible system in Australia for all the attendants at all the different tracks? This would assist them to do a better job.

Last season's champion jockey, Hugh Bowman, fresh from his honeymoon, has put on a bit of condition, but looks in remarkably good fettle. South African rider Glyn Schofield trotted in wearing a glorious pair of red riding boots – I'm sure Dorothy would have eaten her heart out in *The Wizard of Oz*. Kathy O'Hara loomed large with a photo on the front cover of *Racing NSW*, the industry magazine, and I noted with interest her right foot barely touching the stirrup iron.

The American barrier staff is going great guns – Roy and Ken are just brilliant with the horses. Best Of Memories, Mount Olympus, Millennium Express and Bank Robber, who all have records of being slowly away or difficult to load, have come before these masters. My private barriers were too close to the boxes at the Desert War stable and the boys could see what a danger that could be, so they were moved back about two metres and 'Snowy' (Louise Lloyd) had to remove some of the trees so they wouldn't be trampled on. We started with the Desert War horses, then from 7am moved to the barriers in the bullring on-course.

THURSDAY, JANUARY 14

Danehill Dancer gelding Lorne Dancer was found to have swelling in his off-fore tendon yesterday and was immediately sent to the Randwick Equine Centre for a scan. A small lesion was found in his tendon. I rang the owners to inform them and they were understandably disappointed, but took it in their stride. They asked, "Do we retire him?" He needs to have six months in the paddock and then he will be re-scanned. He is an amazingly tough horse, so there is no reason he will not return to racing. I never thought Lorne Dancer would return after an earlier injury, a slab fracture, but he did in great style, winning and running second in his two starts. He's a warhorse who loves being in the stables and particularly loves his racing. One has to admire his courage and determination – as recently as last Saturday at Randwick he scored a tough all-the-way win over 1600 metres, his eighth from 15 starts.

The barrier work is going super. Roy has 26 years' experience and Ken, as he put it, is only a pup – but a handy pup. Ken was saying that on his trip out to Australia the man next to him asked if he was holidaying in Australia and he told him he was here to work for a horse trainer called Gai Waterhouse. The Australian chap told Ken how his father used to have horses with TJ Smith, my father. Isn't it a remarkably small world?

A young American trainer/breaker called Kellyn Gorder also has travelled to Australia and he told me how the yearlings go to the barriers at his farm 70-80 times before leaving to go to their respective trainers. This constant practice at the barriers with the breakers is then reinforced on the track and I'm sure that makes the American horse so at ease with the starting stalls, which in turn makes him break quickly. If anyone has experienced racing in America or watched the races on TV, the main thing is they hit the ground running.

Now, don't think I'm having a love affair with America – I'm just trying to bring back what I feel has been lost, jumping clean and fast. It's amazing with my (and other trainers') horses that they are so highly strung when they visit the jumpout stalls in the bullring. Their eyes are wild and nostrils are flaring – one would think they are on some sort of substance. In just four days under Roy and Ken I have seen a huge transformation. One particularly difficult soul was End Of Time (by Anabaa) and even the dual winner Power And Glory was wilful and not responding to the handler. The boys said this doesn't happen in America.

Denise Martin purchased the best value money can buy from the Magic Millions last week. Knocked down to Star Thoroughbreds were three cracking colts by the hot young stallion Snitzel, a magnificent filly by Charge Forward, a truly lovely colt by God's Own and a gorgeous chestnut colt by the great More Than Ready – let's hope he emulates the deeds of the other superstar colt by More Than Ready syndicated by Star Thoroughbreds, the magnificent Sebring, who has done an outstanding job in his first season at Widden Stud. I believe Denise has bought some absolute future champions. See you in the winner's circle in 12 months' time!

CHAPTER 8

Sandals off, and pink stilettos on, at the track

MONDAY, JANUARY 18

noticed young Caitlin Rawiller (Nash's daughter) had cast both plates and was running around barefoot in the downstairs members' section at Rosehill on Saturday. "Where are your shoes?" I asked. "They hurt the back of my feet," she explained. The mobile chemist shop (my handbag) opened up and two Band-Aids were produced. I left mother Sarah in charge of applying them. I was pleased to see Caitlin with her pretty silver sandals back on later in the day.

It was a frustrating meeting at Rosehill where the fence was no good at all. Why do tracks have bias? Nash realised the problem, dictated in front on our winner Rabbuka and kept off the rail in the straight. Rabbuka looked like a young Desert War coasting through the race before upping the tempo at the 500-metre mark. In the last race, Music Maestro was not as fortunate when he was unable to race on the pace. I do believe top-weighted horses are much better when ridden on the speed instead of cuddling them back in the field and taking a sit. Letting them bowl along in front makes it much easier to gradually increase their tempo, rather than asking them to sit and sprint.

The barrier boys gave a display, using Rock Of Gibraltar two-year-old Besieged, to owners at Tulloch Lodge yesterday morning. Roy explained and Ken worked with the horse in the yard. Everyone was fascinated and took a keen interest.

This morning we were cooking with gas at the barriers. Steve Dennett my stable manager and organiser extraordinaire organised a float to the bullring with staff unloading then saddling the horses and two riders coming over to ride them. Ken and Roy assisted the riders by squaring the horses up and making sure the riders were happy with them before opening the front gates and letting the horses come out at their own speed. If a horse was being difficult in the outside barrier, Roy and Ben moved it into the running rail then back to the outside. If he didn't want to go forward he'd swing his rump to knock the barrier attendant out of the way. The tried-and-true trick by the equine boys was to place one hand on the shoulder then square the horse with a piece of rope swinging around behind their legs – no hitting, just constant, steady pressure moving the horse forward into the gate.

Star Thoroughbreds' Kinnersley has been in great form on the training track and is on target for his trip to Tasmania to contest the $200,000 Group 3 Tasmanian Derby (2200 metres) at Elwick in Hobart. This son of Al Maher has made a complete transformation and will take a power of beating. Vet John Peatfield came to inspect the Gooree horses and commented to me, "I don't think I've ever seen your horses looking better, Gai."

Ben Looker took Joku out over 1400 metres and went too slowly, which made me sick watching him. I'm sure he felt like digging a large hole when I let him know on his return to the middle. Next he rode Stratofortress and I told him to bowl solidly over 1400. He certainly did that. Thank goodness Stratofortress is an extremely fit gelding!

Trackrider Nacim Dilmi, with his beautiful French accent, told me how delighted he was with the Red Ransom-Leveller colt; Blake, with his Aussie accent, said Charing Cross was going great.

I got this letter from a part-owner, Gary Beecroft, about Besieged and the barrier display at Tulloch Lodge on Sunday:

Hi Gai,

We were all fascinated in listening to Roy and Ken, real masters of their trade. It is great that our favourite trainer is always pro-active in giving our horses the best education possible. We appreciate your dedication greatly.

Was good to see Besieged in his acting role ... we may have to put him into showbiz after he finishes his racing career. Was great to see how he responded to Ken's instructions, and was good to see him in the limelight.

All the best to all the crew at Tulloch Lodge.

Regards,
Gary

After morning trackwork I had the pleasure of catching up with the editor of the *Sunday Telegraph*, Neil Breen, who is 110 per cent behind the Pink Stiletto event at Randwick on February 26. There is an advertising video out with top jockey Corey Brown declaring to all he is not gay, but happily married; the scene has to be seen to be believed. Doing things outside the box and looking at a new demographic in racegoers is so essential to keep our heads above water. I don't think people in racing realise how unbelievably successful Pink Stiletto day will be, and not even the AJC has fully taken on board the interest that will develop around this race date.

FRIDAY, JANUARY 22

Neil Breen said yesterday at lunch there was a report that a famous jockey, apparently Edgar Britt, had passed away, but Britt's family responded by saying Edgar was alive and well, living comfortably and happily at Avalon. Neil, to his credit, sent a journalist to interview Edgar and this most revealing and entertaining interview will be seen in the *Sunday Telegraph* and is well worth a read.

While inspecting horses at the Classic Sale at Inglis' Newmarket property, Antony Thompson of Widden Stud informed me of three great examples of why the Classic Sale has great value for money and potential Group 1 winners. "I've sold three Group 1 horses at this sale," he said. "Whobegotyou ($20,000), Triple Honour ($50,000) and Typhoon Zed ($65,000)."

Antony also told me that in tomorrow's Inglis Classic race for two-year-olds, three of the 10 runners were sold by Widden last year – yes numbers 2, 3 and 7 were bred at this famous stud. There you go, back the trifecta! (No. 2 Ilovethiscity was second, No. 7 Spot The Rock was third, but No. 3 Testarhythm finished last in the race won by exciting filly Chance Bye.)

WEDNESDAY, JANUARY 27

I've been off the planet the past couple of days – not resting on my laurels, but I've been at the Classic Sale and, more importantly, training your horses. I made only one purchase, a Snippetson colt, who is a big, strong, strapping fellow bred by Judy Marheine of Stratheden Stud. Denise and I were underbidders on about 12 horses. It was a hard sale to buy at, but it's terrific to see the market so strong.

At yesterday's Randwick meeting the filly Modonna won impressively when ridden by Kody Nestor. It was quite amusing – as I walked out of the weighing room I saw this strapping young boy in colours I recognised and thought, "He's too big to be riding my horse." He smiled at me and I did the same, but walked straight past him. He must have thought *The Lady Trainer* was going senile. He followed me to the owners and, again, I looked at him blankly before I realised it had to be Kody. He might be tall, but he can certainly ride. He used Modonna's speed, took control of the race early, before booting her wide on the turn to get the best running and motoring down the rise, looking a sure bet for those who had placed money on her. They are tough breed, the More Than Readys – when you buy them as yearlings they quite often look lean and weak, but the more you give them in training, the more they respond. This filly is a perfect example. A month ago she was struggling, highly strung and living on her nerves, but she has settled with the work and now all she wants to do is win races. One of the owners suggested she go on to the Light Fingers Stakes, a Group 2 race over 1200 metres at Randwick on February 13. I reminded them that little fish are sweet and while we are winning Benchmark 70s we should enjoy that glory and wait until she matures and comes back as a four-year-old. Whatever she does now, I can assure you she will do far greater things as a four-year-old mare.[46]

Denise, Greg Nash and I met at the airport and flew to Perth last night. The heat hit us as we got off the plane and I was dreading today as our inspections started for the Perth Magic Millions sale. They are being held for the last time at Belmont racecourse – from next year they will be staged at the Ascot course.

THURSDAY, JANUARY 28

Budding star stayer Kinnersley arrived at Ensign Lodge at Devonport, the Tassie stable of Barry Campbell, who so capably managed my Brisbane yard for three years. Barry reported that the gelding has settled into his temporary surroundings especially well and in his first work handled the reverse way of going with ease. I know Kinnersley's Tasmanian connection Phillip Evans and all the visiting owners are hoping for a Group 3 Derby win with their boy when he races on Saturday with Nash Rawiller in the saddle.[47]

---

46 The stable was to win the Light Fingers anyway, with the star three-year-old filly More Joyous.
47 Kinnersley was second as the $1.90 favourite, picking up a $36,000 cheque.

Back at headquarters, Gold Water is coming up a treat after her return from a failed stud career. This Group-winning mare, owned and bred by Gooree, will have an easy trial next Tuesday at Rosehill. Montana Flyer enjoyed her final gallop with Kathy O'Hara in the saddle. Kathy was extremely happy with the way this winner of the Group 2 Roman Consul Stakes (1200 metres, Randwick, October 4, 2008) felt. Unfortunately, Montana Flyer didn't kick a goal at her last couple of preparations, nor was she ready for motherhood. The Towell family, of GT Park spelling farm at Kulnura, sent her back to Tempest Morn Lodge at Doncaster Avenue and she will resume in the open 1100-metre race at Randwick on Saturday.

Roy Williamson, our New York starter, returned home yesterday morning. Kenny Retzel is staying on for another two weeks to get my team trained and ready to carry on the brilliant work these American guys have done with the horses. I know that both Heath (Farish) and "Fox" (Graham Howard) will be better horseman from the time they have spent with Ken and Roy.

We have many owners in Perth – Julie Donnan and her brother John are two. They own the talented two-year-old Actrice, a filly that will trial in heat 14 at Randwick tomorrow. (Actrice won her 740-metre trial.) Julie and John visited us at the sales last night and told me how they and their co-workers are keen readers of the blog. Julie works on an oil and gas exploration ship in the Indian Ocean, where she is catering manager looking after the culinary needs of 50 staff. John is a part-owner of Solitarian, an unraced two-year-old Fastnet Rock gelding, and he is a crane driver with one of the ships just off the coast of Western Australia. Both thought it very amusing when I said it was a little like McHale's Navy! They love their racing and enjoy being kept abreast on what is happening through the website. Barry McGrath, part-owner of Epsom hero Rock Kingdom, was also in fine form at the sales. And it was great to catch up with Michelle and David Bishop again. Michelle does an amazing job transporting show horses across the Nullarbor in their remarkable horse float.

The sale in Perth has been very strong. Denise and I tried hard to secure Lot 1, a beautiful filly by More Than Ready, but she went for $230,000 so Denise called a halt.

Greg, Denise and I started early this morning, enjoying a lovely walk along the river. I was interviewed on the Andrew Bensley radio show while we were pounding the pavement and enjoyed a great chat with Malcolm Johnston, discussing how best to ride the daunting rise at Royal Randwick. It certainly isn't on par with the inclines we see in England and Ireland, but by Australian standards it has to be taken seriously. Malcolm knew what speed the horses could travel and he utilised it perfectly in winning three premierships in Sydney in the 1970s and '80s with TJ, who was known as The Little General and won 34 premierships in total (the first 33 on end), unmatched anywhere in the world. I like speed jocks – it makes no difference riding in a Cox Plate, Melbourne Cup, Flight Stakes or Golden Slipper, it is the speed and the way the jocks apply it that wins the races.

FRIDAY, JANUARY 29

Denise, Greg and I struck gold at the Perth sales, purchasing Lot 165, a colt by Fastnet Rock from Munchie. He had everything I look for in a yearling by this sire – big, loose-framed and moves freely. Out of a young mare by a highly fashionable sire (Snippets), he was marked highest of the horses we had inspected. Most importantly, he passed the X-ray with flying colours. I am constantly amazed how many of the attractively-bred, high-priced yearlings have major X-ray issues.

I don't want to wait four-six months to break my yearlings in, so have gone back to the days of TJ when all our young horses were broken in directly after the sales; on to the breakers they would go, and on the track they would be within a week of being purchased. That's why TJ dominated the two-year-old races, including the Golden Slipper.

I'm heading back to my beloved Sydney tonight, only to catch the 6am flight to Auckland tomorrow.

TUESDAY, FEBRUARY 2

Tindal is "two stone lighter" than when he raced in Melbourne and his attitude has changed since Lloyd Williams and Tony Santic sent me this colt in the spring. "You know how to train sprinters Gai, so see if you can make a horse of this boy?" Lloyd said. Six weeks later I said to Lloyd, "I will, but not while he is a colt." We gelded him and put him in a pony paddock at the back of Bounding Away stables, where he fights for his tucker and, boy, has he changed. Originally he was so timid and he looked at everything. Now that he's a gelding all he wants to do is get on with the job of being a racehorse. He will trial in the next week or so.

On the way to the airport on Saturday we were just about to turn on to the highway when Robbie called and asked, "Do you have your passport, darling?" I replied, "Of course not." He immediately jumped in the car and met me on the road to pass it on. What a sweetheart. I'm like a puppy dog that quickly gets lost once let off the leash. Luckily I was still able to make the plane.

I love the difference in the two countries that goes far deeper than the cold and the accent. I don't think there is anywhere in the world quite like this glorious land of New Zealand: the many volcanic eruptions that have occurred over millions of years, the greenness that reminds me of Ireland, and the sunlight on a Saturday morning beaming through our window.

Everyone is at Karaka. When the sale circuit starts you feel like you're a gypsy. Owners, breeders, trainers and agents all pile into the same complex to find their jewel in the crown.

My husband's racing formula when backing horses in staying races is to just look for the NZ suffix. In anything over more than a mile, these initials dominate. My Australian team and I have one brief only – to find Derby, Oaks and Melbourne Cup horses. Any Australian-bred yearlings are not on our radar. The supreme master of Karaka, Peter Vela, was slightly surprised I only wanted to see his New Zealand-breds.

Joe Manning of Littledale Lodge, who has been a family friend all my life, jetted in to buy a stayer in partnership with his great mate, Peter Falk. Joe has not been to the New Zealand sales for more than 30 years. Lea and Bruce Stracey joined Amanda Skiffington, Kate Grimwade, vet Greg Nash, Rob and me. The Henderson boys, David, Luke and father John, were also in attendance.

We are staying at glorious Mollies, overlooking the Auckland Harbour Bridge, as usual. I wouldn't do the place justice calling it a B&B – the rooms are beautifully appointed and the view is breathtaking. Run by Frances Wilson and Stephen Fitzgerald, Mollies has a great parade of magnificent opera singers performing every night. Last night we were joined by David and Angela Paykel, great family friends of mine who have the champion filly over here, Zarzuela, who is being set for the AJC Oaks.

New Zealand sales hype is always high and it is no different this time. I tend to get a little highly strung, to say the least, while Kate and Amanda cope well with the pressure of trying to get the best.

WEDNESDAY, FEBRUARY 3

The sales finished with a real bang for Team Waterhouse yesterday. We had identified the top lot as No. 470, a colt by Zabeel out of the stakes-winning mare Just A Tad – it was interesting that of all the horses at Karaka, he was the only colt marked on top by the whole team of Amanda, Greg, Kate and yours truly. He's so special – big and leggy – and, more importantly, he's a real physical specimen. I left the business end to Amanda and Kate and their one bid secured the colt for $NZ425,000. The New Zealand dollar provides a nice little comfort zone.

Back to Mollies last night and into the bath I plunged (something I never do at home). About to walk outside starkers and there in front of me was a "rent a crowd", including Bob and Rosemary Scarborough from Woodnock Stud, Lea and Bruce, Amanda, Greg and the Henderson boys, John and Marilyn Baxter, John's brother David, AJC committee representative Alan Osburg and Joe Manning and his merry band of men and women. Two of the most exquisite singers, a soprano and a baritone, sang some of the classic songs by Andrew Lloyd Webber. Frances Wilson, who makes this wonderful hotel move and groove, was on keyboards. By the way, most rooms have their own baby grand. It is artistry in the most tasteful and sophisticated manner.

Back to reality today and the phone is ringing and I'm constantly chatting to owners to see what interest there is in the yearlings I have purchased. Like most trainers who go to the sale, I put my money where my mouth is, "specking" the horses that I think will be supreme athletes. I have to work with these horses over the next few years and have to like them. I compare it to seeing Robbie every morning and waking up thinking I don't like my partner any more. I like to relate to my four-legged children and get a positive feeling about them.

These were some of my purchases, and what the buying team thought of them:

LOT 103 – B C ZABEEL X POWER AND GRACE (HENNESSY). NZ$475,000.

By the champion Group 1 sire and out of a winning half-sister to a Derby winner, this colt is very closely related to Might And Power.

GAI: tall, leggy, good shoulder and rein, good girth. Handsome. AMANDA: lengthy colt. Lovely in time. GREG: solid colt, good hindquarters.

LOT 144 – B C ZABEEL X SARAJAY (DANASINGA). NZ$270,000.

A son of the mighty Zabeel and the first foal of a multiple Group-winning mare. He is tall, scopey and looks a lovely stayer in the making.

GAI: well grown, solid. Will be good size. AMANDA: very strong body. Walks well. GREG: deep girth. Nice colt.

LOT 153 – CH F BACHELOR DUKE X SERENITY PRINCESS (ENCOSTA DE LAGO). NZ$80,000.

This filly is an Oaks type. Out of a winning daughter of Queensland Oaks winner Mon Meki and champion Australian sire Encosta De Lago, she is impeccably bred. Bachelor Duke is New Zealand's champion first season sire and is throwing quality in abundance.

GAI: well grown, quality filly. Good nostrils. AMANDA: Just like dad. Good walk. GREG: Good hindquarter. Solid filly.

LOT 165 – BC O'REILLY X SIENA (VOLKSRAAD). NZ$200,000.

A scopey, athletic son of New Zealand's champion sire, this colt is exactly what I look for when I come to New Zealand. His dam is a multiple winner and related to no less than four black-type winners, by the seven-times New Zealand champion sire Volksraad. GAI: good size and length. Strong forearms. Good bone. AMANDA: Great substance. Walks well. GREG: Solid colt. Good walk.

THURSDAY, FEBRUARY 4

Foreman Dave Meijer and I have worked together for a long time and I'm a great admirer of this athlete, who has been clocking up the miles preparing for a marathon run in Rotarua, New Zealand. Last week Dave did 180 kilometres running around Sydney – no wonder More Joyous and his other charges win so many races!

Interesting to see I was not the only trainer to complain bitterly about some of my horses being balloted out of the trials at Warwick Farm next Monday. I wrote to acting CEO Darren Pearce and told him that balloting out these horses could disrupt their autumn carnival preparations and this matter should be taken more seriously. Grahame Begg rang Darren and voiced the same concern. I am taking my 12 horses that were balloted out at Warwick Farm to Hawkesbury to trial on the same day.

FRIDAY, FEBRUARY 5

I'm pleased with Redoute's Choice three-year-old Bassoon, whose nickname used to be Buffoon. I'm sure he got wind of it and changed his tune. Wearing blinkers, and with one trial under his belt (second over 740 metres at Randwick on January 29), he was more tractable and found the line strongly with Flying Spur filly Sarah Can Fly. Making sure that I pair equally talented horses is my most important job. If they are beaten in their gallops, I need to swap them with another horse around the same mark.

MONDAY, FEBRUARY 8

There is absolutely no truth in reports that Blake Shinn is no longer my stable rider. TVN mentioned that Blake did not ride for my stable on Saturday. Well, I chose Chris Munce for Kontiki Park, as we have had a long association and I thought he would suit the horse. Jockeys are like trainers – they can hit a flat spot and when they've worked out what they are doing wrong they just need to tune themselves and get back to basics; just like me.

Cannonball, trained by the brilliant American Wesley Ward, arrived at my Flemington stable today. Rob, Wesley and I got to know each other when Rob and I travelled to Miami in December to study his training methods. Cannonball will be floated to Sydney so I can have a good look at him and prepare him for the Group 1 Newmarket Handicap (1200 metres) at Flemington on Super Saturday, March 6. The five-year-old was ninth in the Lightning Stakes (1000 metres) at Flemington on January 30. He has raced 21 times for four wins and eight placings, including an eye-catching second in the Group 1 Golden Jubilee at Royal Ascot last June. I'm very flattered that Wesley and owner Ken Ramsey entrusted the horse into my care.

There seems to be a multitude of birthdays, including Kate's boyfriend Luke and Tom's girlfriend Hoda. We are all going for tea, starting at 5.30pm. Rob and I will catch the ferry in and then get a water taxi home. Such fun. We always feel like James Bond and his bird.

TUESDAY, FEBRUARY 9

Manhattan Rain produced the best work I've seen in a long time. He ran down half a mile (800 metres) with Montana Flyer, who is no slouch on the training track and a Group 2 winner against the boys in her own right. It was as though she was stuck to the running rail as the colt exploded away. The three-year-old will make his exciting return to the track on Saturday in the Royal Sovereign Stakes, a race I think he will win in easy fashion.[48]

Not to be overshadowed by his juniors, Theseo bowled solidly over 1200 metres. It was only over the last furlong that he changed stride when he got a little tired. Also working solo was Viking Legend. It was his second time in blinkers and he ripped up 800 metres. He is a hard colt to get fit, but he really enjoyed working on the cushion surface of the Kensington track. He will wear the blinkers in the Royal Sovereign on Saturday, as he needs to be sharp for the 1200-metre sprint. They will not stay on him for the whole preparation; when we have achieved the desired result over the shorter distances they will be cast aside.[49]

WEDNESDAY, FEBRUARY 10

Yesterday was presentation time in the TJ Smith room at Tulloch Lodge, with all the boys and girls from the yard in attendance. The trophies are given out to strappers and riders as a way to say thank you to a very dedicated team. Everyone was interested

---

48 Manhattan Rain was fifth at $1.70 favourite in the Group 2 race after rearing at the start. Shoot Out was the winner.
49 Viking Legend, $21, finished third in the Royal Sovereign.

in what the others received and there was great chitter-chatter amongst the team. It's a nice way to say thanks for the long hours and hard work under sometimes difficult conditions.

Nash Rawiller gave a big tick to the Kiwi import Herculian Prince, who has been a bit of a nightmare for *The Lady Trainer* and his owners. At his only start he went so-so, then to the paddock he went before returning and pulling a shoe off on the float on his way back to Randwick. He was lame and rested in his box for two weeks, but is back on track now. It took him a little time to acclimatise to the Sydney scene. Nash said he felt great this morning, when the massive-striding bay found the line well alongside the lovely mare Maybe I.

As an ambassador for David Jones I attended a fashion parade where Miranda Kerr looked divine with her petite figure and adorable dimples; a dream model for any designer. Megan Gale was looking extremely sexy in a well-designed, fitted, little black number, while daughter Kate was wearing a postage stamp. Interestingly, Dad didn't like the little black dress, as it reminded him of funerals. After he died, Mum bought her first little black number.

THURSDAY, FEBRUARY 11

This morning we received outstanding reports from breaker Trevor Sutherland on our Magic Millions purchases. Trevor was particularly delighted with the Encosta De Lago colt out of Orderly, describing him as very, very athletic and saying, "This colt is very forward for his foaling date. He is big with a lovely easy stride." He is out of a sister to the outstanding Excellerator, so I am not at all surprised that he is so forward-going. A $320,000 purchase, he is outstanding value and has fantastic stallion potential. Another to catch the eye was the Gerry Harvey-bred Redoute's Choice colt from Platonic. This colt stood out like a neon light when I first saw him at Baramul Stud in November. He developed well through his preparation and I was delighted to secure him for $400,000. Trevor said: "This colt is big, strong and forward. He loves his food, is amazingly powerful under saddle and I expect him to come back outstanding from his spell."

FRIDAY, FEBRUARY 12

I'm not sure who named Once Were Wild, John Singleton, Mark Carnegie or Trevor Kennedy. At a guess I would say 'Singo' – he might have been the wildest of the group; he's certainly the most volatile. John and Mark were coming to Canterbury today to watch Once Were Wild run, but at the last minute had to pull out for important

THE ACTRESS GAI: this photo was taken in 1975 for Gai's portfolio before she left for the UK, where she acted in television's *Doctor Who* and toured England and Canada on the stage alongside Trevor Howard in *The Scenario.*

PHOTOS IN THIS SECTION:
GAI WATERHOUSE
FAMILY COLLECTION
(unless otherwise named)

MOTHER AND DAUGHTER, 1: Val Smith with tiny-tot Gai.

MOTHER AND DAUGHTER, 2: "Fix your lippy, darling," are Val's motherly words of wisdom to ensure Gai puts on her best face.

AT SCHOOL: Gai in communion dress and the uniform of the Convent of Sacred Heart in Rose Bay, Sydney.

STAR SELECTION: Gai with June Salter in the 1985 production of *Crown Matrimonial*; and Gai's autograph book from the 1960s with the signatures of actors Greer Garson, Chips Rafferty, Jimmy Stewart and Roy Rogers (and his wife Dale Evans and horse Trigger).

THE FAMILY: Tom, Gai, Kate and Rob Waterhouse dressed to ski in Aspen, Colorado.

ROYAL ASCOT: Rob, Gai, Hoda (Tom's girlfriend) and Tom, dressed for the occasion at the 2010 Royal Ascot meeting.

GREAT MATES: (clockwise from top left) glamorous couple Rob and Gai on their wedding day, December 14, 1980; Gai with fellow David Jones ambassadors Emma Freedman (top) and daughter Kate; and Kate with Jock Rorrison, with whom she had a special 'grandfather-like' bond. Jock died in 2008, aged 101. FASHION PHOTOS: COURTESY DAVID JONES

SPOTLIGHT ON TOM: Gai, Bill, Tom, Rob, Louise (Raedler, Rob's sister) and Kate pose during a stylish photo shoot to promote Tom's internet betting business. PHOTO: FENTON STEPHENS

ROYAL OCCASION: the Waterhouses attended the induction of King George Tupou V in Tonga in July 2008. Here Gai, Rob and Tom congratulate His Majesty. Kate and her boyfriend Luke Ricketson are at left. Gunther Raedler, Louise's husband, is in the background.

THE LADY TRAINER: Gai in pensive mood
'at home' on Randwick racecourse.

business in Queensland. Ben Looker was at his best in this apprentices' race and simply outrode his fellow jockeys, taking the lead before stacking them up in the middle stages. He scooted the filly away, easing well clear of the fence to find the best going and winning by almost two-and-a-half lengths. It was the third success on end for this combination. I rang 'Singo' as soon as the filly passed the post only to hear that he and Mark had watched it in some pub. "Don't even know the name of it," he screamed down the phone. I love owners who are enthusiastic about their horses, and 'Singo' loves racing with a passion.

Racecourse whispers have it that the powers that be at the AJC are feverishly interviewing potential chief executives. I can't help but think they have such an excellent man in Darren Pearce as their acting CEO. He might not quite fit what the committee think is the perfect CEO, but in my opinion the best people are those who roll up their sleeves, get their hands dirty and understand the business of racing. They get in early, work through the day and don't leave until their job is done. Darren does that. Come on ladies and gents, get on with the job and give him the position.

Darren has advertised Pink Stiletto day in several magazines. These mags are not our normal reading material, but the advertisements have been well placed. Robyn (Hartney) and I have been reviewing which horses will be racing on the day – which ones will be "coming out", as the amusing ad for the fun day says!

MONDAY, FEBRUARY 15

It was great to see More Joyous ($2.20 favourite) blitz her rivals on Saturday in the Group 2 Light Fingers Stakes (1200 metres, at Randwick). In the morning before her race her ever-confident handler Dave Meijer told me he was concerned about the wet ground. Next my husband questioned whether she had made the weight-for-age improvement needed, and many more were to question the ability of this lightly-framed, athletic filly. I assured all of them that she had gone ahead in her true professional manner. Nash rode her an absolute treat and he was able to use her speed to great advantage and she went on to win in a canter.

TUESDAY, FEBRUARY 16

Looking at the program for the talented Gooree middle-distance gelding Joku, I completely understand why so many horses remain in Melbourne. If Joku were to contest the Group 2 Blamey Stakes on March 13, he would be running in a race worth $300,000; our equivalent in Sydney, the Randwick Stakes, is worth just $125,000. I am as concerned as others who ask 'where is the money going?'

I enjoyed an interesting meeting with agent Harry M. Miller and his lovely daughter Lauren, who now runs the business in partnership with her father. I met Harry many years ago when I was just a young girl still at school doing a show for the Black And White Committee. He said to me, "You should be in theatre, Gai." This was music to my ears. It didn't take much to get Gai to tread the boards, as I had nurtured that aspiration from childhood. When I returned from overseas Harry became my agent and he and Lauren still manage the work I do for David Jones and any TV appearances I might be called upon to make. There aren't many, but I like his shrewd wisdom and knowledge of the industry that makes him a great negotiator.

WEDNESDAY, FEBRUARY 17

Today at Warwick Farm the members' section was thrown open to the public, just as they do at Randwick during the week. It gives the feeling the crowd is better than what it is. We were able to park under the old Leger bookmakers' stand and the atmosphere was lovely and relaxed.

John Singleton texted me the other night to ask if we could speak and I told him I was busy getting Rob's dinner. When we spoke the following morning I had to laugh when he asked where my priorities were. I replied, "Well, maybe that's why we've been married for 30 years." I had a giggle, too, when he asked about backing up a horse twice in the one day. I explained that was no longer the practice, as in 2008 a rule was introduced in NSW banning any thoroughbred racehorse from racing twice in the one day. 'Singo' wants his talented filly More Joyous to run in the Group 1 Doncaster (1600 metres) and I suggested the Oaks (2400 metres). 'Singo' is the owner and pays all the bills, so I will let him have the last call.[50]

THURSDAY, FEBRUARY 18

Good to see Robyn Freeman back at Randwick during the week. This well-travelled and extremely talented jockey hasn't changed a bit and still looks as delightful as ever with her beaming smile. Robyn has ridden for me successfully for a number of years, but has been missing in recent times as she has been travelling overseas and then riding in the country. She's back and planning to marry in November and I know we all wish her well.

She told me a couple of interesting stories, including how there were some remarkably unsound horses racing in Macau. On one occasion, she told the trainer

---

50 As it turned out, More Joyous won the Group 1 Surround Stakes, 1400 metres, at Warwick Farm on March 6 and went for a spell before the Doncaster.

the horse felt very scratchy in his action. "No, no, no," he replied. She rode the horse on the Saturday, and he snapped his front leg. Then she went to South Africa, where they work on the heavy sand and only go three furlongs – but they go like bats out of hell and then, to pull them up, they whistle. How amazing is it to think the jocks and attendants whistle and the horses know to stop?

I was looking at Theseo this afternoon after he had completed four laps of the pool and I asked that he go back and do another two. It's important to get these older horses as fit as possible, as we certainly want him running well on Saturday.

I have removed the blinkers on the Secret Savings gelding Al Muhanad, who blotted his copybook at Kembla Grange on debut on Saturday when 13th in a Maiden. Interestingly, track rider Nacim Dilmi thinks he gets very tense when he can hear the horses coming behind him, then he half wants to bolt.

This morning Dave Fenning, who has been a good mate of mine for a couple of decades and very kindly clocks the horses, told me that my "boyfriend" Geffen, whom I have a bit of a soft spot for, clocked a slick 11.3 seconds with Cap Dancer as his mate. I said to him, "Look whose head is in front." His reply? "Well, he should be running on the Pink Stiletto day!" Very unnecessary comment I thought.

Speaking of Pink Stiletto, I'm in the midst of decorating my house. Nothing flash, maybe a paint job. I said to the young decorator who recommended I get rid of a certain chair, "It's very comfortable, why don't you sit on it?" "I've got a bad back," he replied. "No wonder with those tight pants you have on," I declared. I asked him if he was coming to the Pink Stiletto meeting at Randwick and he said he was thinking of it. I can't tell you the number of people who are coming racing next Friday, the 26th, so come along and join in the festivities!

MONDAY, FEBRUARY 22

Daniel Ganderton came back to earth with his disappointment in finishing a close third on the favourite Beneteau in the Group 1 Blue Diamond Stakes (1200 metres) at Caulfield on Saturday, but he's a terrific young guy and it's a credit to him that Arrowfield Stud engaged him as their jockey.

Last Thursday night's Canterbury meeting exposed a particularly talented filly in Kiss From A Rose, by Encosta De Lago from Comical Smile. When she came into the yard I asked Andrew (Baddock, Gooree's racing manager) where he got the name from and I think he was quite offended. I felt quite ignorant as he explained it is the name of a most popular song by Seal. Kiss From A Rose indicated she's a very smart filly in the making, getting the "hurry up stakes" from Nash after taking a few strides to muster speed in a hot tempo race. She wobbled a little around the tight turn at Canterbury and, for a second, it looked as though she may have been found wanting, but Nash balanced her up, got busy on her as only Nash can do, and she put her mind straight back on the job. The rest, as they say, is history.

Cannonball is doing exactly what I look for in an older horse coming under my care, transforming noticeably in the short time he has been with me. He is settling down, his coat is gleaming and he is enjoying his regular swimming and work on the High Performance Galloping Machine, as well as his trips to the beach – all the little added extras that keep them happy horses.

Once Were Wild glided to the line and will run on Pink Stiletto day in the 1800-metre three-year-old race. 'Singo' has promised he will dress as me. Gosh, I hope he doesn't want me to dress up as him!

Talk about having a nasty dig. Heaven knows how I've offended Richard Callander, but on Thursday night on TVN he made a very under-handed comment, basically saying 20 per cent of my horses are going okay and 80 per cent of the stable are not. I think if Richard has a gripe he might at least have the courtesy to make his comments to me face to face – man to woman. I'm fully aware that the stable, like many other stables, has disappointing times, but that is part and parcel of this wonderful world of horse-racing. I would hate to think Master Callander might be speaking through his pocket.

TUESDAY, FEBRUARY 23

Last week my darling husband looked at my hair and said, "You look middle-aged," to which I replied, "Well, I am." As soon as my hair stylist Christine returned to Valonz I was in there like a shot and now Rob's a much happier man.

Jockey Tim Clark celebrated the birth of his first baby when his partner Jayde Parr (Josh's sister) gave birth to a baby girl, Ellie Grace, last Wednesday. Tim capped this most memorable occasion with a winning double on Saturday at Rosehill. He is probably one of the most underestimated jockeys in Sydney. He is also one of the few who has kept his weight down.

Foreman Mel Norton has a theory on how to get four-year-old mares back in form in her Tempest Morn Lodge. She has three of them who were served, but did not get in foal and the owners sent them back to me. They are Maybe I, who had not won a trial before she went like a rocket on Friday to win at Rosehill; Montana Flyer, with two seconds from two starts; and Gold Water, who has a similar story. It does say a lot for having a full sex life.

I had so much fun going on the Alan Jones breakfast show this morning on 2GB. I was invited in to discuss my involvement in the Pink Stiletto race day at Randwick on Friday. Watching Alan in his glass tank (studio), I saw a very precise, professional person with an impeccable appearance and a voice that goes out to millions of Australians every day. We had so much fun and we talked about racing and how he has five runners trained by Paul Messara that will be racing on the day.

We mere mortals often wonder what committees discuss when they come together. The fact is last Friday the AJC debated in great depth the lavatory situation for the Pink Stiletto day – they were in a dilemma: what to do with the mums, dads, kiddies, gays and drags. I'm happy to say they have come up with a very simple solution, with unisex loos. Well done! I'm sure it will be a huge success and, certainly from my perspective, very entertaining!

WEDNESDAY, FEBRUARY 24

An owner asked me today why his horse Viking Legend led first up in the Royal Sovereign this month. He said, "You're training him to stay, so why is he showing so much gate speed?" I told him that over the shorter distances, with the blinkers on, it is great to see him show speed, but as he jumps up in distance we will take the blinkers off. The colt will still be able to race on the speed, but at a different tempo. I love horses that possess great gate speed and I can assure you, as a trainer, I love horses to jump and take a position.

Home to change after trackwork, then it was on a flight to Melbourne to inspect the yearlings at the Inglis Premier sale that starts on Monday. I had seen the full brother to Viking Legend last October and have just inspected him again. He knows he's a lad and a dude, but he's a lovely colt.

MONDAY, MARCH 1

Glamour colt Manhattan Rain (by Encosta De Lago from the Canny Lad mare Shantha's Choice) has been retired to stud. Arrowfield Stud has secured the colt to stand alongside his half-brother, champion sire Redoute's Choice, after an 11-start career that yielded two wins and seven placings with prizemoney of $1.3 million. The wins were the Group 1 Sires' Produce Stakes and the Group 3 Skyline Stakes as a two-year-old. Group 1 placings came at two (the Golden Slipper and Champagne Stakes) and three (the Caulfield Guineas and Cox Plate).

"Manhattan Rain is a lightly-raced Group 1 winner by a champion stallion out of a champion broodmare," Arrowfield's chief, John Messara, said. "We are delighted that Mr Yaseen has seen fit to place this colt's stud career in Arrowfield's care."

I feel like I've been away forever, but it has only been a couple of days visiting Melbourne for the Inglis Premier sale. Denise has bought some great bargains. I thought there was terrific value at the sale and some lovely horses went through at remarkably sensible prices. It just shows that if you do the shopping like Denise did, it's amazing what you can come up with.

I purchased an imposing Danzero colt, Lot 136, for $130,000. Vet Greg Nash and I marked him this way –

GAI: good style of colt, nice broad head, strong shoulder, relaxed walk, three-quarter brother to Kingda Ka. GREG: solid colt, strong, good bone for bulk.

While inspecting the yearlings last week we went out to visit Tony and Deslee Santic at their Makybe Stud. On the way, we saw a forlorn male goat turned upside down. Kate (Grimwade) insisted we stop, so Jim (our driver) put his foot on the brakes and we came to a screaming halt. Kate and I jumped over the fence and into the paddock we ran. The goat wasn't too sure if he should be happy to see us, or terrified. Kate grabbed his hind legs while I turned the wire mesh upside down and, yahoo, little Mr Goat trotted off. He was very lame, so I fear he had been in that position for some time. She's a grand girl, Kate, so caring of animals. Most people would have driven past, but not Kate.

Blake was impressed with the Kiwi horse Descarado this morning, saying that the blinkers should be added as he is such a laid-back character. The son of High Chapparal is set to make his Australian debut at Canberra in the Guineas on Sunday.

Montana Flyer produced an enormous effort to win the Group 3 Millie Fox Stakes (1300 metres) at Rosehill on Saturday. She was all set to stride to the lead early, but Bejewelled persisted in keeping her out. The two set a solid pace in front and it was sheer toughness that kept Montana Flyer going while the leader tired to finish fifth. It says a lot for the daughter of Flying Spur and she has been nominated for the Wiggle Handicap (1400 metres) at Warwick Farm on Saturday – after much discussion with owners Ron and Mark Towell, and after some gentle persuasion from *The Lady Trainer,* they are considering the Wiggle as a good option, with the thought of going to Adelaide for the Group 1 Robert Sangster Stakes (1200 metres) also on the agenda. If she stays in Sydney, the Group 1 Coolmore Classic (1500 metres) could very well be on the cards.[51]

---

[51] Montana Flyer was sixth in the Wiggle and ninth in the Sangster two weeks later.

I am determined to change the recent stable stats, as I've been a bit disappointed how we've performed of late. I met with my senior staff to discuss the predicament and each one, including Lofty (Brett Killion), Steve (Dennett), Tania (Rouse), Jane (Abercrombie)and Dave (Meijer), all gave such sensible and valid points. Mark Newnham and I had a chat the week before and it's amazing how easily a trainer can go east or west of the dial. You know that you're doing something wrong, but are not able to change it. The most important thing is my responsibility to my owners and the many people who work with me. I also have to satisfy the harshest critic of all, Rob. Some nights I tell him to zip it when he goes on and on, but I know that he always means well and wants me to be successful.

Why did Joku run so badly in the Futurity Stakes (1600 metres) at Caulfield last Saturday? Well he was up dramatically in class and it is always hard to cope with the speed and pressure of a weight-for-age Group 1 race. He has plenty of wins in him, but not at Group 1 at this stage.

American horse Cannonball will run in the Newmarket at Flemington on Saturday. He has done a treat and reminds me of All Our Mob, who won the race for me in 1995. Cannonball will travel south in the trailer on Thursday with a stopover of six-seven hours at Tarcutta, where they have time to have a drink, a lie down and walk around, making the trip less strenuous.

I had an intense discussion yesterday with 'Singo' about the weight of More Joyous in the Doncaster and a jockey for the filly. He, with very strong views, said, "You know lady jockeys can't ride and ladies can't train well." I know him well enough now not to fall for the bait and his evil delight in geeing me up. He said he was going to ring the handicapper and the chief steward to ask them to lift the weight. I told him that most trainers and owners dream about receiving the luxury weight of 49.5kg. No hope for Nash Rawiller to ride at that weight, so John wanted to book Corey Brown. I told him Corey would have to cut both legs off. I have seen many times experienced jocks waste severely, and it's not good for anyone. There were three obvious choices – Kathy O'Hara, Glen Boss and Craig Williams. I was relieved to hear Boss had been chosen. He is a great big-race rider and he partnered Sebring to win the 2008 Golden Slipper.[52]

Great to see Nacim (Dilmi) pretend to "come out of the closet" on Pink Stiletto day at Randwick last Friday, the meeting promoted to attract Sydney's Gay Mardi Gras

---

52 The engagement, as it turned out, was for nought – More Joyous went for a spell before the race.

fans. The outgoing and effervescent "blonde" was a stark contrast to the quiet and shy and very straight Nacim we see riding trackwork every morning. Nacim even had this to say about the day: "A big thanks to all who supported me on Pink Stiletto day. Will wear a dress more often! Sorry to Nash Rawiller for scaring him and to Ben Looker for the embarassment I caused! Thanks to Gai for a fun and great day, and I hope lots of money was raised!"

The AJC should get the biggest pat on the back with the way they went about the Pink Stiletto day. It really was a most joyous affair. Everyone was in great form, including all the staff. AJC vice-chairman John Cornish, whose brainchild it was, normally has white hair, but he had an enormous pink stripe through the centre. Chairman Ron Finemore wore the pinkest of shirts and creamest of suits. John Singleton wore a really frilly evening shirt with a bow tie. Several ladies serving in the Champagne Bar sported pink eyelashes and sequin eyebrows. The fashions-on-the-field contest for best-dressed male and female and best costume was held at the back and was a fun affair.

Funniest site of all was young Nacim. Not a bad figure and beautiful shoulders, but he had hideously hairy legs and I told him he should've shaved them. Foreman Steve Dennett was delighted that all our barrier work had obviously paid dividends, as Nacim broke quickly and bolted in, despite his dress falling down.

The Champagne Bar looked divine and each table had a lovely Star Thoroughbreds brochure explaining how owning a racehorse can be affordable.

THURSDAY, MARCH 4

After the track this morning, my driver Damien whizzed me to Royal North Shore Hospital for a stress test. I'm sure all the people I work with think it would be a better idea if they went for the test! On to the treadmill I jumped. It was elevated and increasing speed; I thought how the devil do I cope with this. Next thing I know the speed increases again and I am run off my feet. I can't run, although I'm a fast walker, but I can tell you I was hanging on for grim life, terrified that I was going to fly off the back. There was a cartoon on the wall in front of me showing a poor person on the treadmill, then a cleaner coming in and pulling the plug so he could start vacuuming. I won't tell you what happens to the patient. The doctor asked me if I would like the fan on and, with sweat pouring down my face, the answer was a definite "yes". Thank goodness the agony came to a stop. I must say I was very glad to go home.

Descarado is heading to the Canberra Guineas on Sunday. The ex-Kiwi lines up for his first Aussie start following just the one barrier trial at Rosehill where he finished a most creditable second to the Group 1 winner Triple Honour. Descarado will wear blinkers, as he did in New Zealand. Several of my readers have been giving me a bit of flack over my "black book" specials, but I like Descarado very much and think he will be very competitive on Sunday.

In my role as an ambassador for David Jones I wear many different hats. Today I did a segment for *A Current Affair* with fashion designer Alex Perry and the store's racewear ambassador Emma Freedman. Joining us were three ladies of different age groups with $1000 to spend — we had to suggest to them their outfits. We all had great fun and the ladies adored choosing hats and dresses. My chosen lady, Colleen, selected a Trent Nathan suit and she looked super. All the girls had a ball.

MONDAY, MARCH 8

Some of Theseo's owners wrote to say thanks after our champ won his fourth Group 1 race, the Chipping Norton Stakes (1600 metres) at Warwick Farm on Saturday:

Dear Gai,

This is just to say a very big thank you to everyone in the stables, in particular Gai and Irish (Steve O'Halloran) for the wonderful job you have done with Theseo. Saturday was a fantastic day; he looked magnificent, plaited up by Steph, and Nash rode him to perfection.

Many, many thanks,
Sue Hardie

Dear Gai and team,

Just a note of thanks to all of you at Tulloch Lodge and Desert War for the great job you have done in bringing Theseo back to the top. Sure, the horse ran the race, but he could not have done it without Steve, Steph, Nash and all the other guys and gals who assist in the everyday chores around the stable. It goes without saying what we owe much to Gai and Denise, but it's you guys who keep the wheels on and the place humming. You have all brought us a huge amount of fun and knowledge and are glad you are with us for the rest of the ride.

Best regards,
Ron and Jill Nathans

Successful West Australian breeder Craig Thompson, who is a part-owner of Theseo, sent me this text about his horse on Saturday night: "You would take him as a mate in the trenches at Gallipoli."

Steve Dennett returned from Melbourne with Joku and Cannonball, who disappointed in their Group 1 runs. Both horses will be spelled. Steve said he has not seen such a volume of water before as there was when he passed through Wagga on the way home – he should know as he has been going this route for the past 17 years.

The stable is back on track, winning three of the five Group races on Saturday at Warwick Farm, and they were all courageous wins. Dreamscape, who was a little inconsistent as a younger horse, has matured into the real thing. More Joyous was exactly that, giving 'Singo' something to be happy about. Theseo, apparently beaten off by Rangirangdoo in the straight, fought back like a caged lion, aided by superlative riding by Nash.

Randwick trainer John O'Shea's filly Solar Charged is the real thing, and her owner Peter Horwitz knows exactly how to win a Golden Slipper – he won with Sir Dapper in 1983 and ran a close second to Dance Hero with Charge Forward, sire of Solar Charged, in 2004. I rang Peter this morning and asked him if he bought or bred Solar Charged and with great pride he told me he had bred her and had raced her mother and grandmother. What a remarkable effort, and I know how he feels as my father, TJ Smith, had the great pleasure of owning, breeding and training Bounding Away, the 1986 winner. I remember bloodstock agent Richard Galpin rang TJ days before the Slipper, offering a huge amount of money for Bounding Away to go to America. It did not take Dad long to make his decision – he said that he had waited his whole life to breed, own and train a champion. No sale transpired.

Many of you may have noticed Singo's filly More Joyous and More Strawberries wearing different colours at the weekend – the black, pink and pale blue, instead of the usual royal blue and white, represent the Gut Foundation, an organisation trying to raise money for colon cancer. 'Singo' and Gerry Harvey feel passionate about this cause and want the public to become more aware. As John told me today, this cancer kills more people than any other.

There was only one jockey, Mark Newnham, on hand for this morning's gallops. Nash was stuck in Goulburn because a bad road accident blocked his way home from Canberra races, where Descarado was fourth in the Canberra Guineas. He didn't get home until midnight. Poor Blake rang to say his car was stolen from out the front of his house with all his riding gear in it.

Herculian Prince put in a super gallop this morning. The Kiwi import will have his second Australian start on Wednesday at Canterbury with Nash in the saddle, and I couldn't be happier with the way he is going.[53]

TUESDAY, MARCH 9

My boyfriend, as I call him – Geffen – greeted the judge today at Gosford and I could not have been more delighted. I must say there have been a number of people in the stable who had been pulling on his tail; one even went so far as to suggest he be nominated for the Pink Stiletto race! Ben Looker showed faith, winning two trials aboard the son of Flying Spur and declaring, "I want to ride him, Gai, wherever he goes." Well young Ben did us proud with an excellent ride, taking the sit in fourth position before peeling wide to score by a short neck. Ben is looking further afield and tomorrow moves on from his three months on loan at Tulloch Lodge. He's unsure of his future and has been a little homesick for Grafton, but what a lovely thank-you to the boy that he was able to ride a winner as a departing gesture. He has always been a fan, like *The Lady Trainer*, of Geffen and always had great belief in the gelding's ability, so it was with great satisfaction we watched him win. Riding a winner at his first ride for the stable, then riding a winner on his last day are nice bookends. All at the stable wish Ben the best of luck.

WEDNESDAY, MARCH 10

I have said little about Blake Shinn and me apparently parting company, but this is definitely not the case. Blake came to me and said he felt he needed to be riding for other stables. I told him it was an excellent idea and a great way to get his confidence back, as he was feeling the pressure of being under one master. He gave me a kiss on the cheek and said I would always be his boss. Blake is so committed and focused and has been working out in the gym with Mark Newnham. Most people don't realise that being a champion jockey takes a lot of hard and consistent work and riding with confidence is one of the most important attributes to a successful jockey.

Lack of confidence even applies to the trainer; there have been many times when the winners aren't rolling in and one is in the doldrums. One gets to the stage where one is not even enjoying going to the races. Facing disappointed staff, jockeys and owners is not a pleasant experience and no one likes it, but it doesn't take long for things to turn around.

---

53 Herculian Prince won the 1550-metre race as the $2.35 favourite.

Extremely busy week with winner after winner! Oh, of course I'm being facetious, but we've certainly turned our form around. We have made a few changes and I have to be around to make sure they are all fitting into place. A young protégé, Kane Simpson, has come over with Laurie Lynch and will work at Tulloch Lodge as our in-house farrier. I have long wanted the stable to have its own farrier and I have the greatest admiration for Laurie, who has revolutionised shoeing in Australia.

Aren't the Brits fabulous! Check out their amazing advertisement for their wonderful Cheltenham race carnival – Chelt'nham, sung to the tune of Petula Clark's *Downtown*. Rob went to Cheltenham last year with a group of his punting pals and said the four-day meeting was absolutely top class!

Last week it was my stress test; this week I had my blocked ears checked. Because of a sinus infection I got while I was in Aspen, *The Lady Trainer* has not been able to pop her ears for the past few months. On Tuesday I visited a Chinese gentleman, Dr Phillip Chang, at his St Vincent's rooms. He had a delightful habit of tapping my arm when he spoke. After a moment I tapped him and asked why he did that and he told me it was to get the patient's attention.

Chief steward Ray Murrihy might be interested when I present myself at the next meeting, as Dr Chang has placed me on a course of steroids. I asked why I was not given antibiotics, and he said they would not have the same effect in opening my sinuses. He told me I would have more energy and I must say I'm definitely feeling that way. I told him I would be keen to stay on this for the rest of my life, much to the amusement of my driver Damien! He quickly shot me down and told me it was just for seven days.

One interesting comment that Dr Chang made to me was one should never fly with a sinus infection as one in 20 people lose their hearing when they fly with heavy colds or the kind of sinus infection I had.

Trials today at Randwick and Star Thoroughbreds' Fusakeo bowled along for young Jessie Whipp, who started riding out for me one day a week just this week. She is a talented young jockey showing oodles of ability.

Great morning at Randwick with lots of jockeys on hand and everyone was in a buoyant mood. Carnival time and all the stables are happy as the best horses are out and gracing our tracks. Tim Clark is coming to ride one morning a week, as is my former apprentice, Daniel Ganderton. Tim felt that three-year-old Supertrooper had definitely improved since his trial, when he was fourth of five at Randwick on Friday, but was still soft. Tim said he felt like a middle-distance horse. Remember this son of Rock Of Gibraltar is out of the Australian two-year-old champ Hasna.[54]

I like the way Just A Blaze, our cups chance, is coming up. Aren't all potential stayers cup hopes? He worked solo, so I placed him in blinkers. Nash said he has a super stride.

Distant And Lovely and Fictional Romance were a lovely pair partnered by Neil (Paine) and Tim, who commented how both horses were very bad kickers – they claimed one victim on the way out on to the track.

It's quite amusing how the superbly-bred filly No Choice, by Redoute's Choice from Get Around, got her name. Rob Dulhunty and his group could not sell her at two different sales and, after deciding to race her themselves, thought the name very appropriate. We all know yearling inspectors can, at times, end up with egg on their faces and I hope, for the owners, she turns out to be a champion.

What a great result on Saturday for the Punters' Club with two-year-old Brightexpectations, who almost stole the show in the Group 3 Skyline at Rosehill when finishing a most tenacious short-head second behind Hichinbrook. Our colt will line up again on March 27 in the Darley Stakes in his quest to make the Golden Slipper field. He had not raced since the Magic Millions on January 9, and then he enjoyed two weeks at GT Park spelling farm. With just one 740-metre trial under his belt, he came out and gave all bar Hinchinbrook a donkey-licking.

Flemington trainer Mat Ellerton's filly Crystal Lily was most impressive, winning the Sweet Embrace by many lengths. We won't see her again until Slipper day, April 3.[55]

A glorious morning was enjoyed by all at Randwick with all the horses nominated for the black-type races on Saturday eligible to use the course proper for gallops.

Steve O'Halloran was very pleased with More Joyous, but I have decided not to run her on Saturday in the Coolmore. Her last run took quite a bit out of her and

---

54 Supertrooper left the stable after running last in a trial on March 26.
55 Ellerton co-trains the filly with his cousin, Simon Zahra.

I thought the extra two weeks until the Queen Of The Turf would be most suitable. I thought if we ran her on Saturday we may not get through to Singo's desired race, the Doncaster.

Once Were Wild is absolutely flying; she is such a happy filly and was Mark Newnham's best of the morning. Theseo is thriving and it will take a very serious horse to beat him on Saturday. He just loves being on the course proper, thumping his chest and letting everyone know he's the boss.

Another Star Thoroughbreds horse, Charing Cross, was a standout dashing home his final 200 metres in 11.1 seconds alongside the super-talented More Strawberries. Nash declared after the work, "She (More Strawberries) is one of the best two-year-old fillies I have ridden in some time." The penny hasn't completely dropped with Charing Cross, but they'll know he's there on Saturday in the Group 2 Todman Stakes at Rosehill. (He finished eighth.) More Strawberries will be seen next in the 1200-metre Group 2 Magic Night on March 27 before, hopefully, going into the Golden Slipper and I can assure you there will be no missing the start this time. (On her debut at Warwick Farm on March 8, More Strawberries jumped awkwardly and had to be steadied twice before finishing second to Obsequious.)

Unfortunately our talented three-year-old colt Viking Legend has a tendon injury and will be out of racing for the next 12 months. He has done a grand job, winning the Listed Dulcify before running Group 1 placings in the Spring Champion Stakes, Victoria Derby and Randwick Guineas. He certainly strikes me as a colt who would suit a boutique stud. He is on the market.

Golden Orient has shown she can be quite quirksome, but over the last week she has settled to the task and has been much more tractable. Not all the jocks like to ride her, due to that chink in her armour, but it didn't stop young Jessie Whipp jumping straight into the saddle and I'm happy to say the two of them were like a pigeon pair.

Queensland's top rider Stathi Katsidis made an appearance and was very impressed with Lord Drinkcard, saying, "He is a very strong two-year-old, Gai."

Once again we're on the road doing the stud tour. First stop was Reavill Farm, the home of John and Sheenah Rippon, run by their son David with Danny Swain, along with an excellent team of young horse people. A very nice draft of consistent boutique yearlings was presented and we enjoyed a delicious lunch under a glorious tree in the prettiest of gardens.

On Monday, Kate (Grimwade) and I visited George Altomonte's Corumbene Stud where we saw the full-sister to Sebring who is still nursing on the mare.

She's a beautiful, compact filly and very typical of the More Than Ready breed. We also saw the half-sister to Sebring, by Choisir. She is a lovely, big, leggy chestnut just like her sire.

Tyreel Stud's draft was superb, with John Vincent and his newly appointed assistant Rob Sims leading the way. They have produced a few near and dear to me, including Bentley Biscuit's half-sister, a big girl by Redoute's Choice out of Tycoon Joy. It's funny – the page is full of horses TJ or I trained, and it's certainly easier buying from families you know intimately. The draft is made up mostly of fillies and John explained they pin-hooked (bought to sell) a colt by Fastnet Rock and, boy, is he a hotpot sire now. Kate, Hugo (Palmer), Lea (Stracey), Damien (Gaffney) and I commented on the remarkable condition the horses were in with their beautiful coats gleaming in the sunlight. John doesn't feed them more than 500 grams of hard feed a day, but when you look at the river flats you understand why they are producing such quality horses.

I love my little trips to the studs, where we try to find next year's champion and, yes, they are there to be discovered. Each sale has its stars and Easter this year will be no exception.

CHAPTER 9

Expectations bright on track and at sales

I am delighted with the way Gooree's Group winner Dreamscape is going. He's a cool dude. He's laid-back and he never knocks himself about. He has great ability, as will be seen on Saturday at Rosehill and more than likely he will head to Queensland for races such as the Doomben 10,000. He's certainly a commercial stud proposition when he finishes racing, being by the Coolmore sire Choisir from Faith In Dreams (USA), by Ferdinand (USA).[56]

At Newcastle on Wednesday the gates to admit the customers were not opened until half an hour before the first! What has gone wrong with our provincial racing? They should have the gates wide open from 10 o'clock in the morning. This once grand meeting has been reduced to a one-day event, which is quite sad.

Where are the three-year-old fillies' races? We have a rising star in Once Were Wild and we have to wait three weeks for a run. Newcastle could easily have had a Group 2 2000-metre race as a lovely lead-in to the Adrian Knox and Storm Queen and then on to the Oaks. Come on Racing NSW, wake up and get together with these provincial clubs and work on the race-day programming.

Road Safety Week got Damien and I chatting about when we learned to drive. Everyone drove as soon as we were old enough to get our licence and then we clocked up plenty of miles before driving on our own. It appears today that kids have to do 100 hours

---

[56] Dreamscape was seventh to Hot Danish in the Group 2 Canterbury Stakes, 1300 metres, at Rosehill.

of driving, either paying for it or finding a driver with the free time to take them. The more practice the better, I say. Kids think speed is great, but our road toll tells us a completely different story.

Bit of a production at the track this morning, as key man Dave Meijer is away and one can really notice the difference. He has gone to New Zealand to race in a 60-kilometre distance run. Then he and another foreman, Lofty (Brett Killian), are going to Hawaii, where Dave will tackle the 120-kilometre run and Lofty the half-marathon. Both are very fit and switched-on men. Mark Newnham, his wife, Donna, and Lofty's girlfriend, Dominica, are going along as their cheer squad.

Just finished the day with 'Damo' behind the wheel, taking Kate and me to Twin Palms Stud and Evergreen, which was exactly that. Both have good drafts of yearlings and a couple of standouts.

Joining the team in Sydney this week is Bruce Slade, who has travelled from New Zealand to be with us. Bruce grew up with thoroughbreds on the South Island and, after completing a commerce degree, he was awarded the 2008 Sunline Trust Management Scholarship, which allowed him to travel and learn from some of the best breeders in the world at Cheveley Park Stud (UK), Coolmore (Ireland) and Taylor Made Farm (USA). On return to New Zealand, Bruce took up a position with New Zealand Bloodstock's marketing department, which saw him heavily involved in promotion of the Karaka sales, where he was well known for his bid-spotting energy and antics. Attracted to top quality Sydney racing, Bruce can now look forward to using his energy in assisting Kate and I in the office, at trackwork, on sale day and on race day.

Warhorse Theseo thundered in for his fifth Group 1 victory in the Ranvet Stakes (2000 metres) at Rosehill on Saturday, beating Rangirangdoo again. The brave six-year-old took his earnings past $3 million.

Despite the great result I feel obliged to record my disappointment with the track. Put simply, it was vastly over-watered. I suspect that curator Lindsay Murphy, who I think is the best in Australia, has succumbed to the "watering lobby". Some people foolishly object to the best horses winning, often by leading on the shortest way home – the fence. Sounds normal and good to me. Leading jockeys Nash Rawiller and Craig Williams said the track was most unsatisfactory with significant inconsistent soft patches. When a horse hits a soft patch, he won't stretch out. The jockeys of The Jackal,

Phenomenal Lass and Star Witness – all trained by others – told the stewards that the artificially-affected going compromised their chances. Bad for racing. The punters, our only customers, hate it.

Nash had worked out the track bias by the time Theseo's race came around. He hugged the fence and came off it on the turn – you would have seen he rolled out markedly at the top of the straight to move off the chopped-up fence. His move was positive and the winning stroke. For Denise and our Star owners it was a moment of triumph. After the race I rang one of them, Craig Thompson, in Perth. He could hardly contain his excitement, but he did say, "Two weeks ago he had three Group 1s, now he is the winner of five." Theseo moves into the elite group of my great gallopers – Grand Armee and Desert War are two others to flash to mind: similar racing styles, big and bold, they get their competitors off the bit and win with sustained stamina.

Kate, Lea and I are on the road again, this time to Scone. Our first day has been a most memorable one, starting with Emirates Park, where many of the great mares I trained for His Excellency Nasser Lootah have yearlings entered for the Easter Sale. On to Goodwood Farm and Kerrie Tibbie knows how to produce a great horse – it was from Kerrie's draft a few years back that our team purchased the great sprinter Dance Hero. On to Cressfield, and it is always a pleasure to drive into this immaculate farm. Owner Bruce Neil is a perfectionist, with the farm and in the mares he has acquired through agent Kieran Moore. The latest of these is Star Satire, the dam of Zarzuela, whose recent third in the Group 1 New Zealand Oaks and fourth in the Group 1 New Zealand Derby makes her dam most valuable.

On the way back we dropped into the Kerv Espresso Bar in Scone for a caffeine fix. There, we met up with old friends William Hastings-Bass and Debbie and Kieran Moore and their young son Billy, who I hear is treading the boards in a school play.

Willow Park was a delight. Glenn Burrows and partner Joan Faras do an amazing job preparing quality yearlings. As with Cressfield, the draft includes many owned by some of the most renowned breeders in the southern hemisphere. Moving right along, Arrowfield and Bellerive were next. We saw a quality draft of fillies, slightly superior to the colts perhaps, but overall they were consistent in height and size – it was a real smorgasbord. Now I am finishing the day at Sefton Park. Colleen and Peter Boyle have a boutique stud and it is not easy competing against major players, but they are there with 11 at Easter, which is a great credit to them.

Tonight we return to a favourite watering hole, Strathearn Park Lodge, where we are treated like royalty. Kate will enter the data and we will chew over what we have seen. Hopefully we will be able to pull it all together as it is only two weeks until Easter.

According to Steve O'Halloran, Brightexpectations, the punters' pal, worked as strongly as he did on Saturday, and yes that was a winning gallop. The rematch of the people's champ with Hinchinbrook at the weekend is especially exciting for all, including yours truly, who have a piece of the colt.

The English import Casilda made vast improvement in work this morning. The lovely, big Cape Cross mare is owned by Glenlogan Stud and has come from Andrew Balding's Lambourn yard. Some Kiwi and English stayers can take time before the penny drops – Australian tracks are hard and fast, so horses need to be near or on the speed on many occasions.

Daniel Ganderton partnered Common Objective and was delighted with the way the gelding performed. The big burly son of Redoute's Choice disappointed last preparation, as I was hoping he would make the quantum leap, but he is back to prove himself this time. He will trial at Randwick on Friday and resume racing in three weeks.[57]

The Randwick dirt has been inconsistent in readings over the past 24 hours – as track manager Dave Hodgson said, "After a renovation (which happened on Saturday) the dirt's readings throw up dramatically until it settles." My concern when I wrote to Dave this morning was how long until it settles? We are in carnival mode and no horse should be put in jeopardy of breaking down because of track inconsistency. I woke early and saw on my pager my man Arthur Buxton's daily readings. I immediately messaged Tania (Rouse, assistant trainer), who is at the helm while I am in Scone looking at yearlings, to change the work of horses galloping on dirt. We just brought them back a notch.

Yarraman Park's Easter yearling draft is a creamy one. Harry Mitchell is a great horsemen and he always has a nice colt or two. Daintree Road was home-bred at Yarraman for Yvonne Smith and he will win the Class 1 1400-metre handicap at Newcastle on Saturday with Mark Newnham aboard.[58]

Today's studs also included Attunga and Glastonbury, where Charge Forward's half-brother, by Redoute's Choice, will be keenly sought. Kia Ora has a boutique draft and stud manager Eric Foster and his team do an excellent job.

The next stop, Kitchwin Hills, some 10km from Gundy and its Linga Longa Hotel, under Mick Malone and his team of talented young people, had a very hard act to follow – lunch. I had to have a 10-minute snooze so I could be at full focus for the

---

57 Common Objective was second in the 1200-metre trial.
58 Daintree Road was seventh, but won his next start two weeks later at Newcastle.

excellent draft. Mick told us hot off the press that Group 1 BTC Cup (1200 metres) and Group 2 Golden Rose (1400 metres) winner Duporth (Red Ransom-Staging, by Success Express) would stand alongside Dane Shadow at Kitchwin Hills next breeding season.

Then it was on to Stuart Ramsey's Turranga Farm, across the road from Arrowfield. Stuart's horses always grow good bone and toughness, and he breeds a lot of Group horses. We finished the day at Segenhoe, up the road from Darley.

THURSDAY, MARCH 25

This reply came from AJC track manager Dave Hodgson after I complained about Randwick's dirt track renovation:

Hi Gai,

Unfortunately, we had no choice other than to do the renovation to the dirt track last weekend.

At this time of the year with high rainfall through the latter summer months a larger amount of organic matter is displaced from the surface of the dirt track into the drains. Moisture retention is then more difficult and the dirt track becomes firmer at a quicker rate than normal.

Last weekend the readings on the dirt track left Turnpoint (which manages the track) with no choice other than to do the minor renovation, as the track would have become much too firm for horses to gallop on this week.

The dirt track will become more consistent as the week goes on, although it does tend to have a better consistency once the optimum range of moisture is applied to it. Unfortunately, the predicted rain didn't come to our aid over the past two days, but I can assure you that the (maintenance) team have been doing all in their power to get the track back into its best condition in the meantime.

I understand your concerns about renovating the track at this time of the year, but the process we have followed is one that the AJC has historically followed ... as per (American expert) Steve Wood's recommendations. By renovating on Saturday we were able to have a three-day break until Tuesday's fast work day. This enabled the team to get more moisture into the surface.

As Tuesday was special gallop day we were also able to offer two grass tracks (the Kensington and steeple grass) for horses needing to gallop in their preparation.

The AJC and Turnpoint always do everything in their power to produce safe and consistent training and racing surfaces at all times, and decisions on the maintenance of tracks are treated as a top priority at all times.

I hope that these facts help you understand why we needed to renovate the dirt track at this time.

Regards,
Dave

FRIDAY, MARCH 26

Jump-outs promptly followed trackwork this morning. I gave all the jockeys a sleep-in, but Mark (Newnham) would never take it up. Nash asked for the morning off so he would be fresh for the trials, also at Randwick, and Neil (Paine) did the same thing as he knew he was going to be kept busy riding the Gooree horses there. Mark, as professional as always, turned up to trackwork where he gave his usual great feedback. He is a pleasure to work with.

Polar Eclipse hit the ground running in his jump-out. This Stratum colt is massive, but you'd swear he was a light filly the way he scooted across the ground today.

We went to nearby Allpress for a quick coffee and a bite, but there was no time to stop as Damien (Gaffney) and I were a man and a woman on a mission – the Randwick trials, where two-year-old Touch Of Greatness, by Don Eduardo, was very impressive in Gooree's red and black over 740 metres. She jumped, took control and said "see you later alligator". She has lots more to learn but did everything today in great style.

It was pleasing to see the Gooree-owned Stage Performer, by Encosta De Lago, win nicely at Wyong today. I received a message from Andrew Baddock, general manager of the fine breeding establishment, saying the boss, Eduardo Cojuangco of the San Miguel Corporation in the Philippines, who is holidaying at his Mudgee property, was very happy, particularly with the big odds ($8 in a Maiden for three-year-olds). Stage Performer can be a handful to train and just last week she refused to go on the track. Thanks to Steve O'Halloran and Mick Stanley, the AJC's clerk of the course, Stage Performer made it ... eventually.

I cannot describe how good it was to be back at Randwick after four days on the road on our stud tour. It is like a drug – I cannot keep away. I really miss my beloved turf. Just A Blaze and Show Dancer really pleased this morning. Both are lovely staying types from the Land of the Long White Cloud. They worked super together and will head to the trials at Randwick on April 12.

No active sire in Australasia has left more Group 1 winners than Zabeel, the Cambridge Stud stallion having produced 39 individual winners at the elite level, 27 of them colts or geldings, including Might And Power, Octagonal, Sky Heights, Efficient, Maldivian, Mouawad, Railings, Fiumicino, Savabeel, Vengeance Of Rain, Zonda, Dignity Dancer, St Reims and Reset. I purchased two colts by Zabeel at this year's Karaka Premier Sale and both have arrived safely in Australia. The colts are from young, winning, well-credentialled mares, Power And Grace (by Hennessy) and Justa Tad (by Istidaad). Breeder Sir Patrick Hogan will retain 10 per cent of the former, given his high regard for the colt. My sales catalogue comment on the latter was: "Attractive, will be big."

The NSW stud tour came to a close yesterday. Our last stop was Bylong Park, where we enjoyed the boutique draft and excellent lemon water and cupcake. Lunch was with Katie and Antony Thompson of Widden, the oldest breeding ground in Australia. Early into the parade I was standing close to the barn opening when an Anabaa colt came out, his heels high in the air, missing *The Lady Trainer's* head by centimetres. On with the work, as we had to get through these yearlings, although poor Antony nearly had a heart-attack as he reeled in horror. The Widden yearlings were a top bunch and they will again make top dollar this year. Driving out we were fortunate enough to see plenty of wildlife, including a couple of magnificent emus whose plumage we will get used to seeing on well-dressed ladies over the autumn carnival. We also spotted what I thought was a wild dog, but Kate believed was a dingo, and Lea a fox, stopped on the side of the road with another for afternoon tea.

During the tour we had the privilege of visiting Coolmore Stud at the same time as distinguished guest Jacqueline O'Brien. How great it was to view Royal Academy with her, but a shame that her husband Vincent O'Brien is no longer with us – the former great Irish trainer died in June last year. Jacqueline, of course, is the grandmother of Coolmore Australia's Tom Magnier.

We saw the yearling drafts of Monarch Stud, Brooklyn Lodge and Edinglassie Stud before arriving at Coolmore and all made us feel most welcome. Their Easter-bound prospects set the bar for a top-notch day of yearling inspections.

MONDAY, MARCH 29

The punters' pal and the people's champion Brightexpectations booked his place in the $3.5 million Golden Slipper with a dominant three-and-a-half length win in the Group 2 Pago Pago Stakes at Rosehill on Saturday. By the sire of the past two Slipper winners, More Than Ready, Brightexpectations rolled along in front for Nash before unleashing a finishing burst that caused a roar from the crowd in the grandstand.

One of the jubilant owners sent this e-mail:

Dear Gai,

Could I pass on my family's thanks for a great day on Saturday? That was truly a stunning performance by Brightexpectations – out of this world!

If I forgot to thank anyone at the presentation, please accept my apologies and consider yourself well and truly thanked now. I was so stunned that my friends said I was as white as a ghost several hours later.

Again, thanks for a great day. I would heartily recommend the experience to anybody – it's about as much fun as you can have with your clothes on!

Cheers,
Keith Farrell

Everybody was in grand form this morning, I think as a result of the success of Saturday. The stable had three runners in three consecutive events. Before Brightexpectations raced, I told Nash, with a steely look on my face, "You are on a moral, ride him as such." Nash understood the brief and the colt donkey-licked the opposition. In the next race, More Strawberries' slow jump cost her a winning position, but she is certainly not short of tenacity, fighting gallantly to run second to Willow Creek. I advised John Singleton's manager Duncan Grimley to run her in the Sires' Produce, not the Slipper. Duncan was going to break the news to me gently on Sunday, but I had already rung John on my way home. "Don't be ridiculous," he said. "One is worth $3.5 million, the other $300,000." The decision was made immediately, Corey Brown booked as the jockey and history is ready to be made on Saturday if More Strawberries can follow in the hoof prints of Belle Du Jour, who won the Slipper for 'Singo' in 2000.

Rock Kingdom failed to run a place in the next race, much to my surprise and disappointment. The gelding had worked beautifully all week, his coat is immaculate and, as his trainer, I could not fault him. It is hard to understand; he was so fit and well but raced below par. I am a great believer in patience, the horse will tell me …

TUESDAY, MARCH 30

This morning the final gallops were conducted for horses set to race on the Group 1-packed Rosehill card on Saturday. Theseo, wearing a crossover nose band, which he has not worn since last preparation, was feeling fresh and strong. Regular rider Steve O'Halloran felt he needed something to contain him and he worked a treat, breezing over 1400 metres in remarkable fashion. This great son of Danewin found the line with conviction in the style of a six-time Group 1 winner (he has five to date) … let's hope so. I have been asked on numerous occasions about Theseo getting the 2400-metre journey of the BMW, but there is no concern with me.

Dreamscape was partnered by promising apprentice Blake Spriggs, now with the stable as Blake Shinn rides work elsewhere. Dreamscape may have disappointed when unplaced in the Canterbury Stakes, but I can assure you he will not disappoint in The Galaxy (Group 1) next month. Back to handicap races he will be most effective because he really is a tough and cool cookie. People do not realise how hard it is to make the step up from handicap races to weight-for-age.

Mark Webbey, who has recently joined us as race programmer, has a career spanning 34 years in the racing industry, with his roles including senior handicapper for Racing NSW and senior handicapper/racing manager of the Singapore Turf Club. His simple explanation of handicap and weight-for-age racing is:

> Handicap races are conducted with the intent of affording all horses, where practicable, an equal chance of winning a race within a specific grade in which they are eligible to compete.
>
> Weight-for-age racing caters for the top echelon of performers where set weights are allocated relevant to age and sex. As the season progresses the weight allowance for the younger horses (two and three-year-olds) will decrease until they reach full maturity at four. Fillies and mares receive a consistent 2kg allowance from the males.

The three-year-old Once Were Wild is the perfect rags-to-riches story after being purchased at Magic Millions for $50,000. I thought she was a well-grown and strong – just a lovely type of filly – at the 2008 sale and, after five straight wins, I have no doubt this daughter of Johannesburg is ready for the Group 1 race step-up in the Vinery Stud Stakes (2000 metres).

More Joyous, the topic of much conversation, is to race in the Group 1 Queen of the Turf Stakes (1500 metres). She is a serious filly, dubbed champion three-year-old of her year, and she will take a power of beating in the event she has been set for. She has pleased her rider Steve O'Halloran, and her trainer. All she has to do now is run her normal pattern in the race.

I am glad I made the decision on the first Tuesday in November of 2009 to increase the New Zealand presence in the stable. The Kiwi four-year-old Herculian Prince is a surprise package selected by my darling one Rob. In his first Australian race the gelding ran below par, so we pulled the plug and spelled him. I cannot tell you how well these New Zealand horses thrive in their second preparation. They are handy to have in the stable and HP, as some of his owners call him, steps up to black-type level in the Listed Sellwood Stakes (1400 metres) on Monday at Canterbury.[59]

This heart-warming letter was sent to us recently:

Dear Gai and the team at Tulloch Lodge,

After winning a raffle at the races at Rosehill I attended your stables with my girlfriend on Mother's Day last year. I cannot describe the joy and sheer delight that the visit provided me with. I have been a huge racing fan for as long as I can remember, but have had no experience at all like I did that day. My Nan, who I used to bet with every week, was full of questions about what it was like and what Gai was like. Since then my Nan has passed away, and on the 13th of March a race was named after her at Kembla Grange, which Cap Dancer won. I was fortunate enough to have my second great horse-racing experience and a second great Tulloch Lodge experience by getting my photo taken with the winner and giving her a big pat.

I just wanted to write and thank you for raffling those "Day at the stable with Gai" tickets and let you know how much of a thrill and dream that experience provides racing lovers such as myself. I was fortunate enough to see and take pictures of Dreamscape and Swift Alliance that day, both of which I have followed and cheered on winning Stakes races since. I now have another horse to follow, one which will happily remind me of my Nan, in Cap Dancer.

Eternally grateful,
Rhys Gray

How frustrating for owners who have travelled miles and turned up in designer jeans looking fabulous to be told they can't go into the mounting enclosure. Here we are today at Warwick Farm, with owners, and they are trying to tell us you have to be wearing a coat and tie to enter when most people here are wearing shorts, and I am wearing white jeans. Our poor owner was banished, not able to talk to the jockey about the race, or see the horse close-up; just made to feel like a second-class citizen. To add salt to the wounds our owner had contacted the AJC and specifically asked about dress code and was told it would be relaxed at Warwick Farm on a Tuesday. We want people to come racing, not be told 'go away'. People wearing jeans at the Crown casino, for example, are not turned away from spending their gambling dollar.

---

59 Herculian Prince won at Canterbury to make it three from three this campaign.

The AJC committee should be ashamed that the club did not notify trainers, riders, punters, owners and media that the Warwick Farm track had been watered, that 25 horses had galloped on it this morning and that it had been rolled. Local jockey Tommy Berry clearly knew about the rolling and won the first race wide out on the track. Do we really have to go boxing in the dark?

Nash, on one of our winners Autumn Ember, said there was a soft spot at the 600 metres where there was a major fall in the six-horse field. Corey Brown broke his left shoulder and is out of the Golden Slipper, and the chance of him winning the premiership might have disappeared – he is in a contest with Nash. Autumn Ember sustained a nasty wound several inches long on her off-hind leg when she was galloped on and had to be sent to the Randwick Equine Hospital.

I hope the club learns from the incident and gives us better information in the future.

THURSDAY, APRIL 1

As the big Golden Slipper day draws closer, the thought of the competition excites me enormously, as I am a creature that way inclined – I love to see my horses giving their best, finding the line and shaking off the opposition. This morning Bruce (Slade) was looking at the gallop sheet where I had a smiley face beside Descarado. Kiwi Bruce asked, "What does this mean?" I replied that he is pleasing his trainer and rider, and, boy, is he doing that. The leggy, lanky son of High Chaparral is shaping as a wonderful staying prospect. His third place in the Phar Lap Stakes (1500 metres, March 20) was eye-catching and he will run over more distance in the 2000-metre Tulloch Stakes on Saturday, which will suit.

Most exciting news this morning – a new staying star arrived at Tulloch Lodge. Steve Dennett said, "I can't ride that. He bucks like mad," so I called upon Pony Tim (O'Riordan), Craig Messenger and Frank Fitchett to lunge him first ... and with this, Tullamore (by Savabeel) was officially introduced to Randwick. Craig commented that the gelding had a magnificent stride. Rob identified Tullamore through doing his form in New Zealand and is confident he can follow in the hoof-prints of Descarado and Herculian Prince. The new boy is an orphan with no owners.

Two darling little girls, one with her brother, came to the stable to enjoy a photo with Brightexpectations this morning. Both girls are cancer sufferers. On Saturday, Brightexpectations will run for his individual owners Arthur Menzies, Rohan and Kate Aujard, Bruce and Lea Stracey, Joe and Lou Manning, Keith Farrell and his mother Pat, and my daughter Kate, and for the Racing NSW/*Daily Telegraph* Punters' Club, who are donating funds to Redkite, a very special organisation. Redkite has provided support to children and young people and their families affected by cancer for the past 25 years. If Brightexpectations wins, the Punters' Club will donate $250,000 to the charity, as will the TAB in a roundabout way.

Swift Alliance is an unsung hero at Tulloch Lodge. He may not be the biggest colt in the stable, but if you measured his heart you would find it is huge. I like his sire Don Eduardo. I have always been a great admirer, even though I did not train him, and boy is he a lovely stallion. He stands at the Chitty family's Haunui Farm, just south of Auckland. This is the farm that reared and sold last Saturday's Group 1 Rosehill Guineas winner Zabrasive (by Zabeel). The Chittys have brought his yearling half-brother to the Easter sale and I saw him yesterday and thought he was a damn nice O'Reilly colt.

FRIDAY, APRIL 2

'Singo' is so excited about tomorrow: never before has he had three runners in three Group 1 races and never before has he had a horse win five straight with *The Lady Trainer*, as Once Were Wild has done. "Gai, you and I have a strike rate of 40 per cent stakes-winners to runners together," he said. What a partnership!

MONDAY, APRIL 5

Saturday was an enormous day – I was up at 2.30am ready for my call from foreman Lofty (Brett Killion) at 3.10am – but time moves at a very rapid pace on these great Group 1 days. We went into bat at the track at Randwick, where all the charges were happy and healthy, then it was home to have my face and hair made up. What a pleasure to look years younger and feel a million dollars, courtesy of the make-up artist.

When I arrived on course at Rosehill just about the first person I saw was Francoise Naude, breeder and owner of Hinchinbrook. I asked him what he thought of his colt in the Slipper and he replied, "I have expectations." I fired back, "Mine are bright." I was stepping out confidently, but by the third race my stride had shortened and after Theseo's loss it was more of an amble. More Strawberries did not let us down with her third in the Golden Slipper and I thought Damien Oliver was quite brilliant in taking the initiative on the inside. Credit must be given to the very speedy and very beautiful Crystal Lily. Mat Ellerton and Simon Zahra are a great training team and they have a marvellous filly on their hands.

How appropriate that the final race went to Nash and *The Lady Trainer*. It had been such a frustrating day, so thank goodness for the ever-reliable and honest Swift Alliance, who won the Sebring Stakes in brilliant fashion. All the owners of Gooree's mighty young stallion were there to cheer the winner on.

A very tough day at the office. The Inglis Easter sales are buoyant, but there are still plenty of passed-in lots. The UK auctioneer, John O'Kelly, is a star and he is greatly appreciated by our international guests, who are accustomed to his selling style.

Nervous Tony and Deslee Santic scurried into the vendor box before their quality Makybe Diva filly by Fusaichi Pegasus went through the ring. Deslee was clutching her darling babe, Charli Rose, who was as pretty as a picture, dressed in red. When the filly went through for $1.2 million, I thought they were going to go flying in the air with excitement.

The first horse I secured was Lot 48 by the Group 1 winning stallion I trained, Secret Savings. I have great admiration for the yearling's breeder, Emirates Park. The success I have enjoyed buying from them, and training for them, is perhaps only equalled by Gooree and George Altomonte. This colt, a grey like Brightexpectations, brought $110,000. He is a full brother to Cent Per Cent, who won six races up to Listed level. His dam is four-time winning Snippets mare Minnie Me, and all her progeny to race have won.

The sales are always a great meeting place for international players in the thoroughbred game. I had the great privilege of meeting Robert Clay, of the leading Kentucky-based stud farm Three Chimneys. He was speaking with an excited 'Singo', and YES, Kentucky Derby winner Big Brown is coming to Vinery Stud; a real coup.

Later I secured Lot 170 for $100,000, a smashing type by Golden Slipper winner and great producer Flying Spur. He is out of the five-time winner Snipify, and this Danehill/Snippets cross has produced the likes of this year's Slipper winner Crystal Lily and Group 1-winning sires Snitzel and Magnus. This is a cross that WORKS!

As dark replaced light, I purchased my final lot of the day, a full-brother to Racing To Win (Encosta De Lago-Surrealist), winner of the Doncaster and Epsom Handicaps. I have his two-year-old brother, Royal Battalion, in training and I really like him a lot. I saw the yearling first at Coolmore on our stud tour. He is masculine, has terrific presence, covers ground when he walks, and has a lovely pedigree. At $400,000 I thought he was the buy of the sale and he is a real-deal stallion prospect.

The most interesting thing about the sale is that the vendors are screaming that they are not at all happy with their returns. There is a lot of groaning going on, yet overall the sale is up 10 per cent on last year.

Day two of Inglis' Easter Yearling Sale, and I went to $100,000 to purchase Lot 303, a grey Danzero filly that really looks a runner. Bred for speed, she is by the sire of

Dance Hero, out of a Rory's Jester mare, who in turn is out of a Godswalk mare. Being an August 27 foal, she is so well grown and I was amazed to secure her for $100,000. Another filly I secured today was Lot 107 (by Encosta De Lago from Princess Stacey), who was passed in, a casualty of the soft first day of selling. Prepared to perfection by Mark and Shelley Treweek of Lyndhurst Farm, Cambridge (NZ), I adored this filly the moment I laid eyes on her early last week. She, too, looks very precocious and hails from a wonderful filly family that includes the phenomenal Typhoon Tracy and her dam Tracy's Element. Her residual value is enormous and at $300,000 I just had to have her.

THURSDAY, APRIL 8

I started the day very strongly at Newmarket, buying two of the first 10 lots through the ring. Both are by the most precocious sire since Star Kingdom, More Than Ready, the sire of two of the past three Golden Slipper winners. Lot 406 is an early comer and a real running sort. His dam En Bateau (by Dehere) won three races and his full-brother, More On The Toe, had won five races up to this season. Lot 408 is out of Esther (by Fasliyev), who I trained to run a place in the Group 2 Silver Slipper Stakes. This, too, is a particularly early family – the filly's grand-dam is a full-sister to Slipper winner Burst (by Marauding). She was a gift at $150,000. Late in the first session, I added a third yearling by More Than Ready. This colt, Lot 494, is bred on the same More Than Ready/Flying Spur cross as Sebring, being from Group 3 winner Joy Of Flight.

The Easter sales are now over, thank the Lord, but I do believe between Star Thoroughbreds and the horses I have secured for owners that we have a beaut portfolio of both pedigree and type.

FRIDAY, APRIL 9

Last night's races at Canterbury were a frustrating affair, especially being bridesmaid in the fillies' race with Upon This Rock. Nash is such a formidable jockey, I prefer him riding for the stable than against it. The race was won after the horses had gone 200 metres – Upon This Rock's jockey, Tim Clark, eased slightly, giving Nash the advantage on The Last General, trained by Clarry Conners. It was a two-horse duel up the straight and in the final 50 metres Nash threw all his body weight behind his mount, driving her to win by a nose. I must say, however, that it is great to see a true craftsman get some of the action and in jockey Nash Rawiller there is no finer example.

Descarado put in a top performance to finish second in the Group 1 AJC Derby at Randwick on Saturday. The son of High Chaparral played his part in his sire's trifecta in the race, an enormous accomplishment – he split Shoot Out and Monaco Consul. Now out in the paddock, Decarado can enjoy some rest and relaxation before targeting some exciting spring goals.

The Asian Racing Conference started in Sydney today. Rob flew the flag and I will go to enjoy the talks tomorrow. Rob was amazed at how forward-thinking American and other overseas speakers were, and how we Aussies are still talking about the past. Perhaps it is because of our geographic location; we are so far away from all the happenings.

We had a fascinating lunch in Mosman yesterday with ex-trainer and Tapeta racetrack manufacturer Michael Dickinson, one of the most versatile people you could ever meet in racing. He has been successful in every aspect of the sport: he was a champion amateur steeplechase jockey and a champion steeplechase trainer in England; he trained at Manton for Robert Sangster; and he trained in the United States.

On turf tracks, I was delighted to hear his views on the roller being a tool of the devil. "It is an admission of failure of the track curator, who has not done his job correctly, finally using the roller to patch up his mistakes," he said. His next statement made me laugh. "Anyone who rolls a thoroughbred turf track should have their head on a spike as a deterrent to others using the dreadful tool."

Michael explained that if you roll a firm track and get no rain, you get a hard track; if you get a bit of rain, you get a slippery track; and if you get plenty of rain, you have ruined your drainage by rolling it.

It was wonderful meeting someone so full of common sense. There is no one who knows more about tracks than Michael and it is no surprise that his surface is being used at Dubai's new Meydan course, where they run the richest race in the world, the $US10 million Group 1 Dubai World Cup, on Tapeta.

Geffen wowed jockey Peter Wells, who said he went better than excellent, "very excellent" in fact, at trackwork. Not sure on his use of the English language, but he was right in what he was saying.

Gooree's scintillating sprinting entire Dreamscape (Choisir-Faith In Dreams, by Ferdinand) has been retired to the Thompson family's Widden Stud. The winner of four of 11, this is a stallion who has everything. He is an athlete of the highest calibre, he hails from a marvellous sire-producing family, and he has smashing looks. He has a deep bay coat and black markings. He has the most lovely shoulder and is beautifully balanced. I wish him every success.

I am presently sitting at Randwick's swimming pool, which is a great way for me to see 90 per cent of the yard every day because my four separate stables bring horses to the pool around 1pm. They walk around us waiting for their turn in the water. Sometimes I send a horse back for a couple more laps because they are not fit enough or, in the case of Theseo today, had done less work than usual in the morning. Training requires you to watch your stable of athletes closely. They can change so quickly on you, so unless you keep your mind on them every day they can get away.

Recently at Warwick Farm, designer denim was rejected as suitable for the members' section. Thanks to fast-acting CEO Darren Pearce – and I mean acting as in getting things done – the AJC changed the dress code to get rid of the archaic rule. Then at Canterbury the other day a gentlemen and his friend, immaculately dressed with jacket, shirt, tie and, OH NO, a pair of designer jeans, were rejected. Again, the STC, in its wisdom, denied owners entry. Please, ladies and gentlemen, move into the modern world! What a travesty to think people who spend millions of dollar on horse flesh, and wear jeans that are accepted worldwide, are pushed away.

As I was departing the Canterbury trials a lady ran up to me. There was a trade fair taking place and she reminded me that we had met in Melbourne and gave me the most beautiful clutch purse. She is the designer Katalin Csardas. What a sweet person, and what a great idea for the clubs to have trade shows. Yesterday at Hawkesbury races, Rob said there was a seed/grain-growing trade fair. He said there were so many people in the betting ring, including new faces. By having a fair on at the same time racing is marketed to a fresh audience in a natural way. I remember being at Warwick Farm during the Pope's visit and there was a car show. You couldn't move – they should have had the races on at the same time. It's just a matter of thinking outside the box. Hawkesbury gets first-class honours here.

There was much written and said this week about the jockey engagements for the Group 1 Doncaster and about me going to the Supreme Court yesterday. In retrospect, I wouldn't do it again – my mistake, but the owners are always at the forefront of my mind. Owners' rights must be protected and that's my job.

My No. 1 jockey Nash Rawiller and his manager (Glenn Darcy) had assumed that Theseo would not run in tomorrow's Doncaster, and they accepted trainer Chris Waller's booking for Rangirangdoo. The judge was extremely fair. And, it must be said, Chris Waller behaved perfectly in booking Nash and demanding he honour the booking. He was protecting his owners' position.

I think what must come out of it is that jockey managers should take their role much more seriously. They are extremely well paid. When a jockey accepts the rides for a horse's campaign, as Nash had done, they must respect that commitment/booking and "ask Gai the question", not assume that Theseo was going to a different, less valuable race.[60]

I was starting to get very worried that my husband had found another bird, as he would say to me after dinner, "I'm just going out to sit with the bird." Well, I thought, "Aren't I the bird?" He meant the baby cockatoo that he bought and installed as our house guest for the past six weeks. But the bird bolted this morning – I went off to Canterbury trials and Nina flew the coop. She flew over the pool, over the fence and disappeared. Sonia (Dejager) rushed after it, ringing Rob on the mobile to come and help. Anyone who finds a little, baby pink-and-white cockatoo that answers to Nina, please give me a call.

MONDAY, APRIL 19

It was a very pleasant reward on Saturday when Nash won the Group 1 $350,000 AJC Oaks on the $50,000 purchase Once Were Wild. My team, including Amanda Skiffington, an agent from England who assists me at all the yearling sales in Australia, inspected her at the Magic Millions. The filly was knocked down to Amanda. Vet Greg Nash liked her enormously and I recalled her mother Wildesong and half-sister Grand Song, both of whom I trained. The breeder is John Muir, who has been breeding for many a year. Nash rode her very patiently and I must say I was amazed at how the other jockeys let him get away with such slow sectionals. This gave her the ability to sprint and, boy, did she do just that in the final furlong.

Our New Zealand purchase Herculian Prince made it four from four this preparation and signalled his arrival among Australia's top-level stayers when he scored handsomely in the Listed JRA Plate (2000 metres). He will spell before being prepared for spring.

I've seen the most amazing film, *The Girl with the Dragon Tattoo*. There was explicit sex and violence, but boy was it a good story. I'm not one for sitting in a theatre

---

60 When stewards turned down Gai's bid earlier in the week to hold Rawiller to the stable's star, Theseo, in the rich mile race, she took the matter to court. When she lost the case, Hong Kong-based Darren Beadman took over on Theseo – he ran eighth; Rangirangdoo, ridden by Rawiller, won.

for long, but Rob and I were transfixed. Absolutely a Group 1 performance by the young actress (Noomi Rapace). If you can find a leisurely three hours you definitely should see it.

Zabeel three-year-old Show Dancer has been a "Gai deceiver" and he must have known our thoughts because, lo and behold, he put his best foot forward. Stayers take an age to get fit but he and his workmate Maling (by Redoute's Choice) have really turned the corner. I loved Dad's expression as he got older: "For heaven's sake, don't give me a stayer. A man will be dead before it comes right." Dad loved racing two-year-olds. He loved speed and precocity, and he dominated two-year-old racing in Australia.

Yesterday I had a blast from the past. Norman Gillespie, the former AJC CEO, and I caught up and he introduced me to his friend Charlotte Smith. Charlotte's American god-mother has left her a range of vintage clothing, nearly 1000 pieces of which are housed in a display room just above Taylor's Square in Oxford Street, Sydney. What a remarkable thing. Young Kate and I enjoyed browsing through this wonderful collection. Charlotte's book, *Dreaming of Dior – every dress tells a story*, gives an insight into the collection.

Nash said Swift Alliance was shuffly this morning, which is no surprise as he had a hard run when third to Ortensia and Shellscrape in the Group 1 Galaxy at Randwick on Saturday.

I once had an owner who considered his skinny filly fragile. I have found the opposite to be true – thin fillies are usually tough and extremely durable. It is quite interesting that AJC Oaks winner Once Were Wild is far from a thick-set filly, but she is athletic and that is half the battle. If fillies are athletic and not fat, they are lighter on their feet as youngsters and move around the paddock more freely. I am a skinny filly, and as a child I was always running around and climbing trees. Skinny fillies have a marvellous ability to race at the top for longer.

Those who say New Zealand-bred horses don't make the best stayers must have their heads in the ground – the first four home in the Sydney Cup (3200 metres) on Saturday were all bred in the Land of the Long White Cloud. Jessicabeel gave her champion sire

Zabeel his 41st Group 1 winner. Interestingly, he is also the sire of Sahayb, the dam of yesterday's VRC St Leger (2800 metres) winner Exceptionally (by Ekraar), another New Zealand-bred. It is pretty easy to understand the Kiwis' depth in the staying ranks. They have a colder climate and their horses mature more slowly. In Australia it is hot and everything happens quickly, so we breed world-class sprinters while New Zealand breeds great stayers.

Why is there no racing in Sydney today? My husband is taking me to lunch, which is a pleasant surprise, but I feel I should be at the races. People have a free day and they want entertainment. We could have made it free entry and brought in the clowns and marching bands – it is the Anzac Day holiday for yesterday, isn't it? People would love it. Unfortunately once you take racing away, people learn to seek other entertainments. We get no attendance at Friday races, yet on public holidays we can't put a race meeting on. The powers-that-be should be shot.

FRIDAY, APRIL 30

The boys laughed after I told them first thing this morning that I had dreamed about track-rider Nacim Dilmi, who leaves us soon. Eyebrows were well raised and there was plenty of ribbing from the others. Nacim and Craig Messenger, along with their beautiful partners Lauren Taskis and Erin O'Loughlin, are moving on next week as their working visas have expired. It is funny how your subconscious plays games and I often find I dream about things that most concern me. Robbie would sooner prefer I dream of him, but that can't always be.

I received a great email from Nigel Smith, who used to strap Herculian Prince, or 'Butch' as he was known in New Zealand:

Hello. My name is Nigel Smith. I was a trainer in the UK for the best part of 25 years, flat and jumps. I went to work in Beijing for the now defunct Beijing Jockey Club in 2005. From there I ended up in New Zealand with a Kiwi partner and a beautiful daughter (long story).

When I was in NZ working for the McQuades (Karyn McQuade is a Matamata trainer) as chief cook and bottle washer – you would call it foreman, driver, race-day attendant, yardman, feed man, etc. You have the picture I am sure – I had the pleasure of looking after 'Butch' (Herculian Prince).

He won me a shed load in his first win and was obviously a tough character, plus a class act. I saw his picture on your website and he looks fabulous. Surprising what a bit of time will do, is it not?

Good luck with 'Butch'. He is my sort of nag to go to war with and he reminds me of one I had a few years back by Be My Guest – fast, but stayed longer than the mother-in-law.

Regards,
Nigel Smith.

MONDAY, MAY 3

Off to Bowral we tootled yesterday, rather tired after a long week and the Hawkesbury races on Saturday. (Full marks go to Brian Fletcher and his committee – what a fantastic job they do. A crowd in excess of 10,000 was there. Brian has all the local sponsors on board and next year, he tells me, we will see each of the major races worth $200,000 apiece.)

It was great to see Tanya Cirkovic, a good friend of mine from Melbourne, and we joined Lea and Bruce for a hilarious weekend. First, there were drinks and appetisers with John and Trish Muir at their delightful Burrawang farm. Trish has been an artiste in putting together her garden and making her home quite special. In fact, their farm featured in Peter Fudge's *True Form*, a must purchase for any coffee table.

You know I have two left feet. Well, I really got the award for it yesterday when we journeyed to downtown Bowral to have lunch at the Journeyman. Carla Zampatti, Australia's greatest fashion designer, was joining us and had asked if two of her friends, Lizzie and Barry, could join her. Knowing Lizzie's maiden name was Spender, I thought they might be Carla's children (Carla's husband is John Spender). Anyway, Carla arrives, then a very tall and most attractive blonde comes in looking nothing like Carla and I thought to myself, how can they be related? Then, phew, moments later the Barry arrives, and it's actor/comedian Barry Humphries. I then realise they are not related, but just good friends. We had an uproarious afternoon, fuelled by in-house raconteur Warwick Vyner and our fine group of friends.

It is such a small world. Lizzie knows horse whisperer Rob Horne, who has done work for me. Lizzie went to the Kimberley and identified two or three wild horses to bring back to NSW, and Rob had helped her break them in and handle them. Barry and I found we had a friend in common also – when I was much younger I travelled through Europe and stayed in Vevey, Switzerland, with famous English actor James Mason and his wife Clarissa. Barry said James would come to many of his shows and was always so complimentary, always having a bouquet for Barry afterwards. I must say it was a great highlight to meet this wonderfully talented gentleman.

A lovely misty morning at Randwick and Glyn Schofield was delighted with Casilda, Glenlogan's staying mare who will have her first Australian start at Randwick on 15 May.

She worked over seven furlongs (1400 metres), with the conditions very different to those she was used to in England at Kingsclere, Andrew Balding's stable.

I have changed the way I am training Fusakeo (by Fusaichi Pegasus), sending him over four furlongs (800 metres) in blinkers with Glyn piloting him. This fellow can flick his head when he works, which is irksome for the jockey and distracting for the horse. This morning he did not go on at the mile-and-a-quarter entry as usual, which made him think twice. I will do the same training pattern, but I like horses to use their head; I hate to hear from jocks that "he was just going through the motions".

What a lovely day at the races at Canterbury. Owner and friend Yvonne Smith (no relation) and I purchased a yearling, by Flying Spur from Corporate Queen, at the 2007 Magic Millions sale, paying a king's ransom of $400,000 to breeder Stuart Ramsey. I can't tell you how much I loved the colt. He broke in well, but he was not growing so I suggested to Yvonne we have him gelded; although not impressed, she did eventually consent. Geffen – we named him after David Geffen, who co-founded the film studio DreamWorks – returned from the procedure to an abysmal start to his racing career, finishing seventh at Newcastle on debut.

In the meantime the Punters' Club had come on board, leasing a share of Geffen. They must have thought, "What is this woman doing?" Geffen came back not much better next prep, but this time the real Geffen stood up to be counted. He had become the stable joke. "Hahahaha," people would laugh. "What an average animal," they cried from one side of Randwick to another. Yvonne reminded me today that when she asked should we sell him, I replied, "He is hopeless, but has shown me a glimmer." I don't think I have had more enjoyment out of winning a race than when Geffen greeted the judge over 1900 metres today.

This morning the breeze came up strongly causing Kate Grimwade to close the windows to the Randwick trainers' hut so she would not catch a cold. The unlikely pair of Antiguan and All Good Things went super. Both can hang on, a term used by the jockeys to describe horses who pull in their work. I wanted to give them strong exercise, so I worked them over six furlongs, finishing strongly over the final two furlongs, and there was nothing between them. I don't think Mark Newnham will want to partner Antiguan in company again for fear of getting extender arms. Standing Ovation, a high-priced son of Sadler's Wells out of Group 1 Golden Slipper winner Ha Ha, has come into the yard. He wanted to do things his own way, which did not suit *The Lady Trainer*, but one of my track riders, young Irishman Rob Rafferty, has done a grand job settling this gelding. In his pacework this morning, fellow Irishman Steve O'Halloran said Standing Ovation was soft but had a nice idea of things.

Courtesy of owner John Camilleri, the Encosta De Lago-Merlene yearling filly will be named by you, and trained by me. Yes, lucky blog readers, John has said you may name his regally-bred filly, so put your thinking caps on and think of something very special. John will make the decision on her name and the winner will receive a bottle of champagne for his/her efforts. The filly has broken in superbly at Tim Boland's Limitless Lodge, and her full-sister Merlene De Lago was a South African star, so you might just be naming a future Group 1 winner. Merlene, of course, won the Golden Slipper in 1996.

CHAPTER 10

Conduct unbecoming, according to trainers

I am shocked that NSW trainers could be so foolish to even consider signing the outrageous document that Racing NSW calls a CODE OF CONDUCT FOR LICENSED TRAINERS. I wish we could be spared the wearisome, nothingness "motherhood statements".

Apparently, the code seeks to promote and strengthen the good reputation of thoroughbred racing in NSW and Australia, and establish appropriate conduct and standards of behaviour for all trainers licensed by Racing NSW. Adherence to the code is a condition attaching to the licence issued to the trainer and a breach can result in the trainer being penalised under the Australian Rules of Racing and/or the NSW Thoroughbred Racing Act.

Racing NSW already has in place rules to regulate trainer behaviour. As one legal person said to me yesterday, "Why do they need more?" And why do we need to tie the noose around our own necks!

The code says, in précis – that licensed trainers should:

be professional in all racing matters; maintain, protect and promote the brand and reputation of racing; observe the Australian Rules of Racing; and observe legislation relating to anti-discrimination, health and safety, and employment. It says that trainers should maintain the highest standards of professional conduct, not in a manner that has an adverse effect; and must comply with the code during the course of any activity or function associated with the industry.

It says the following are breaches: offensive behaviour, discriminatory behaviour, harassment, intimidation of racing officials and other participants within the industry; a criminal offence; other behaviour likely to have an adverse effect on the industry. (And it says) trainers should try to ensure that their employees (whether licensed or not) and apprentice jockeys adhere to these principles.

It really concerns me that if I was charged (and not convicted) for drink-driving, a criminal offence, that I could lose my trainer's licence. Even if a trainer was to swear, he/she could lose his/her licence. Is it not interesting that only this week a university student called a policeman a "p-r-i-c-k", and when it was heard in court the judge threw it out – no doubt the student was referring to an unpleasant thorn.

The code also says –

a licensed trainer must not make any statement in public, including any contribution to television, radio, print media or electronic media (such as Facebook or Twitter) that is disparaging of a racing official or participant; or comment on any matter that is the subject of a current inquiry or appeal; and should try to ensure employees also don't comment disparagingly.

Racing in NSW suffers from too little criticism. We need more!

The code says –

licensed trainers should, where practical, generally promote racing and attend media-related activities ... and present themselves in appropriate apparel.

From what I can gather, trainers always present themselves well, but even if we think something is inappropriate should it cost us our licence and livelihood? In this day and age we want people to go to the races and, at the moment, there are enough regulations on dress-code. I'm pleased top-class restaurants don't make the same demands now-a-days.

And the code says –

any alleged breach of the code shall be investigated by the board or chief executive of Racing NSW, the stewards or any other person delegated by Racing NSW. The trainer may be charged under the Rules of Racing for any breaches.

A breach – in whose opinion? Any right to appeal would be denied and I think this is certainly the greatest injustice in the code. We live in a free country, not Nazi Germany. George Orwell must have had the code very much in mind when he wrote his best-selling novel, *1984*.

When the two-year-old filly Forward Love raced at Canterbury on debut last preparation she was slow to jump, ran like a drunken sailor and, eventually, finished fourth. Today's win at Gosford is a result of plenty of hard work at the barrier with the Charge Forward filly and Craig Messenger, one of my senior riders, partnering her in all her work until she came to hand and did what we wanted. Then Neil Paine was the only jock to ride her in the lead-up to the race. The result of this careful management was there for all to see today when she won with Glyn Schofield riding. I could not be more delighted with the way she won, and all the thanks and praise go to my extremely capable staff.

FRIDAY, MAY 7

We have gone back to having the horses ridden and led in the afternoon, as we used to do. I get the ponies out with the bigger boys aboard, all great horsemen, and they lead the horses around the pool. This gets them to settle down and also teaches them to be user friendly. It is so important for racehorses to have manners when you are trying to train them.

This is one of the e-mails I received about the code-of-conduct idea:

> Congratulations to Gai for her response to the unbelievably ridiculous Code Of Conduct proposed by Racing NSW. Thoroughbred trainers are not only an important part of racing, but as a group they are responsible for their own professionalism. The suggested code is an intrusion on their rights and belittles the professionalism that, almost without exception, these persons show.
>
> Jack Denham (the media-shy trainer who died late last year) and what his response to such drivel would have been, was the first thing to cross my mind. My next reaction was a sustained belly-laugh at the thought of Racing NSW determining what *The Lady Trainer* should wear. But then I remembered how their predecessors tried their level best to prevent her from being a trainer.
>
> Brian McInnes

The board of the NSW Trainers' Association will meet next week to discuss advising their members not to sign any code of conduct. Talk about rules on rules – the bureaucracy gets thicker every day. It would freeze free speech, stifle new ideas and restrict information to the public, as no one would dare make comment as they would be terrified about being fined or losing their licence.

The other afternoon Rob and I had a most delightful time as we were invited on a beautiful boat cruise around Sydney Harbour inlets with an interesting group of people.

Mary Hambro is a friend of ours visiting from England – she knows everyone and is a trainer in her own right. She was very kind to me when I was not very well over there some years back. Anyway, we enjoyed the fine dining, wonderful wines and excellent company on one of the truly beautiful boats, owned by a well-known Sydney identity.

The life of the trainer can sometimes be very tough, ha ha. But normally it is business as usual, watching the horses walk around the pool in the afternoon – there, I can see them exercise and speak to the boys and girls. Today Damien (Gaffney) and I did something different, setting up a card-table and fishing chairs right next to the pool. Darren Pearce, CEO of the AJC, joined me and we were able to have quality time catching up after the carnival. It is so much better than being stuck in a stuffy office and, more importantly, to be on mutual ground. I like Darren because he takes the time to listen to ideas and he always has his finger right on the pulse.

MONDAY, MAY 10

The laugh was on *The Lady Trainer* at Rosehill on Saturday. Common Objective can have his moments and has been a handy gelding, but the winners' circle has eluded him for some time. I had suggested that the owners think of selling him, as we had received a fair offer. Tom Hedley was the only one who said no, as he was keen to race Common Objective around Northern NSW and Queensland with another trainer. When he said this I said no, preferring he stay in the stable where he will earn more. The gelding must have got whiff of the talks, and he strode to victory in the Lord Mayor's Cup, ridden brilliantly by Kerrin McEvoy for his first win in the stable colours. Kerrin was so proud to be wearing TJ's colours. One tends to take these things for granted, but I think Kerrin has been brought up seeing the green and blue win Derby after Derby, so he took great pride in winning the cup.

Two interesting horses in the stable are by the great sire Sadler's Wells and both were bred by Strawberry Hill Stud. I purchased Seventh Reason (from Sunday Joy) at the Magic Millions for $2 million. He has probably been slightly disappointing with two wins from 11 starts, but he has been very immature and, only now at four, do I have a colt whom I can say is special. The other horse came to me second hand, yet my owners and I were under-bidders on him several years ago. His name is Standing Ovation and I had the pleasure of training his dam, Ha Ha, to win a Golden Slipper for Rob Ferguson and John Singleton. When he arrived he was a bit of a rogue, wanting to rip and tear around the place, not eat his tucker, and, in general, if I told him to go left he would go right. So I thought, ha ha (excuse the pun), this is my kind of horse as I love a challenge and he is certainly that.

I utilised the services of a very capable horseman who has come to the stable from America. Rob Rafferty, who was born in Ireland, has lovely soft hands, a good seat, and he is heavy enough to make horses concentrate. Every day, Rob and I did something different with Standing Ovation, including hill work, and foreman Mel Norton informed me he had started to get on his food. He has now been here three weeks and is a totally different horse. Darshan (Prakas), an Indian-born rider who also came via America, commented to Mel, "The horse is like butter … that is what we say in India about a horse whose action is so smooth."

I have just finished the most entertaining hour at the "Bill Whittaker Award for Racing Books" lunch held in the AJC committee room at Randwick. The finalists were: *Etienne De Mestre – The Master's Touch*; *Bart – My Life*; *What Are The Odds? The Bill Waterhouse Story*; *Phar Lap – The Untold Story*; *A Brush with Horses*; *Harnessing a Legend*; *The Cup*; *Dan O'Brien – Carbine*; and *Takeover Target*. Of course I was there with our supporters hoping that *What Are The Odds?*, my father-in-law's book, would be first past the post. The winner, however, was *Harnessing a Legend – The G.A. Lang Story*, written by Max Agnew about the great harness racing horseman Graeme Lang.

There was a great feel about the function, but I do think the AJC needs to tart up the rather tired committee room. Many people commented to me that it was like stepping into the past. It is our most important function area and all the VIPs are invited to lunch here at Randwick.

The trainers' association board will meet trainers on Wednesday to discuss the outrageous code-of-conduct document. I was not surprised to read in yesterday's paper that the very same document was sent to the veterinary association to sign, but they rightly tossed it out the window.

TUESDAY, MAY 11

Nash Rawiller enjoyed 10 days shooting the breeze in Fiji. The Pacific island was the venue for the 50th birthday party of Tony Noonan, which does not surprise me because Mornington-based Tony loves to travel as a trainer. Nash certainly looks refreshed and I was tempted to say to him, "Boy, you have done well with the spell."

I was at the bullring watching some of the yearlings going around, all recently arrived from breaker and pre-trainer extraordinaire Trevor Sutherland. It is so much fun to be able to recognise them after not seeing them for four months. The Encosta De Lago-River Song colt is such a lovely horse. Another colt I have a lot of time for is the Encosta De Lago-Orderly, whose dam is a sister to a great sprinter I trained,

Excellerator. The More Than Ready-Perfect Evening colt is so typical of his sire's progeny – leggy, loose on the move and just a cracking type. The Rock Of Gibraltar-Professional Lady is all chestnut in colour and is such a well-put-together youngster. The Redoute's Choice-Platonic grabbed my eye, as he did at the sales. I really think we bought very well this year. Round and round the yearlings went and all of them were super tractable for top riders Steve (O'Halloran), Ranjeet (Singh), Darshan (Prakas) and Alex (Jenkins).

Randwick is very good about allowing horses racing interstate to use the "Kenso" (Kensington) track and course proper for fast work. Mark Newnham gave Swift Alliance the thumbs-up this morning, saying he felt fabulous and that he was back on track. He will race next in the Group 1 Doomben 10,000 on May 29. He will remain in Sydney for as long as possible before travelling for the race.

THURSDAY, MAY 13

Members of the NSW trainers' board met yesterday. It was unanimously agreed that the proposed code of conduct is unacceptable, as rules are already in place that trainers have to abide by. We did agree that there should be a motherhood statement that sets the standards a trainer should adhere to without being specific to media appearances, dress code, etc.

I produced a very smart colt yesterday at Randwick, Star Thoroughbreds' Polar Eclipse (by Stratum). He has one of the most beautiful jowls I have ever seen on a youngster and only race inexperience stopped him winning on debut when he was second to Golestan over 1150 metres. The track was in good condition but it was stated on TVN that it was much worse than the announced Good 3. In my opinion the bias was not created by the track but by the extreme wind, which meant if you were not sitting off the speed, with cover and wide, you had no chance of winning. By the fourth race Nash had worked it out perfectly. Positioning our Redoute's Choice three-year-old Maling just behind leaders with cover, he then angled out and used his genius hands-and-heels riding to make him the winner over 1400 metres. Part-owners of Polar Eclipse are Ryan and Kim Faulkner, who run a wonderful breaking, pre-training and spelling property called Two Mile Lodge at Bowral.

The Merlene filly has a name. Her breeder, John Camilleri, kindly gave all blog readers the chance to name his beautiful yearling and the response was enormous with more than 100 names put forward. John decided that his filly by Encosta De Lago would be called Costa Serena, sharing her name with a luxurious cruise liner. The winning suggestion came from Mark Evatt, of City Beach, Western Australia, who we know through his ownership of two horses at Tulloch Lodge, Sincerity and Catanooga. Bravo Mark! We will all cheer frantically when she wins her first Group 1. John kindly gave a bottle of the premium Veuve Clicquot Ponsardin NV Brut champagne to Mark.

Damien gets married tomorrow to his darling Corinne. Batman is going to miss her Robin, but Arthur Buxton has kindly stepped in to drive me. It was so funny this morning – there has been a routine in place for several years now, but today was like wearing a new pair of shoes for the first time. I must say I did feel I was in safe hands.

Bart Cummings has always been known for his prowess in training stayers, but Tulloch Lodge is home to our very own long-distance star – foreman Dave Mejier ran fourth over 60 kilometres in New Zealand a few weeks ago and since then he has trained even harder. In the Blue Mountains at 7am tomorrow Dave will jump from the barriers in a 100-kilometre ultra-marathon. Like a good Waterhouse galloper he will be quick out of the gates, as we are told that early in the race there is 5km of stairs where the field can bottleneck and back-markers can encounter interference.[61]

I would not call myself superstitious, but I never put a hat on the bed – as Dad never did – and I always put my hat down brim up because, as Fast Eddie from Aspen, Colorado, would say, "Don't let the luck fall out". The other thing I don't do is offer cheers with water; I would sooner have a small bubbly in my hand.

Frank and Tony Mittiga and their wives, part-owners of Falvelon two-year-old Extreme Mover, who raced at Randwick on Saturday, visited a clairvoyant last week and somehow racing came up. After informing the seer that their horse was running she quickly told them that he would not win as the race would be won by a horse starting with the letter P. Well, what do you know, the topweight Extreme Mover was a courageous third to Parriwi. The clairvoyant went on to say that a grey horse would also win on the day, but she made horrible mistake as the only grey on the day ran last. I just wish she had got the first one wrong, too.

Dave Hodgson, the Randwick track manager, is departing in July after doing an excellent job in bringing the track back to its former excellent state. The only thing lacking in his tenure was that he did not live on course. When the committee makes its next choice it should make it part of the contract to live at Randwick because there

---

61 Dave got to the line 17 hours later. He said he had wanted to pull out with 10km to go, but his family talked him into going on. A month later he was still sore.

is plenty of accommodation available in the refurbished house vacated by former AJC CEO Norman Gillespie. Many things can go wrong on course in the wee hours of the morning – for example, last year a pipe burst and the tunnel flooded.

I got a real kick out of Geffen's win today; he has put together a very decent record with four wins from nine starts. I had to laugh when Tania Rouse and I went for a soft drink after his win. She said, "He is such a funny little horse. I love his receding hairline." Tania referred to the fact that Geffen has only a tiny piece of fluff for a forelock and it never seems to get any longer. It is a little bit adolescent, to say the least, but he does have a great set of nostrils and a big hindquarter. He will now enjoy a well-earned spell at Joe and Lou Manning's Littledale Lodge.

Canterbury racecourse could be such a special place. If the threat of selling it does not eventuate I am sure the STC will make it into one of Australia's loveliest racecourses. At the moment it feels more like a retirement centre than a racecourse. All the punters are old and, if you are lucky enough to see anybody, you have usually seen their faces before. This centre of western suburbia should be teeming with young people, but the stands are empty and the bookmakers look forlorn. They should have a park in the centre of the track, include childcare facilities and make it free entry to ensure that racing is a place for families with entertainment for all generations. How do we train people for the Sport of Kings if they don't know it exists or how wonderful it can be? I am worried that in the next 20 years people will not be used to going to the track and the problems will be bigger than they are now.

Winter Olympian Jeremy Rolleston, who is writing a book on what drives successful sportsmen, visited Randwick this morning. He asked me if Luke Ricketson and Kate, our daughter, were still an item, to which I replied, "From what I last heard, yes". Jeremy explained that he used to play footy against Luke, Jeremy being a Barker boy and Luke a Waverlian. The title of Jeremy's book is *A Life That Counts*.

Only the other day my American mate Wesley Ward – what a remarkable man – dropped me this email in reference to our visit last year:

> Tell Gai that those wild brumbies she saw – five are going to Royal Ascot. One of them just broke the track record at Woodbine in Canada.

I was chatting to Ray Thomas, racing editor of the *Daily Telegraph*, who was very excited at the prospect of going to Royal Ascot to cover the Royal meeting for his paper. He also mentioned that he had read that the first race meeting was held at Randwick on May 29, 150 years ago. Ray mentioned it to the AJC and, to his surprise, the club was not aware of this. Full credit to the powers-that-be, as they immediately took up the important date and I believe much will be made of it at Royal Randwick on Saturday week.

FRIDAY, MAY 21

Crossbow annihilated his competition in a barrier trial at Warwick Farm today to win by four-and-three-quarter lengths, with Blake Spriggs looking over his shoulder as he cruised to the winning post. I advised Blake after the trial that this was not acceptable in our stable.

Tomorrow all eyes should be on the mighty Gold Water in the Group 1 Doomben Cup. The bonny mare has her foot well and truly on the Group 1 till. The distance (2020 metres) is no problem and she has shown on numerous occasions that she is right up to this company.[62]

WEDNESDAY, MAY 26

A slightly older statesman was partnered by one of my senior assistants at the track this morning. Ex-Yankee horse Cannonball was ridden by Steve Dennett. Last prep Cannonball could be quite boisterous, but Steve said he could have ridden him on a silk thread this morning. I said, "Steve, you old cotton fingers," referring of course to the nickname given to the famous and most talented jockey George Moore, who was Dad's champion rider in the 1950s and '60s.

There was great cheering and hilarity after race three over 1300 metres on the Kensington track at Randwick yesterday. Star Thoroughbreds' filly Anniversary greeted the judge after fighting off her main danger Palomares, who made a game challenge in final 100 metres. Nash decided the game plan after walking the track, which was a 'heavy 9', and having a discussion with me about where the best going was. Nash said he would elect to steer Anniversary to the far outside fence on the home turn, and at first I was a little surprised, but once he described how he would do it I told him to go for the doctor. The More Than Ready filly won by three-quarters of a length.

Anniversary reminds me very much of a doe – she has a wonderful loping action. I said to co-owners Bill and Geraldine Bozinis-Wendt, that she could be an Oaks filly next season.

---

62 Gold Water ran second, beaten a nose by Metal Bender.

It is getting so hard to program races for my two-year-olds. How do I get through to the Racing NSW programming board? On Tuesday, Anniversary greeted the judge first up over 1300 metres. For her to race in a distance equal to or greater than this, I have to back her up quickly to run at Rosehill next Saturday over 1500 metres or she does not get another suitable race until June 26 or 29. Then yesterday, Snippetson gelding Fast Clip won over 1250 metres at Canterbury. He is now either forced back in distance to run at Randwick over 1100 metres or wait until the same dates as Anniversary.

We have the most absurd situation during the month of June where the programmers have scheduled within the metropolitan and provincial areas a surplus of Maiden events. Surely with the simplicity of Benchmark ratings it cannot be too difficult for the handicappers to attach ratings to all horses that have raced. If that was the case we could then run all metropolitan races late in the season as Benchmark races, with a genuine spread of weights. First starters could begin off a specific weight, dependant on the quality of nomination. In this scenario the entire horse pool is catered for, otherwise we have this ridiculous situation where horses are unable to be programmed.

All we are doing is pushing horses interstate when most are not good enough or seasoned enough to make the trip, itself a huge cost to the owners. All two-year-olds should be given an opportunity to progress through the classes before they turn three. Progressive action must be taken.

Wonderful 150th year celebrations will take place at Randwick on Saturday. The AJC is getting right into the swing of it, as can be seen by the list of highlights on a briefing document Bettina Brown so kindly sent me. They include: free entry; a commemorative racebook based on the oldest book in existence at the AJC (1869); the first 3000 people to purchase a racebook will receive a "150 Years of Racing at Royal Randwick" cap; a memorabilia room and exhibitions; an antique car display; kids' entertainment; mounting yard presentations; a parade of ex-champions; and a farewell to retiring bookmaker Bill Waterhouse.

We had the pleasure of having a mate of Bruce Slade's, Patrick Hunt, at trackwork this morning. We had dinner with Patrick and his grandfather, Sir Patrick Hogan, just the other night and young Patrick was keen to see how the operation worked. I think he found the morning very interesting and it was not long before he and Bruce were competing, each trying to see who could get the most accurate sectionals on their stop-watches. Nothing is more pleasant than to watch the enthusiasm of youth.

After reading a front-page article in the *Sydney Morning Herald*, I wonder if in the next few months we will see a merged STC and AJC headed by a prominent breeder. I have nothing but respect for John Messara and his business acumen, I like him very much and I know he believes he has racing's best interests at heart, but I know that most people in racing fear a man with such extensive stud interests being in control. No one could expect him to dispose of his stud interest to take the job, but most believe that his interest compromises him.

Huge amounts of money appear throughout the article. I cannot see any way of it being generated without the sale of a racecourse, the last thing we want. Board members of the clubs are in unpaid positions and they represent a cross-section of people in racing. I hope it stays as it is.

The best part of another glorious morning was to call in and see Theseo, along with staying stars Descarado and Herculian Prince, who have all arrived back at Tulloch Lodge in preparation for spring. These boys are just shooting the breeze until they tone up enough for three-quarter pace.

MONDAY, MAY 31

Tania Rouse, we all know, is a champion, but she was awarded the title publicly by Sydney's surf lifesaving community over the weekend – she is Sydney's champion lifesaver. Any of you thinking about going for a dip must just hope that Ms Rouse is not far away. Tania will now go on to contest the NSW championships.

Neil Paine was in New Caledonia on the weekend and his French is improving out of all knowledge. He won on a mare called Crepes, by Commands, his seventh win on her this season. The previous preparation he partnered her for six wins.

My father-in-law, Bill Waterhouse, had his final day as a bookmaker at the races at Randwick on Saturday. It was an emotional time for my husband Rob, Louise (Bill's daughter) and Susie (his wife). Bill would still be at races today but the years have crept on and his family thought it best he retire. I thought his speech was fantastic, so I have included part of it here:

> I can't believe that today at Royal Randwick will be my last day fielding as a bookmaker. I am 88 and how my life has flown – just like a bullet train.
>
> As I look back on my lifetime career in bookmaking and betting, which started more than 70 years ago when I was just 16, it is incredible how racing has changed. We had hand-written ledgers and, at my peak, I could write 4800 legible tickets in

STAR RIDER: Gai Waterhouse's stable jockey Nash Rawiller returns to scale on Theseo after winning the Group 1 Mackinnon Stakes at Flemington in 2008. PHOTO: SLATTERY MEDIA GROUP/ MICHAEL WILLSON

METEOR STRIKES: Northern Meteor wins the 2008 Group 1 Coolmore Stud Stakes at Flemington for Nash Rawiller and Gai Waterhouse on the same day as Theseo won the Mackinnon Stakes. PHOTO: SLATTERY MEDIA GROUP/MICHAEL WILLSON

WINNERS ARE GRINNERS: Gai, Nash and Gooree Park racing manager Andrew Baddock celebrate Northern Meteor's Group 1 breakthrough at just his third start for Gai.
PHOTO: SLATTERY MEDIA GROUP/MICHAEL WILLSON

GOLDEN MOMENT: Glen Boss drives Sebring to victory in the 2008 Group 1 Golden Slipper Stakes at Rosehill. It was Gai's third Slipper success. PHOTO: LISA GRIMM

STAND AND SALUTE: Glen Boss celebrates Sebring's Slipper win as part-owner James Hazzisevastos leads the colt back; and, clockwise, other Star Thoroughbreds owners Luke Henderson (holding trophy), Brian Leonard, Margaret Butler, Denise Leonard and Anne McDonnell pose after the presentation. PHOTOS: LISA GRIMM

HE WILL ROCK YOU: Blake Shinn acknowledges the cheers after Rock Kingdom's win in the 2009 Group 1 Epsom Handicap at Randwick.
PHOTO: BRUNO CANNATELLI

one day – still a record! We enjoyed huge crowds every week with over 350 bookies at Randwick. The races were places of great excitement and the racegoers were punters looking for action.

These days are long gone with only a smattering of bookmakers and everything computerised. Most bets are placed by phone. Punters don't need to come to the track to place their bets, removing that on-course flair and excitement.

What can be done? To me it's simple: give the punters a reason to come back to the track with better odds – either through the bookie or the Tote by reducing bookmaker taxes and lowering Tote deductions on course. If you bring the marketplace for betting back to the track, then the crowds will follow.

I love racing with a passion. It has always been in my blood, with the odds never far from my mind since I was a little boy. Through my mathematical leaning, I developed a keen gambler's instinct and learnt how to 'make my own luck' ... and I became known as the world's biggest gambler.

It was said I set the Melbourne ring on fire with the exploits of the 'Hong Kong Tiger' (Frank Duval), who had me gobsmacked by placing a series of bets to win $1 million on Oaks day in 1966 when $20,000 would have bought you a good house in Sydney.

One of the biggest of them all was the 'Filipino Fireball', Filipe Ysmael who bet in telephone numbers. Nothing was as unsettling as when he set me up to lose over $1 million in a hotel room in 1967 ...

I learnt early on that a man's word is his honour and a gambler who doesn't pay his debts is not worth a grain of salt – unfortunately, I could line my office walls with worthless cheques, sometimes from pillars of society.

I made mistakes too and one of the biggest was letting a young Kerry Packer ring my office one Saturday afternoon to bet with my secretary, as he couldn't make the races. He lost $1 million that day, but brassed me! I guess it served me right for bending the rules.

The Fine Cotton betting scandal cruelly and unfairly took away my livelihood. I knew absolutely nothing about the 'Fine Cotton ring-in' but was wrongly denied my passion for racing for 17 years through a trumped-up charge of 'prior knowledge'...

After my long exile from the course, I still wanted to come back as a bookmaker in 2002 so I could teach my grandson, Tom, the classic art of bookmaking. Tom was 20 and I was 80 and he took to the races like a duck to water. Together we fought our way on to the interstate rails, became the number one holders and the Waterhouse name was back at the top. Tom moved to the Melbourne ring because of the more favourable betting regulations in Victoria and is now the biggest individual bookmaker in Australia and is launching his betting site *www.tomwaterhouse.com* so everyone can take him on …

Now that I am a senior octogenarian, I find it's time to hang up my shingle, although I still go to my office seven days a week, wanting to stay sharp and be around my tireless working family.

I feel so fortunate to have lived the life I have and thank racing for everything it has given me over the years.

My biggest wish? That racing in NSW would put the punters first by bringing in a better playing field for its bookies – and Tom could come back and work at home in Sydney!

TUESDAY, JUNE 1

Although bred in Ireland, Princess Tracy (by Ahonoora) has left her biggest mark on the Australian breeding industry. Tulloch Lodge, I believe, has the next success story from the prolific family with a filly by Encosta De Lago from Princess Stacey (by End Sweep from Princess Tracy). The dam of seven winners, five at Group level, Princess Tracy's best progeny include triple Group 1 winner Tracy's Element (Last Tycoon) and Group 1 Stradbroke winner and successful sire Danasinga (Danehill). Every single one of her producing daughters has left a Group 2 winner or better, with their progeny including Typhoon Tracy (winner of five Group 1 races), Red Element (to stand at Glenlogan Stud in 2010), Prince of War, Prince Arthur (to stand at Think Big Stud in 2010), Suntagonal, Happy Morning, Fatal Attraction and Kylikwong, who was placed in Group 1 races at two and three. The family has recently been in the news as it is responsible for producing Snitzel's first winner in Japan, Floreal (from Floreana) – the filly didn't just win, she bolted in by eight lengths.

I purchased the filly from Princess Stacey at the Easter sale in Sydney. At $300,000, she was great value. She is a stunning sort, looks an early comer (born September 28) and is being broken-in at Muskoka Farm where she continues to do everything asked of her.

Glyn Schofield rode Extreme Mover this morning and was delighted with the way he found the line. I gave the owners the choice of taking him to Queensland for the Inglis race for two-year-olds worth $100,000, or staying in Sydney to race at Rosehill this weekend for $70,000 over 1400 metres. Understandably, they chose to stay home and cheer their horse in Sydney, where he will have every chance of greeting the judge.

Fast Clip is in the same race. This lovely gelding by Snippetson won at Canterbury last Wednesday and he steps up in class and distance, but he is more than capable of both. It is always hard when you have two or more in one race, but we try extremely hard to place them where they are best suited to winning. Of course, there can only be one winner, but I will leave it to you readers to decide which to back.[63]

I think the AJC and the STC should put in time and effort, with Events NSW and Racing NSW, to making the 200th anniversary of racing in NSW later this year a real celebration. My racing manager Kate Grimwade said that in England, when the Queen Mother had her 100th birthday, most people in the different towns dressed in period costumes – what a great gesture to the grand lady. Wouldn't it be a hoot if everyone tried hard and people in period dress and carriages flocked to Hyde Park where it all began? What a great way of telling people about the Sport of Kings.

WEDNESDAY, JUNE 2

Late last night we received a star Kiwi recruit, Beloved (by Ustinov), from over the Tasman. A three-year-old filly with strong form around her, Beloved has been sent to race in Sydney by her owner Andrea Craven. The name Beloved is taken in Australia, so we need to help Andrea select a new name. She would prefer a name with seven letters and has offered a bottle of champagne to the winner via the blog.

I have just been told by Dave Fenning, who has kindly taken over chauffeuring me while 'Damo' is off on the longest honeymoon in the world, that it is his mum Pat's birthday today. I am sure you all wanted to know! Birthdays are important, not because you get a year older, but because it is good for people to recognise and celebrate that you are alive. They say happy birthday, step back and appreciate your presence, and then wish you good will for the future. I have a birthday book at home that Sonia Dejager fills into the top of my diary page each day. Everyone thinks I have this marvellous memory, but really I just have a great whipper-in (a hunting term used for the second-in-charge huntsman who rounds up the hounds).

My darling one has developed a lovely habit of buying flowers for me each Friday. The greengrocer asks him each week, "Are those for your wife or your girlfriend?" Rob says, "A bit of both."

A tip for anyone who enjoys cut flowers in the house. I enjoy getting them and I purposely make a great fuss when they arrive, but I notice the roses usually die within 48 hours. Thankfully the greengrocer gave Rob this tip: bang the bottoms

---

63 Extreme Mover, $5.50, was third; Fast Clip, $4, was fifth.

of the stems and put a spoonful of sugar on the damaged parts, then the roses will stay alive longer. I can tell you the tip is the best I have had in years. Only last night I thought the roses looked droopy after four days in the house. So I banged their bums, added sugar and, voilà, they stood to attention.

THURSDAY, JUNE 3

Star Thoroughbreds' two-year-old filly Anniversary was well matched with Catbird filly Suki as they glided around the B grass over 800 metres this morning. Anniversary, by More Than Ready, treks south for a 1400-metre race in Melbourne next weekend because, as I have mentioned before, there is nothing for her here. Nothing, that is, until the end of this month – for horse, owner and trainer it is a long time between drinks.[64]

FRIDAY, JUNE 4

Had the very important pick-up of my Royal Ascot outfit from David Jones' designer Alex Perry today. I must say I was truly impressed with the detail he had gone to. What colour you ask? The dress is aqua, very 1960s, very 'mother of the bride'. I also got my Neil Grigg chapeau; you cannot go without a hat and gloves to Ascot. How does one transport this hat on the plane? Very simple. You buy yourself a drum box – people will think you are in a band, but who cares – and then you put it with your main luggage and don't worry about it until it reaches your port of call.

At lunchtime Peter Carrick, breeder of the Redoute's Choice gelding Crossbow, visited the yard. We adjourned for a bite of pasta at Lucio's in Paddington. I am not a wine buff, especially at lunchtime because it makes *The Lady Trainer* sleep, so I left the drinks decision to Peter. He has a three-quarter sister in blood to Crossbow and I will be training the youngster. If Crossbow can live up to my expectations, his sister certainly has great residual value.

I couldn't leave Sydney this weekend without visiting my favourite place, the hairdresser Valonz. There at the basins was the trifecta – Charlotte Inglis, Carmel Size and yours truly. Well, you can imagine what the conversation was. Yes, "What are you wearing to Ascot?"

There has been a false start. Under 'riding instructions', the filly from New Zealand, Beloved, was to have a name change before racing in Australia. Feverishly, my readers racked their brains in search of names that owner Andrea Craven would find acceptable. Lo and behold, Racing NSW raised the flag, allowing Beloved to race as Beloved. Andrea said, however, that she liked the names so much that she would still

---

64 Anniversary was fourth as the $2.80 favourite at Flemington on June 12.

award a bottle of champagne to the person who submitted the best name. Her choice? "The winner is Won Love because I indicated a preference for seven letters and One Love by U2 is one of my favourite songs, together with the connotations in racing." Mark Evatt, who won the last naming contest, wins again. Bottoms up, Mark.

MONDAY, JUNE 7

How small is the world? We have just landed in London, and on the flight next to us was Nick Solley, who has a number of horses with Star Thoroughbreds, including the Jet Spur colt Mikoyan, who will trial at Warwick Farm on Friday. Heathrow is full of a multitude of different nationalities and cultures; it makes Tulloch Lodge look so microscopic.

I thought it must have been one of those bad Irish jokes when we went to check in for our flight to Dublin on Air Lingus. The computer check-in system was not working – the last thing you need after flying halfway around the world.

I am so looking forward to catching up with friends in the Emerald Isle. Visiting Ballydoyle and seeing genius mastermind John Magnier and his maestro trainer Aidan O'Brien will be a special highlight. We have four days in Ireland, then it is on to Bristol to catch a train to Newmarket. Rob and I love to travel by train as we get time to talk, take in the countryside and catch up on plenty of reading. I am enjoying reading Rob's *The Economist*, a magazine he always has tucked under one arm. Also, after decades of not touching George Orwell's *Animal Farm*, I am finally getting stuck in and enjoying it.

The team at home got through the trackwork in grand fashion, I am told, with Tania Rouse very ably steering the ship.

THURSDAY, JUNE 10

Where do I start? Since landing at Shannon Airport on Ireland's west coast I have found Ireland remarkable. The roads are tiny, but once you are on the freeway it is pretty good travelling, despite the weather being changeable. It is not just the greenness that makes this place, it is the people. Everyone is just lovely – they are interested in what you are doing, and are always smiling. The grand live in a style we all only dream about, while the rest are more humble. Since Rob and I were last here, the Irish economy has taken a pounding.

Staying with our great friend Silla Harrington in County Limerick was a true joy – she and her wonderful husband Bill looked after 'the little Aussie' many decades ago and they ensured I had the most wonderful time. The hunting was superb, the parties memorable and the people just wonderful. That's why 30-plus years later Rob and I look forward to visiting Silla's most glorious home on the farm known as The Glen.

The trees are lovingly cared for, the garden is unique with its little wood area, and all Rob and I could do was marvel at the flowers, especially the peonies. We had a quiet dinner at the Dunraven Arms in Adare and I thought back to the jars we had after days out hunting when I was younger. Jetlag quickly caught up with *The Lady Trainer*, but this did not worry Silla, who chatted away to Rob while I dozed. Next morning Silla woke at the crack of dawn to make us breakfast. I don't think I have drunk so much English Breakfast tea in all my life.

On the road again and off to Longfield to visit the training establishment of David and Kate Wachman. David trains mostly fillies, all beautifully bred with Danehill Dancer blood in abundance, and there were some cracking sorts among them. The coats and condition of his team were excellent. We watched lot after lot go through their paces and asked many questions. David is bright, keen and extremely competitive, all the elements necessary for a good coach because, essentially, that's what trainers are.

Breakfast was with Tom and Sophie Magnier and their son Charlie. (Tom and Kate Wachman are brother and sister.) We chatted horses before it was out again to watch the second lot, finishing around midday. Then it was in the car and on to the road again, following Tom at a frantic speed.

Coolmore, Ireland – of all the studs I have visited in Australasia, America and Europe, I don't think I have ever been in a more impressive establishment. They have wonderful statues of the great stallions placed through the grassed laneways and gardens and a beaut bronze of the boss himself, John Magnier. Into the summer house we tumbled for lunch. I know this sounds like a gourmet traveller's tour, but the cheese soufflé rising inches high was a delicacy to make one drool. The pea soup or salmon to start with was mouth-watering and then I followed Tom into some apple pie for dessert. Susan Magnier, the matriarch of the household, was so happy to be surrounded by her grandchildren, especially Charlie, whom she does not see often because Tom and Sophie live in Australia.

Off to the stallion barn it was, with Tom and Shane McGrath, who is over from Coolmore Australia. Sadler's Wells is showing his age, but wouldn't we all at 100-plus (he's 29, actually). The grand stallion of stallions has not covered a mare since 2008, but he is happy and, as his attendant, said, "He is such character". His sons Montjeu and Galileo looked in superb condition. The Danehill stallion Holy Roman Emperor is not big, but he has powerful quarters and a wonderful top-line. His progeny are the same and they are burning up the tracks here in Europe. Tom informed us that another rather impressive son of Danehill, Aussie Rules, is going very well with his first crop in Europe. He is a great sort.

We are staying in a large manor house in Ballingary, Tipperary. Last night we caught up with the Lillingston family and New England stud's Peter Stanley, who was visiting Ireland. We will be staying with Peter and his wife Frances in Newmarket from next Friday. Everyone was in champion form. We had many a laugh and then I could see my darling one fading quickly. He had done all the driving and deserved not too late a night.

We are on the road again after another early rising. We are heading to Coolmore's famous training farm Ballydoyle, which is headed by the masterful Aidan O'Brien. We have to be there at 7am sharp as Starspangledbanner, the wonderful Australian colt, will gallop at 10-past and, yes, we are extremely excited.

Garry Frazer has been breaking in horses for *The Lady Trainer* since the very early days. One he remembers particularly well was a Fasliyev filly called Esther. Being by a European champion two-year-old and out of a sister to Australian Two-Year-Old Triple Crown winner Burst, he held high hopes for her. She beat Fastnet Rock home when third in the 2004 Silver Slipper behind Ballybleue and Dane Shadow. Sadly an accident prevented her from fulfilling her potential, but her daughter by More Than Ready can make amends. Garry is breaking her in. "She is coming along really well," he said. "She feels like she'll go early. She's very well balanced and reminds me very much of her mother."

The experienced Jamie Innes was on deck at trackwork at Randwick today, as was young Jason Collett, a leading New Zealand apprentice who is in Australia on scholarship for a couple of weeks gaining experience.

Fusakeo jumped logs this morning to engage his brain and keep him fresh for his 1400-metre race at Randwick on Saturday, where an improved performance is expected on his last-start eighth.[65]

FRIDAY, JUNE 11

Ballydoyle is a hard place to describe, but it is a truly remarkable one and home to a remarkable trainer. On arrival you sense the aura of the place, its organisation and the people who run it – Aidan and Anne-Marie O'Brien are special people. Ironically, they share the same surname as Aidan's predecessor, Vincent, the late father-in-law of Coolmore principal John Magnier.

The horses are turned out immaculately. Everything here is in place; and not for show – it is just that Aidan is a master horsemen and absolute perfectionist.

---

65 Ridden by Blake Spriggs, Fusakeo ran fourth to Lebrechaun.

Tom took us to the training barn and indoor riding arena, which you find in Europe because of the harsh winter. Eighty-plus older horses walk one behind the other while the small bird-like figure of Aidan O'Brien stands at the entrance with a nod of morning recognition to all his riders, each known by first name … Seamus, Liam, Rory, etc. One senses a great and kind warmth towards his large team. They walk for 20 minutes, then what starts is amazing – the horses in the arena all get organised into a big figure-eight circuit that, in full swing, looks just like a long, winding snake. This is the first lot, another four or five will follow. Of course, we are all keen to see Starspangledbanner, bought from Australia after winning the Group 1 Caulfield Guineas and before he won the Group 1 Oakleigh Plate.

After another 20 minutes they depart and on to gallops the next lot go. We jump in the four-wheel drive along with the No.1 jockey, Johnny Murtagh, who has his name embroidered on his jacket (not that you would forget it). He has the firmest handshake on meeting; you have to try not to whimper when he shakes. A very nice man.

Also joining us in the four-wheel drive is Jenny, with video in hand. She videos all the gallops for the 'lads' (John Magnier and his group of owners), along with the jockeys' comments, which are directed at Aidan. This part of their system reminds me of our set-up at Randwick. I think it is very important that the jocks' comments are recorded after trackwork and trials, so I was delighted to see that the maestro does the same. Important things can come out of what the jockeys say, and it is best to talk to them while the horses are fresh in their heads.

They work on a wood-fibre track here, but they also have plenty of grass tracks available. Cantering up in twos and threes they pass us and riding out is Aidan's oldest son Joe, a bright-eyed, eager and enthusiastic 17-year-old. He has a great seat and hands. When the horses have finished they walk down, are hosed off and then go to their boxes.

We adjourn for breakfast and Aidan tips the porridge, which I have not had for years. His wife Anne-Marie is so supportive. It is interesting that whenever Aidan has a runner he is seen on the phone afterwards and, it is said, he is speaking to Anne-Marie. They live and breathe their training and that is why they have been so hugely successful. The pressure must be enormous, being Ascot eve, but you would never tell; he is polite, astute and very helpful.

Back to the barn and leading the group is the grand four-year-old Rip Van Winkle, a most beautiful athlete. He will start in Race 1 at Royal Ascot on Tuesday, the Group 1 Queen Anne Stakes (1600 metres) and the hottest event of the five-day carnival.[66]

---

[66] Rip Van Winkle started 4/1 third favourite in the Queen Anne and ran sixth behind 11/8 favourite Goldikova.

Third down the line is a handsome chestnut with a funny white marking under his belly. Yes, it is Starspangledbanner. Walking past he certainly did not grab my attention, but when he went out I could not get over how powerful his hindquarters are. He had his head down and was breathing rhythmically as his hooves pounded the turf. It was simply exhilarating to watch him.

Johnny jumps out of the vehicle and hops on to Age Of Aquarius, who was second to Profound Beauty, Dermot Weld's Melbourne Cup entry, at Leopardstown last month. It is interesting that they work with a lead horse here and when they race – it is seen as quite acceptable for a front-runner to set a genuine speed without being a real winning chance. We learnt from speaking to Aidan that the lead horses' heart-rates do not increase at all when put under pressure and asked to stretch out; they have learnt to be cunning – they look the part, as if they are under pressure, but they don't really try because they know they will always be beaten.

Each jockey wears an earpiece so Aidan can speak to him; there is no shouting out the window here. I must say we were travelling at a solid speed next to the gallop, not dissimilar to what Melbourne Cup-winning trainer George Hanlon used to do on his property near Geelong. Video rolling, we were bouncing along to get set to see the final furlong, which I found fascinating. At this last stage of the gallop you can see that the lead horse is under real pressure. He gets picked up with ease by the classy partner, who pulls up hardly blowing at all. Johnny Murtagh explained that Haradasun did similar work over a mile before he won the Group 1 Queen Anne in 2008. He said that he finished so strongly at the end of his gallop that it took him so long to pull up.

The training regime in Ireland and England is so different from that in Australia. The fitness levels of the horses, who have to cope with the undulating conditions of the tracks, is far greater than 'Down Under'. The jockeys, too, are fitter. These boys ride at four to five meetings a week and are expected to be at the gallops at least twice a week. From what I saw yesterday, and from having walked the Newmarket and Ascot courses, there is great undulation. They even climb in the sprinting races.

We had lunch at Cashel with Luke Lillingston and Dr Emmeline Hill, an acquaintance of Kate Grimwade. Dr Hill, a famous geneticist, has discovered the genes that identify sprinters and stayers, even as foals. We'll be hearing more about this when she comes to Australia this year. It was then back home to freshen up before a delightful finish to the day with the Magnier family at Coolmore. Visiting Ballydoyle was a delight.

We flew into Bristol last night; what a joyous town. Kate and Tania (Rouse) were both born and raised near here. I took particular delight in winding through the roads to find the Bristol Old Vic. In my theatrical days when I trod the boards, I always had the great wish to act in the hallowed theatre, but it was not to be. The streets are cobbled in this large university town, which is a great fishing port. We enjoyed the catch of the day and wandered hand-in-hand back to the hotel, which is named Du Vin. All the rooms are named after famous wines, ours being Laroche, a very good chardonnay. It is definitely worth a visit.

We took a train to Newmarket today to stay with Peter and Frances Stanley. Tomorrow Sir Michael Stoute's stables are on our agenda – Sir Michael has the great pleasure of training Workforce, this year's Epsom Derby winner.

THURSDAY, JUNE 17

Since we have arrived in Newmarket the time has flown and a whirlwind of horses, trainers and gallops has passed by. I am staying with Peter and Frances, who only a few years ago bred the mighty Ouija Board for Peter's brother Lord Derby. This is a family steeped in history with their ancestors having fought with the Kings of England. They are bright, intelligent and heavily involved in the sport we love so much through their work with the Jockey Club.

On Saturday we visited Michael Bell's yard. He is a wonderful trainer married to Georgina, with whose relatives we had dinner in Ireland – the Lillingstons. Michael has a lovely yard and some very nice horses, including a couple of Ascot hopefuls. We walked along the July Course at Newmarket, Rob bringing Michael's car so we could be in position to watch the gallops and then drive back to the stables.

After a hearty breakfast with Michael and the team, it was over to Sir Michael Stoute's and his partner Coral. It was an absolute joy to see Workforce, a gorgeous creature – big, strong and enormous bone for bulk. His strapper changed his rug conveniently when we were watching him in his round wire pen, about 12 metres in diameter, which can be moved from grassy patch to grassy patch. The young strapper said his Derby "sling" would pay off his mortgage – the success of really great horses on the racetrack really does give people a better lifestyle.

After Michael's we had a lunch engagement with Johnny and Susie McKeever. Johnny is an excellent chef and his roast beef on the Weber was delicious, and we enjoyed the company of their friends, also racing people. Then it was back to Peter and Frances' New England Stud and a hot bath, as showers in England just seem to dribble out.

Most of our friends are going to 50th and 60th birthday parties, so Rob and I were delighted to be invited to the 21st birthday party for Archie Stewart, son of renowned

English trainer Alex Stewart. There, I had the pleasure of sitting next to Luca Cumani, well known to Australians with his Melbourne Cup attempts that have brought two seconds, and we discussed the same dilemma that besets trainers as their children grow up: do you retire, as Ian Balding did for Andrew at Kingsclere, or do you have your son or daughter training under you? Or, do you buy a small yard for the next in line? Or do you go to the small yard yourself? As Luca pointed out, he is passionate about what he does and still loves it very much, so the decision can be very hard. In Australasia, trainers can train in partnership, which is quite common, and this is a wonderful way of sharing responsibility and bringing new blood into the family business.

I have decided that racing in England is unhealthy. At every function you attend there is thick, billowing smoke. How damaged their lungs must be, I dread to think. Cigarette after cigarette devoured with such delight is a real worry. It was very amusing at a Sydney party I recently attended when a guest complained about a person smoking indoors – I know this sounds prudish but I think banning smoking indoors is important so everybody can enjoy themselves without the smoke signals. These experiences are half the fun of being in different a place, though.

On Sunday we visited Adrian Beaumont who has the huge responsibility of organising visiting trainers. This year he was responsible for trainers from South Africa, Hong Kong, Australia and the US, not to mention European countries. The first person we saw was American Kenny McPeek, who remembered us well and was only too pleased to show us his two Ascot charges, Noble's Time and Tiz My Time, both in remarkable condition. We then bumped into Wesley Ward's foreman and their gelding Metropolitan Man, who we had seen as a yearling in the US last November.

Out on to the gallops and Sydney trainer Gary Portelli and his team of owners were watching Gold Trail with such excitement before the day dawned. Gary brought his mum and dad over for their first trip to Europe. Paul Messara's Alverta was enjoying the sun in her paddock and, even though the reports say she has lost plenty of condition, I thought she looked remarkably healthy.

We adjourned for coffee and I said to Rob that we should call Sir Mark Prescott, the eccentric and genius trainer. He never allows owners to ring him on any day other than Sunday, but being cheeky I gave him a call. I said, "Mark, it is Gai and Rob and we are on your doorstep. Can we visit?" He replied, "For you, Gai, of course."

His yard at Newmarket roundabout has a newly surfaced indoor training area, a swimming pool and exquisite boxes with hunting scenes painted on each, including the hares being chased by the hounds, and the fighting cock. Sir Mark is a man who loves his blood sports, which are very much looked down on these days.

I found out through Mark that the expression "well-heeled" actually came from cock fighting. The attendants of the cock would place a man-made spur to the back of the tendon of the bird, slightly to the left or right to ensure a lethal blow, depending on the cock's gait. Interestingly, the first fleet of people to arrive in Australia were given cocks as part of their rations; everyone enjoyed cock fighting then, but things are now more civilised. We made a date with Mark to follow the bullfights for four days in Spain with him next year, as all his stories of the event are vivid and capture you in the moment. His ideas on racing and training are revolutionary and his strike rate is outstanding.

The Royal Ascot meeting commenced on Tuesday and what remarkable racing we saw. There were only six races and the time seems to fly between them. In the Group 1 King's Stand (1000 metres), Frankie Dettori told me Nicconi, David Hayes' horse, missed the start. Consequently, he was pushed hard early so his effort to run fourth was great. He is clearly a horse with plenty of ability. Gold Trail seemed lost on the straight course and was bumped left and right and never appeared comfortable.

The winner, Equiano, won the race two years ago when he was trained by Spaniard Mauricio Delcher-Sanchez, after which he was purchased by clients of English trainer Barry Hills. By Acclamation out of an Ela-Mana-Mou mare, he is the perfect sprinting type for England; short-coupled but with leg. The result was an all-family affair, as Barry's son Michael rode the winner.

We caught the train to Ascot, but you have to get out of the gates like Dance Hero to get there before the traffic, which is atrocious. After racing it was back to our London hotel, our first time at the Dorchester, which is a glorious and exclusively decorated hotel perfectly located in Park Lane. We finished the evening with lovely, quiet, family dinner at one of London's finest restaurants, Le Gavroche.

TUESDAY, JUNE 22

I was delighted to see that Starspangledsbanner won so impressively at Ascot on Saturday. We had seen the colt at Ballydoyle only 10 days previously and Aidan had said he needed another gallop or two. Well done Aidan, what a master trainer. It is interesting to note for the future that both Haradasun (who won the Group 1 Queen Anne Stakes at Royal Ascot in 2008 after Coolmore bought into the horse and Aidan took over the training) and Starspangledsbanner had a barrier close to the stand side and were able to utilise the fence as a guide, a great help for horses having their first run up Ascot's long straight.

On Friday, Robbie took my girlfriend Silla Harrington and me off on a train to Kent, which only took 15 minutes, and from there it was on to Down House, in Downe, where Charles Darwin used to live. This is the remarkable place where the great scientist developed a theory that changed people's thinking on evolution. Charles Darwin was married to his cousin Emma Wedgwood, whose family developed the famous blue porcelain pottery. Rob admired the beautiful old mulberry tree growing against the window, the same one Darwin wrote about so lovingly. Silla and I walked the well-kept garden, which is open all year.

Rob, coincidentally, met up with Robert Ford, who he had never met but had corresponded with. Both are keen maths and form students and have admired each other's work for years. They were in deep conversation for an age.

Back to London and Rob and I had a lovely meal at Claridge's. The standard of food and service makes this one of the top hotels of England – you can't find this level anywhere else.

On Saturday we made our way to Gatwick to catch a flight to Verona, of Romeo and Juliet fame, in Italy. There we met up with great friend Jenny McAlpine. Jenny spends part of her life in Verona and the other part working with David Hayes in Australia. She takes tours around the studs of Italy and England and knows every inch of beautiful Verona.

On Sunday we caught up with Agnes Waser, whom I have written about in the blog. We "picked up" Agnes at the opera in Sydney and she stayed with us for nearly six months after that. She made the pilgrimage to Verona to meet up with us.

Yesterday, for Rob's birthday, we went to a beautiful restaurant called Arquade, in Villa Del Quar, just outside the town, an absolute must if you are in Verona. It has not stopped raining since we arrived, which is strange, as I have never been to Italy and experienced anything but sunshine.

Jenny tells me there is little money in training in Italy. She purchased the 2010 Oaks winner Contredanse for a client and she says there were only 1200 people at the track on Oaks day. I am to meet a young trainer in Milan today – he is coming to Sydney to work with me. He is struggling to make ends meet, but is young and talented. We don't know how lucky we are in Australia. Jenny highlighted this when she told us that the average monthly wage in Italy is 800-1000 Euros (about $1220-1400).

WEDNESDAY, JUNE 23

England's *Racing Post* is a worldwide industry leader. The articles are informative and the punting material is most valuable. One of the paper's features is the rail reading, which sits alongside the weather forecast. This reading gives three separate penetrometer scores for different parts of the track – for example, Ascot ranged from 9 on the stand side to 8.8 in the centre and 9.2 on the far side. The round course had an 8.5 reading and the going was given as "good, good-firm in places". Why can't the AJC and STC give out readings for particular parts of the track? I watch AJC course manager Dave Hodgson walk the track with penetrometer in hand, so why not give the public this information as they do in England? The more information there is the more people are willing to gamble. Less information means a punter will keep his cash in his pocket for use on other entertainment.

Sir Mark Prescott told us the most interesting story when we visited the other day. Sir Mark used to breed greyhounds and he would divide each litter, half going to a professional dog handler where they would be taught to lead, chase and be well-mannered on the whole. The other half went to a Mrs Peabody in Yorkshire, where the natural athletes were allowed to run wild in the fields. They would chase behind the tractor and dive and weave at the small animals churned up and chased out by the tractor's deep murmur. Yes, she lost some but they were extremely well fed and they lived outside in a shelter near the kitchen. As Mark said, when it came to coursing you would back Mrs P's dogs every time to be more effective.

The reason was that they could naturally change strides and they used their killer instinct out in the wild, whereas in the other establishment they were held in yards and were not moving about. It is the same with thoroughbred foals and yearlings. They are far better out in the field, developing muscles and running diagonals. This has to be the better horse as opposed to those who are reared in a small yard. The Mrs P comparison can be seen so clearly amongst thoroughbred breeders of Australasia – you know pretty well where the winners come from.

Here is one for anyone who can understand dreams. I know you think I am too tired to dream, but I always do and they are always about the people coming in and out of my life. The other day in 'Dreamland' I was at Warwick Farm, which had built a new stand close to the rails. My friends Len and Jane Pochley were there too. As Len departed life some time ago, how or why he was in my head you would not know. Anyway, as we walked down the stand together we got to a fence, which I was going to hop over, but then I thought I'd better go around as I had the elderly couple with me.

Now this may not seem strange to you, but it was the first time I had made a decision in a dream and I woke immediately after in astonishment and told Rob. Readers, I would like you to tell me have any of you ever made a decision in your dream? Or, like with me, do things normally just happen. Please, is there anyone who can help the poor *Lady Trainer* whose sub-conscious plays tricks on her? What is the meaning of this?

THURSDAY, JUNE 24

Yesterday's debacle back home was the two-year-old event at Gosford, which was won by the stable's Crossbow in dominant fashion but declared a no-race because the gates opened as the result of an electrical fault before the starter took his stand to press the button. What disappointment for the owners of the Redoute's Choice gelding, and the stable. We identified him early at Magic Millions in the draft of his breeder, Peter Carrick's Grange Farm, and he has continued to impress ever since. I love the neat Redoute's Choice youngsters and Crossbow is nicely coupled and has a lovely alert head. I always look for an intelligent head. (Interestingly, Rob chose our dog Bello – by the way, I am missing him terribly while on holiday – because he looked the smartest in the photos of the litter we were sent.)

I composed this diary entry while sitting in a coffee shop in Milan, a city of business and fashion. The coffee is almost as good as it is at my favourite Sydney haunt, Allpress, and they do freshly squeezed orange juice. Every Italian seems to eat gelato mid-afternoon and every man, except the tourists, is dressed in a suit – grey, white, cream, single-breasted or double-breasted. Even in this hot and sticky climate the men wear suits and ties. In Australia everyone wears a black suit. It is so ho he, ho hum in comparison to Milan. Where is the imagination?

It is a pleasure to walk the streets here through all the frantic shoppers, and I was one of them. The stores all have sales pending, but if they are kind it is nothing to get 30-40 per cent off, especially with my VAT form. The rest of world may be in recession, but Milan is oblivious.

Our holiday draws to a close and Rob and I are keen to sink our teeth into some work. Tania and the team have done a sensational job while we have been away. We speak every day to go through the work sheets, answer any questions, reply to notes, and give direction for things to be done. Horses need 24-hour attention.

FRIDAY, JUNE 25

Australia, as a part of the Commonwealth, has the Queen and the Governor General; NSW has the Governor and the Premier; Sydney has the Lord Mayor; and now we have a new Prime Minister. What do they all have in common? They are, of course, women.

The Randwick track was open for fast work today after a week of showers. The fast workers included the rising three-year-olds, headlined by April's Golden Slipper runners Brightexpectations and More Strawberries. Alex Jenkins said the grey Brightexpectations was one of his best two-year-olds of the morning, while Nash said the same about More Strawberries, the half-sister to Arrowfield's new stallion All American. She worked with Dance Hero's three-quarter brother Tango Valentino (by Redoute's Choice), who Blake Spriggs said "worked terrific". And Blake loves Blue Lotus (also by Redoute's Choice), a daughter of Group 1 sprinter Our Egyptian Raine.

The older horse ranks were dominated by the return of Herculian Prince, who worked over 1200 metres in fine style for Alex. It is scary to think that these horses will be beginning their spring campaigns with trials in the next two-three weeks. New Zealand stayers Descarado (by High Chaparral), Just A Blaze (by The Gladiator) and Tullamore (by Savabeel) bowled along, covering "acres of turf" with each loping stride. Star Thoroughbreds' Theseo was his usual impressive self, even though he is still building up with three-quarter pace.

TUESDAY, JUNE 29

American sprinter Cannonball was partnered on the track by Nash, who was so impressed he labelled him the best of his morning.

WEDNESDAY, JUNE 30

The Catbird two-year-old Suki, a winner on the Kensington track yesterday, is a homebred of owner Yvonne Smith. Yvonne came into my life as bright as a button many years ago and was very keen to get involved. Eilatan (Yvonne's daughter's name backwards) was Yvonne's first horse and, even though he showed ability, Dad suggested she move him along. "Not quite good enough, Yvonne," he said. However, she was very protective, like most new owners, and insisted on keeping him. Only later did Yvonne agree that TJ was right. Yvonne, like everyone else who had anything to do with my dad, very quickly realised he was never very far away from the mark when it came to spotting the potential of horses.

Assertive Lad was Yvonne and her family's greatest excitement in racing. He had brilliant speed as a two-year-old, finishing third to Belle Du Jour in the 2000 Golden Slipper before winning the AJC Sires' Produce and the Champagne Stakes, and he cemented himself as a top older horse by winning the Doncaster in 2001. After that, Yvonne decided to breed from fillies she purchased and Suki is a product of such a mating. Harry Mitchell of Yarraman Park does an excellent job advising which stallions to choose and whether they should be keeping their mares.

Back in Europe, it's our last day in glorious Taormina. It has everything you could possibly want on holiday, a beautiful view and tiny beaches with little boats bobbing on the water, all in formation. Here the moon seems to shine constantly every night, making a pathway to heaven. Now, perched under umbrellas, are almost naked people getting the most of the gorgeous sun.

Rob and I made the pilgrimage to the small island of Lipari yesterday. The trip there takes an hour with breakfast portside halfway along. I had the most delicious chocolate croissant straight out of the oven, with an OJ to go. All the locals also move from island to island – seven islands dot the Aeolian Sea, which is clear blue and just magical. Ulysses, in his travels, would instruct his men to fill their ears with hot wax so not to hear the sensuous sounds of the Sirens luring them to the rocks. He took no chances either, strapping himself to the mast.

But none of that yesterday. The highlight was the lunch on the top of a mountain on Lipari. We were the guest of a young restaurateur and his wife, locals who are thinking of moving to Australia. To get to their place you have to be a mountain goat. The house was a joy, modern yet traditional. It is not big, but typical Italian and immaculately clean. The first thing I noticed upon entering was the aroma of the lunch we were about to enjoy on the balcony after we gazed over the azure of this magical sea.

We had fried aubergine with the view and once seated at the table we were served the lightest entree, delicate white sheep's milk ricotta with the tiniest tomatoes. At this stage I was careful not to eat too much with so many courses after. We then had pasta and squid followed by swordfish with onions in a sauce to die for. All absolutely delicious and truly Sicilian dishes, with fish and aubergine the main ingredients of so many of the meals we have eaten. Just when I was starting to flag, on came dessert and a famous Sicilian one at that – cannelloni, a biscuit filled with sweet ricotta cheese. Watching Sasha in the kitchen lovingly squeeze sweet ricotta into biscuits is really a work of love. A very sweet coffee followed and more, a traditional Sicilian dessert of ricotta covered in green and white marzipan icing. By this time I told them I needed to run up and down their steep driveway a few times to work some of it off. We left them with a fond farewell and promised to reciprocate their generosity when they arrive in Sydney. Eating is a major part of everyday life here and I am reminded of the men of Milano eating their gelatos from their little buckets each afternoon.

We start the morning in Taormina by walking up the hill, puffing frantically as we speak to the office at Randwick. There are nearly 200 steps up to Taormina from the beach, where we are staying in the Sea Palace in Mazzaro. By the time we arrive in the city at 9.30am the residents are feverishly sweeping the streets in front of their restaurants, boutiques and little produce shops. Every piece of small rubbish is swept up immediately, the locals clearly very proud of their beautiful town.

A brioche, a soft breakfast roll, a granita of crushed raspberries and an OJ is my normal breakfast delight; so different to what I have at home, but that is what makes a holiday so delightful. Then down the hill we come on our way home and we always buy fruit at the little cart half-way down. We always stop and have a chat to Guido, the gentleman who hires the cars and mopeds. Before we leave on each holiday daughter Kate always says bring me back a Guido story, as any time he has taken us out we have got horribly lost, or run out of petrol, or there has been some sort of mechanical failure; but he is such a joy to be with.

I am going to get a haircut today – Valonz eat your heart out. At Elle in the main drag I see my man Ricardo who comes each morning for a coffee while we sit down after the long walk up. Everyone is so casual on this island; time does not matter and patience is certainly a virtue.

The other night we had the pleasure of visiting the owner of all the restaurants and clubs in Taormina, a groovy guy who built an exquisite palace behind the main street. Tom and Hoda and their friends, including *Getaway's* Jason Dundas, have been among our playmates here. Tom arrived looking exhausted, but he has certainly put on poundage since being here.

A chilly but clear July dawn greeted Tania, Kate (Grimwade), Dave and the jocks at Randwick this morning. Dance Hero's half-brother Tango Valentino and All American's half-sister More Strawberries both looked every inch of their superior breeding when working over 600 metres for Mark and Blake. Both riders reported that they were suffering from wind-burn on return to the tower.

Theseo, Descarado and Herculian Prince were obvious best choices from the jocks with Rabbuka (Giant's Causeway) also getting a special mention from Neil. When this group of horses works again on Friday *The Lady Trainer* will be on hand to put them through their paces. I promise I have captured some Italian sunshine to bring home with me.

CHAPTER 11

The next crop of babies put on their L-plates

received this wonderful email from Alastair Forres, whose son Guthrie Williamson is behind a very smart, unraced gelding in the stable by the name of Grandee (Grandera-Archeologist, by Festival Hall):

Dear Gai,

I note that Guthrie's two-year-old gelding Grandee is coming home to the farm for a spell shortly. Guthrie and I will keep your office informed of his progress at Merrigan, between Orange and Canowindra.

It is possibly valuable to outline to you what Guthrie is doing as he is repeating a successful formula used by both my uncle and myself in thoroughbred breeding and selection.

My uncle Edward (Ruby) Holland-Martin, an Olympic horseman, founded the Overbury Stud and bought two steeplechasing mares just before World War II (for 35 and 50 guineas respectively) and encountered success quickly: the Coventry Stakes of 1952 was won by the Overbury-bred Whistler, who went on to be a champion sire of two-year-olds ...

The stud's greatest son, however, was sold for the relatively modest sum of 27,000 guineas: Grundy, Horse of the Year in 1975 and winner of the Derby (by three lengths), the Dewhurst (by six lengths), and a legendary King George VI and Queen Elizabeth Stakes, in which he defeated Bustino in course record time. It is worth remembering that Grundy, as a yearling, jumped out of his railed paddock and landed on a cattle fence, requiring 136 stitches to sew up his belly. Grundy is prominent in Mossman's dam's pedigree, of course – a nice dash of toughness.[67]

In my own instance, I built on Grundy's success by buying (and importing) a cheap Great Nephew weanling in the UK, who you know as Great Klaire. I did trackwork at Grenfell (near Cowra, in central-west NSW) on her and realised that there was a V8 under the bonnet and bought her half-sister Eight Carat. Eight Carat needs no introduction – her daughters Cotehele House (named after our house in Orange) and Diamond Lover (who I bred) started their own dynasties and whose offspring are still winning or being placed in races around Australia most weekends.

The point of all the preamble, is this: Australian thoroughbreds over the past 20 to 30 years have become better bred, better conformed but not necessarily much faster – and certainly not as consistently tough as those your father trained. Merrigan, Guthrie's hill farm, is a throwback in time to days when horses were less valuable and were treated like horses, rather than wrapped in cotton wool. Grandee is not a large horse, but there is much in him that reminds me of horses of days gone by.

Grandee is an important experiment – and should he perform as a three year old and older – he should do you and Guthrie proud. Guthrie has built his stud operation on carefully selected mares (not for price or for fashion, but for hopefully that indefinable trait, "ticker"). After Grandee is spelled, he and I will do long, slow work on the hills (possibly even gentle cattle work) for four to six weeks prior to him coming back to your stables. I will coordinate his diet with that of your horses and will communicate closely with your office. We use a top farrier and vets we have known for many years.

Behind Grandee, are other youngsters, bred with a similar objective – for toughness of mind and body. It is up to Guthrie, a much better judge of strategy than myself, as to how their careers unfold, but my role is in the formative phase. It is my hope that the Grandee experiment shows that lightning can strike in the same place, not just twice but three times – Grundy, Great Klaire and Grandee.

Kind regards,
Alastair (Forres)[68]

---

67 Mossman stands at Vinery Stud, near Scone in the Segenhoe Valley.
68 Alastair Williamson is the 4th Baron Forres

I'm back at headquarters and delighted to be back on track. Good to see carnival horses Theseo, Rock Kingdom, More Joyous, Montana Flyer, Descarado, Herculian Prince and more, some bigger than others. My team has done a sensational job looking after the horses while I have been away. Now it is all systems go for the important time of year – spring in Sydney and Melbourne.

I did see two outstanding movies on the plane on the way home. *Welcome*, set in a French coastal port about friction between the Kurds and the French. You don't realise how important Australian passports are; they allow you to go anywhere in the world and getting visas is no problem. In heart-wrenching *Welcome* this poor young man is trying to follow his heart to be with his girlfriend in the UK, so he attempts to swim the English Channel.

The other wonderful movie was the Australian comedy *Bran Nue Dae*. It was just marvellous. It made me laugh from the moment I turned it on, especially after seeing another Australian film, *Samson and Delilah*, which had no dialogue and was probably the most depressing film I have ever seen. *Bran Nue Dae* on the other hand was joyous.

A big trial morning saw only a few gallopers out and about at Randwick. Gooree's Distant And Lovely signalled she was spot on for Hawkesbury next Thursday with strong work over 1200 metres for Blake Spriggs. The event is the last in the Rising Stars jockey series and if the daughter of Encosta De Lago can win, Blake will be named champion for 2009-10.[69]

Group 1 winner More Joyous' half-sister Joy Toy, by Encosta De Lago, gave young Blake a great feel working alongside fellow Encosta De Lago filly Ice Creme, who Alex said did everything he asked of her. They worked at three-quarter pace.

A mention of trackwork today without noting Theseo would be like having spaghetti without the bolognese. The multiple Group 1 winner charged through his work in terrific fashion, pleasing track rider Alex Jenkins no end.

The trials at Randwick were full-on, with more than 20 Waterhouse runners lining up. The return of Brightexpectations was a highlight in the 740-metre events, the grey Group 2 winner running away to score by seven-and-three-quarter lengths under a good hold. Nine of the team won from 12 trials contested, with some good efforts from those who did not win.

---

69 Distant And Lovely won a Class 1 over 1600 metres as $3.80 favourite.

It was lovely working at the track. Tim Clark was most taken by staying hope Just A Blaze and his huge stride. "Boy, I like him," he said, "What a wonderful character." I have mentioned before about Just A Blaze's long neck. He does not carry a great deal of condition, unlike his work partner Seventh Reason (by Sadler's Wells) who has a beautiful, rounded action. What an odd couple! They bowled over seven furlongs (1400 metres) and were a pleasure to watch.

Dee Bee Nine (by Red Ransom) will race on Saturday over 1600 metres at Randwick. I think he is well-placed in the event, especially with Blake's claim. The apprentice is riding in super form – he has booted home a Saturday winner every weekend for the past five weeks, a great feat with Nash and Corey Brown getting the cream of the rides. (Dee Bee Nine finished sixth.) Nash leads in the premiership, but Corey has a distinct advantage because he can get down to a low weight so he gets a smorgasbord of rides. Nash can ride at only 55.5kg and above.[70]

More Joyous was just that and Ranjeet waxed lyrical. Mark mentioned that AJC Oaks winner Once Were Wild was so much thicker across her wither and I, too, am amazed at how much she has developed.

We had the "three stooges" today – Bassoon (by Redoute's Choice), Power Personified (by Exceed And Excel) and Tullamore (Savabeel). They are all a little brain dead, but that is about to change as working them in company makes them think about their work. They are three beautiful, big, strong geldings and Darshan (Prakash), Ronnie (Nunn) and young Alistair (McAuley) did a grand job with the trio.

Steve thinks American sprinter Cannonball has switched on greatly and I said I hoped so because he needed to improve after his first trial back. Stratofortress (by Stravinsky) seems to be getting ready for a new career – Robyn (Freeman) explained that when he went past the winning post he saw a shadow and jumped high into the air at full speed.

Two stars of the show, More Strawberries (by More Than Ready) and Mutameyez (by Encosta De Lago) matched strides beautifully. Mutameyez is a massive colt who is very light on his feet. The filly More Strawberries is just as big as Mutameyez – the little girl you saw run third in the Group 1 Golden Slipper has been left behind at Strawberry Hill; she is now more like her half-brother, All American.

If you want to back a nice two-year-old, you need to be on Squamosa (by Not A Single Doubt), having his first start on the Kensington track on Wednesday. He was Neil's best and he hit the line with vengeance and looks super.[71]

---

70 Spriggs confirmed his form by riding five winners at the Rosehill meeting on July 17.
71 Squamosa won, starting at $1.70 favourite.

I am reading Freud – no, not psychoanalyst Sigmund, but his grandson Clement, who wrote *Freud On Course: The Racing Lives of Clement Freud,* taken from his articles in the *Racing Post* and published by Racing Post Books, 2010. He is a man for all seasons and he wrote with great wit in the sporting tabloid. I laughed most at this piece: "Sending a child to boarding school costs nearly the same as a horse in training, only children have the edge as they are cheaper to shoe and to transport by train as off-peak they are half price."

Another beauty was: "There are owners who make racing pay, just as there are pawn-brokers who offer customers glasses of slow gin before advancing money on wrist watches, and parking meter attendants who are content to let you park on a double yellow line while you are at the dentist. They are rare breed though."

TUESDAY, JULY 6

It has been a busy afternoon and I am a bit like a cat among the pigeons. I like to see the horses ridden and led, especially the yearlings. Graham (Howard), or "Fox" as he is better known, does a great job on his pony and nothing ever flusters him. At the pool Frank (Fitchett) is in charge of proceedings, but with me about he gets in a flap.

I wanted new Irish boy Alistair McCauley to ride Just A Blaze and lead Blue Lotus (by Redoute's Choice), but the filly did not want a bar of her giant lead-horse, so I made a quick change. Ice Creme (by Encosta De Lago) is a lovely ride and she makes a great pony, although I am not sure her owners bought her for this. Being a big filly, the extra exercise does her good and keeps her mind on the job.

This morning's gallops were excellent. The beautiful filly Zutara (by Encosta De Lago) was Blake's best. She is back preparing for classic spring racing and, yes, there are spoils galore. Melbourne in the spring has phenomenal prizemoney; Sydney in certain races, yes, but the lure is to go south, for trainers and owners.

All my spring horses are in work. Theseo delighted Alex, but his best of the morning was Herculian Prince – that might be because they are fellow Kiwis, or perhaps it was just because he is a sharp dude.

I attended an interesting meeting of the NSW Trainers' Association yesterday ahead of our general meeting next Monday – all trainers must attend as there are urgent matters that must be addressed. Such topics touched upon included the code of conduct put forward by Racing NSW. In my opinion, anyone who signs this is mad. It destroys the protections afforded under the rules of racing.

Workers compensation was another major issue, as were the findings of Justice Perram on betting fees. The most pressing is country racing, which I really feel for.

They race for no money, races are abandoned at the drop of a hat and the cost of getting to the races for such tiny rewards is unfair. The country trainer epitomises the Aussie battler. It would be a cruel thing if they were pushed out of the sport – racing should start in the country, and at present that is not happening.

On the score of handicapping and programming, trainers complained that they were not being listened to and that their objections were not looked into any further. This seems ridiculous, as we are at the forefront of dealing with owners, staff and officials, and we are the ones who have to pay wages and run a business.

Anyway, I am hopeful our plight will be looked at in a new light after next Monday.

WEDNESDAY, JULY 7

Today was truly miserable at the Randwick races, except for Star Thoroughbreds' colt Squamosa, who scored a brilliant win by three lengths on the Kenso track, easily dominating his peers and marking himself an above-average individual. I especially kept him to race on my return. The team had put the polish on him while I was away, Nash put on the finishing touches, and, yes, he was too brilliant.

Nash realised early the fence was no good so he scooted five off the rails in the straight. The second horse elected to be 10 off, but racing midfield he could not make up the ground on the speedy Not A Single Doubt colt. As there is no 1200-metre race in Sydney for him, we have to wait to go to the Rosebud, the Golden Rose lead-up race at Rosehill on July 31. The Rosebud will be a hard race for an inexperienced youngster, but if he is the real thing he will do it with ease.[72]

THURSDAY, JULY 8

While walking on Tuesday afternoon, Squamosa knocked Dave Meijer to the ground. Dave, a long-distance runner, is the fittest man in the yard, but as he put his hand down to break the fall his middle finger was bent over backwards and was dislocated very badly. Still, he didn't let the colt escape. Bandaged and bruised, he came to the track this morning – he said he could not sleep, anyway. He loves his job and the horses.

I asked, "Was it mixed emotions when Squamosa won yesterday?" His reply was, "Not at all. It is great for the colt and his owners." What a wonderful outlook on life. Wouldn't it be great if everyone was as accepting.

On a different note, I was delighted to read that former Australian Jockey Club CEO Norman Gillespie has been appointed the head of UNICEF Australia. I wish him well.

---

72 Gai changed her mind and Squamosa raced – and won – over 1400 metres at Randwick on July 24 instead of racing at Rosehill the next week.

It was great to see the lightly-trained Zabeel gelding Show Dancer break through and greet the judge over 2000 metres at Hawkesbury today. Young 1.5kg (provincial) apprentice Blake Spriggs rode him a treat. He was very strong in the final furlong and I hope the gelding has a future as bright as our young rider.

At Randwick on Saturday we will saddle two rather exciting horses, Fusakeo and Dee Bee Nine. With Fusakeo, the top weight in race three, I will use the expertise of Nash. Through the winter the jock is riding a little heavier than at carnival time, so the gelding will carry only 1-1.5kg dead weight. Dee Be Nine was weighted 1kg above the limit in race four, so with Blake's 3kg city claim he will carry 2kg under the limit at 51kg. Both have a large number of owners and I look forward to them joining me in the champagne bar.

I had a small giggle when reading this in *Freud On Course:* "In other major sports – cricket, tennis and coursing – you know who is in charge by the clothes they wear. White coats and panama hats, short-trousered suits with whistle in gob, purple and green Wimbledon blazer, pink coat carrying two flags and riding a horse (Waterloo Cup).

"Yet stewards and clerks of the course wear hats, suits and ties like the rest of us, though usually better cut and more expensive. This must stop. We have to know who to blame (also to praise if praise is due). I think they should follow the garb of football refs; many stewards have perfectly adequate knees."

FRIDAY, JULY 9

Substitute driver Dave Fenning and I trekked to the Warwick Farm trials today. It was well worth the journey out there. Maurie Hartney and his daughter Robyn, plus a contingent of owners and trainers, made up the ranks in the members' stand. There had been quite a bit of rain and the track was affected. It was rated 'slow'.

Just A Blaze kicked off proceedings with a fourth over 1200 metres. I rang senior part-owner John Cornell, who played Strop in the Paul Hogan television series. His question was, "Has his neck got any longer?" My response was, "He now has to tie it around his knees so he does not trip over it." John and his wife Delvene will come south from Byron Bay to see their mighty stayer have his first start on Australian turf in the next fortnight.

It was then the turn of More Strawberries, who has not improved her barrier speed whatsoever from last season, despite considerable work and effort from my staff. But it was not long before she got into stride and, although not handling the going, she came home to run third.

I have been impressed with the lovely Gooree filly Royal Esteem. Jumping well today, she took control and won by two lengths, and she has plenty of upside. Her mother, Basra, won a Group race at Ellerslie (when trained by me) in front of young Bruce Slade, who tells me that day was his first at New Zealand's premier racetrack and he remembers Basra and the moment vividly. Little did he know then that, out of shorts and into long pants, he would be assisting in running the Tulloch Lodge organisation.

I heard the other day that a well-known country trainer rang Racing NSW and got a bit hot under the collar with the trainers' liaison officer, a former trainer. The liaison officer reported the trainer's rudeness to the stewards and he was fined $1000 for his behaviour. Is it not ironic that this officer is placed there to help, but instead of having a cup of tea and trying to placate the poor frustrated person, he chose to report him? Is this behaviour not just like that of a reformed smoker, always intolerant after having given up the habit?

I feel there is an epidemic of discontent in the training ranks. There is lacklustre prize-money, poor communication, and an inability to see our plight. When will it change? I really wonder if the powers-that-be are capable of fixing the problem.

I think it is well worth the Sydney Turf Club and Racing NSW sitting down to look seriously at changing the date of the Group 1 Golden Rose (1400 metres), because it comes too early in the youngsters' preparation. August 28 is this year's date. Spring three-year-olds are all looking at the Group 1 Caulfield Guineas (1600 metres, October 9) at this time of year, a race that comes some five weeks after the Sydney feature, with some horses looking to drop back to the distance of the Group 1 Coolmore (1200 metres, October 30).

Easter was late this year and carnival races ran through April. Mark Webbey, my race programmer and jockey manager, explained that last year when he was assisting Patinack, he was forced to program three-year-old Trusting in the Group 2 Warwick Stakes (1400 metres) against older horses three weeks into the season. As it turned out, it proved successful. However, most horses struggle to have the proper foundation to be ready for the Group 1 Golden Rose in late August.

MONDAY, JULY 12

I have just left the trainers' meeting with Racing NSW and I assure you that we are a disgruntled lot. Prizemoney is not going up, there is no one willing to listen to our plight, and we are treated with disdain and intolerance. We trainers are a fed-up lot.

We represent the owners, who are the linchpins of the industry. People who invest in horses need to be looked after, thus we are not just speaking on our own accord. We are pushing the cause of the owners, the stable staff and, in many cases, the jockeys.

Many a meeting we have been to at headquarters and nothing seems to come of them. It is really sad to see the discontent. Racing NSW is there to represent the participants; instead we are treated like children who have no idea of the business at hand. I am hopeful things will change in the near future – if trainers can have their say they will get things done.

Damien Gaffney is back from his honeymoon, bright as a button, so Dave Fenning's wonderful driving services have now been put on hold. 'Damo' sure is lucky to have such a great understudy.

The babies (rising two-year-olds) have started to move along. Ron Nunn is in charge of them with the help of Johnny, Darshan and Alistair. They are not far away from the jockeys starting to partner them.

TUESDAY, JULY 13

This morning was the first that "Yankee Doodle" Cannonball has really pleased me in his work. Steve Dennett has done a superb job in settling the seven-year-old and I needed to get his mind on the job to be a competitive Group horse. He went on at the mile and trotted on quietly under the guidance of Alex before exploding up the straight, running his last furlong in 11.3 seconds.

Alex felt Herculian Prince was "awesome"; he really has come back a much stronger gelding than last preparation, and he did a great job then. His owners are so excited about the spring. Where will he start? How many Sydney runs will he have before he heads south? John and Val Heriot and their good friends Alan and Jan Stephens live in Victoria and they can't wait for their boy to be down there. John told me today they were planning an early holiday so not to clash with the gelding's spring program.

Everyone wants to tell me Seventh Reason should be in the Mardi Gras. I do not believe this and the day I saw him at Singo's I fell in love with him. By Sadler's Wells from a mare that could run a trip, Seventh Reason has needed time to mature and get fit. He has turned the corner and has been putting in eye-catching pieces of work. Blake said: "I rode him 10 days ago and was unimpressed, but today he really found the line. He has definitely improved."

Chinkara Dancer used to be difficult to ride, so she had to work solo, but Steve Dennett, who I call Stevie Wonder, has brought her to hand beautifully. She produced excellent and steady work this morning in the company of the filly Crystal Empire (by Statue Of Liberty from My Little Girl).

Rob and I had a grand time at Singo's birthday bash last Sunday. Celebrating his girlfriend Yvette's birthday as well as his, it was a joyous occasion. We all sang and danced along to John Paul Young's band. Some of you may be old enough to remember the hit that rocketed the singer to Australian stardom – *Love Is In The Air*. It really was a blast from the past. The lovely tones did not waver and for one-and-a-half hours they belted out tune after well-known tune. I was most impressed by the dance moves of former rugby league star Johnny Raper; all those quick moves on the footy field have stayed with him. Kylie Gavenlock and husband are smooth movers and so is Sarah Rawiller, who was there while Nash was busy riding in Singapore. Sarah and I were on dance floor grooving away all night. The men were slow from barriers, so the females took to the floor with a vengeance.

One thing with 'Singo' is that he surrounds himself with a wonderful mixture of people from all walks of life, and the sliding scale of rags to riches all seem to gather together and enjoy each other's company. John is a grand host and he certainly has got something to look forward to this spring – More Joyous and Once Were Wild look completely different fillies and each has developed over the shoulder and neck.

His new love is the colt Strawberry Boy (Redoute's Choice-Strawberry Girl). I asked him why he had fallen for the colt and he explained that every time he went into his paddock the horse would follow and he would give him a pat on the nose.

One of John's latest names is Lobster for his filly out of Group 1 winner Universal Queen. "I tried for QE11, but was knocked back," he said. "So I thought, oh well, Lobster." John has a great imagination and makes racing fun.

WEDNESDAY, JULY 14

It was a great morning at the track with loads of jockeys on hand and, boy, does it make a difference. Mark and Neil have held the fort extremely well, but this morning Nash even brought a family member along to help, Stacey Rawiller, just crowned Victoria's Rising Star apprentice for the season.

Breeder Andrea Craven is making the pilgrimage from New Zealand after Bruce Slade enticed her to come to Wyong to watch her darling boy Kontiki Park resume. We are also planning a night out as I think it is so delightful that Andrea gets so involved with her horses. Racing is a marvellous thing for people who enjoy travel and meeting new friends.

The most impressive gallop of the morning came from the unraced Gooree-owned colt Memorable Moment, who was partnered by Nash, alongside Brightexpectations with Alex riding – the son of Encosta De Lago and History Maker had not seen the track, while Brightexpectations is a Group 2 winner. Nash confirmed the rap on Memorable Moment, saying, "This is a great colt." Wonderful feedback from Nash. The colt will have his second trial at Randwick on Monday and is a definite black-booker.

It was an absolutely super win at Warwick Farm today by Antiguan, a rising four-year-old by Danzero, at his first attempt over 1600 metres. I felt the race was won at the 800-metre mark when Nash allowed Sirwinni to lead, settling Antiguan into his comfortable racing rhythm. It did the trick and the gelding relaxed and picked up nicely in the straight. The jockeys' premiership is becoming such an interesting race against Corey Brown, with Nash just ahead. Nash told me early in the season that it was one thing that he dearly wanted to win, and in the time I have worked with him he is not one to be thwarted on the way to achieving his goals. I hope the clubs take advantage of the healthy competition over the final meetings; it will be a leviathan battle.

THURSDAY, JULY 15

I was shocked to hear the other day that Racing NSW is taking six metropolitan meetings to the country. Turnover is far greater in the city and trainers here have a far greater financial commitment than that of their country counterparts. Once you lose a meeting from the city, it never comes back. We have to ensure that Saturday race meetings are at Randwick, Rosehill, Warwick Farm or Canterbury. The major population is in Sydney and the race meeting should be there for the bigger punters to bet on the better horses.

Bruce is heading to Wyong tomorrow with Andrea Craven, and that is a tip if ever there was one. It is a long way to come from New Zealand to watch a horse that you bred, but Kontiki Park is a lovely type by the Stradbroke winner Thorn Park, very much moulded in the Kiwi style. I believe he will stay all day. This will become apparent this preparation because, as a rising five-year-old, he is the perfect age to show his true staying qualities. I chose to kick him off in a 1350-metre event so that by the time he comes to town and steps up in trip he will be super fit and bomb-proof for punters.[73]

I have been in the stables with my sleeves rolled up and my socks pulled up. Greg Nash has been sitting in while stable vet Leanne Begg has been on holidays. I love bouncing ideas off Greg and the wonderful Percy Sykes. It was interesting

---

73 The $2.40 favourite Kontiki Park, ridden by Mark Newnham, was a close second to Gemma's Boy at Wyong.

yesterday as we watched the lovely Encosta De Lago-Mrs. Khan filly Ice Creme trot up. She was ever so slightly off in her action, what we call "half a grade lame". We watched her trot up and back with farriers Anthony Haymer and Kane Simpson. We studied the filly closely and Percy piped up, "Look at her feet, all she needs is a break-away shoe." I have seen this applied to a few of my horses over the years and young Kane found it a revelation. Anthony understood exactly what to make and today he presented me with normal aluminium racing plates with their front ground away so that Ice Creme can break over more comfortably. Straight away she trotted-up much lighter on her feet.

Steve O'Halloran, his wife Stef and their baby Riley had a gorgeous time back home in Ireland. Steve thought it best to have Alex on Theseo for one more time this morning, as he felt his regular rider might have lost some strength on his holiday. Alex said one word, "super". Just A Blaze continues to put in super gallops, so part-owner David Gyngell, head of Channel 9, best get over the pneumonia which has laid him up in bed. Get well soon, David, you may have a cup meeting or two to attend in Melbourne.

FRIDAY, JULY 16

Extra Happy (by Exceed And Excel) put in much improved gallop this morning. When she worked on the heavy grass track the other day it was not to her liking. Percy Sykes, this fragile and diminutive vet, now in his nineties, put his hand down her throat. The young vet Rachel Salz had her arms outstretched behind him in case he fell. "She has couple of rough teeth back there," said Percy as he retrieved his worn hand covered in blood from a sharp molar. I produced a wet wipe on demand to stop the flow of blood.

I said to Percy, "It is a wonderful thing that you come to the stables in the afternoon." He replied, "What would I do if I didn't?" This brilliant vet enjoys being out looking at the horses and his astute observations are a great education for the rest of us.

I am bemused that cash-strapped Racing NSW has thought it appropriate to run an expensive full-page ad in today's *Sydney Morning Herald* describing the outcome of the case taken by Sportsbet and Betfair on betting fees. In it, Racing NSW declares, in Orwellian tones, "Did we win the Court case? Yes, the legislation was upheld by the judge etc."

In reality, and contrary to these wasteful ads, the Sportsbet verdict was against Racing NSW and, in the Betfair case, Justice Perram invited Betfair to make further submissions along Sportsbet lines. It can expected that Betfair also will win. And, you might think strangely for a party that says it has won, Racing NSW is appealing the judgment.

The real problem Racing NSW won't face up to is that, under the judgments, while TABcorp gets an "under the table" rebate of its race-fields tax, Racing NSW will keep losing these cases. The judge hated the secret backhanders. And I don't see how the TAB can afford to pay the full tax – it's virtually 100 per cent of its net profit on NSW racing. Please, let's get away from the "1984 newspeak", George Orwell's fictional language, and propaganda.[74]

MONDAY, JULY 19

A long, pleasant and exciting day, starting with trackwork this morning where there were some lovely pieces of work. The babies are exciting. Steve O'Halloran likes the Strada-Wreckage colt a lot. He's a yearling bought by astute owner-breeder Alan Bell. He matched strides with the Holy Roman Emperor-Nellie De Air colt and the Encosta De Lago-Dorado Deceiver filly, the trio hitting the line together. Boardwalk Dancer (by Strada) is lovely and relaxed and the Redoute's Choice-Egyptian Ibis colt Valleyofthekings is his perfect match.

All Pie Cart (Charge Forward-Betsy Pie) knows is to eat, sleep and run. Robyn Freeman said Pie Cart's work partner, the Royal Academy-Lady Fidelia gelding, is "a darling with a lovely floating action". Aubazine (More Than Ready-Corporate Queen) and Lindstrom (Snitzel-Bergman) are both perfect and Iridesse (Charge Forward-Holly Go Lightly) and the Hussonet-Fountain Of Joy filly are lovely, quiet and good rides.

Three-year-olds Dee Bee Nine, a gelding by Red Ransom, and Ten Seconds, a colt by More Than Ready, made a fabulous pair for Glenlogan Stud, which manages them. They are destined to win races in Glenlogan's maroon and white in the next few weeks. Nash Rawiller cannot believe how the three-year-old filly Little Evie (by Al Maher) has developed. She is quite typical of the breed – give them time and you receive your just rewards. Singo's two-year-old filly More Strawberries (by More Than Ready) has taken time to get fit, but she rocketed back today and her maiden status certainly is in jeopardy this spring.

---

74 The much-awaited Federal Court decision on the challenge by corporate bookmaker Sportsbet and betting exchange Betfair against product fees charged by Racing NSW, vital to the funding of racing in the state, was announced in July – Justice Nye Perram ruled in favour of Sportsbet's claim that the 1.5 per cent turnover fee was discriminatory but dismissed Betfair's application on the same issue.

Racing NSW was ordered to refund Sportsbet more than $2 million, but said its race fields legislation has been deemed valid. Racing NSW chairman Alan Brown said: "The court has found as far Betfair is concerned, Racing NSW has been successful on all counts. It's a mixed day for racing, mixed in having to give back some of the fees but enormous relief that there is certainty, that the legislation fee is valid, as is the regulation."

The sticking point in the Sportsbet case was that Racing NSW does not charge on-course bookmakers the fee until they reach a turnover threshold of $5 million. Justice Perram agreed with Sportsbet the effect was that almost no NSW bookmaker paid the fee and the threshold discriminated against interstate bookmakers, many of whom operate from Darwin. He also found the arrangement between Racing NSW and Tabcorp, which operates the NSW TAB, to be flawed in that the fee paid was ultimately refunded to Tabcorp.

Appeals are pending.

The trials that followed trackwork were worth attending, even if the grandstand at Randwick was rather damp and cold. Memorable Moments and Mutamayez, two outstanding Encosta De Lago colts, won 850-metre trials for Nash. Both are bred in the purple, they ran the same time (52.10 seconds) on a slow track and they looked dominant. These big, strong colts will debut in the coming weeks. The owners and the stable look forward to their races with great anticipation.

Theseo, the champion older horse of Australia over the past two years, had a nice easy trial and Nash was extremely happy, saying the big horse had come back super for Star Thoroughbreds. He was third in a 1250-metre trial behind Cups hope Herculian Prince and newcomer Two For Tea (Drama Critic-Sing). It won't be long before the ex-New Zealander wins on Australian soil under his new name – he was Tea For Two.

The Yankee Cannonball exploded from the barriers in his 1250-metre trial and ran away to win by five lengths. The win was commanding and impressive. He will resume in the Missile Stakes on Saturday, August 7.

Part-owner Ross Herron, who was in Sydney on business from Melbourne, watched Caulfield and Melbourne Cups hope Descarado (by High Chaparral). The further the AJC Derby placegetter goes, the better he goes; and he did it within himself when third over 1250 metres.

San Domenico Stakes contender Brightexpectations (More Than Ready) won his 844-metre trial by a length and he was in charge from the gates to the post. Another two-year-old, Zutara (Encosta De Lago-Matras, by Zabeel), impressed Neil Paine with her win over the same distance. He said, "Gai, you would not believe how much horse I had under me."

The mare Montana Flyer was not going to let the youngsters take the limelight. She won easily over 850 metres in good time (52.10 seconds) and is back as big and as beautiful as ever.

TUESDAY, JULY 20

Ice Creme flew over 600 metres with partner Meditation (Elusive Quality-Up The Hill) this morning. Ice Creme (Encosta De Lago-Mrs. Khan) is regally bred, being a half-sister to Group 1 winner Ike's Dream. Unlike most by her sire she is not big and bay, rather a big, bold chestnut with plenty of white. She heads towards a trial soon, so keep an eye on her.

Really Vexing (Charge Forward-Triangular), owned by international breeder Paul Makin, worked with Fictional Romance (Don Eduardo-Desert Bride). They are fillies with very similar style and lovely ability.

She's A Sure Thing will be that when she races next week. This daughter of Not A Single Doubt and Vital Curves, is above average, but no buyers thought that at the Magic Millions in 2009. All the experts put their line through her as, like Dr Percy Sykes commented, she is weak in the hocks. I said to him, "But she gallops pretty good, Perce." Arrowfield's operations manager Sam Fairgray had confidence in the filly, who he had watched from birth, and he thought she was one of the best of the sale. His jaw dropped when she made very little ($45,000), so he and a group of buddies from Arrowfield came together to race her.

I was asked by Coolmore's Michael Kirwan what I thought of the Holy Roman Emperor youngsters I have in the yard. I told him I could not be more impressed. They have size, strength and lovely bone and they are giving me plenty. I cannot see why they won't win races in the spring. Denise Martin of Star Thoroughbreds has a particularly sharp Holy Roman Emperor colt out of Nellie De Air. He has presence and really catches the eye.

WEDNESDAY, JULY 21

We were a bit short-handed at the track this morning. One of our main riders, Alex Jenkins, was seriously injured yesterday when he fell from one of the 'babies'. He fractured the T5 vertebrae in his neck and broke an ankle and will be sidelined for some time. He is already being missed.

Irish Alistair (McCauley) also was hurt when another of the rising two-year-olds was frightened by the accident. Alistair suffered neck whiplash. He came to the tower at 4.30am today to see the operation from the other side of the fence. He loved seeing the galloping action and 'Damo' took him through the role of clocking and scribing. He also saw Bruce and me take notes on the jockeys' comments; word for word transcribed and sent to the owners, just as Aidan O'Brien does at Ballydoyle.

More Strawberries will trial at Warwick Farm on Tuesday. I was not happy with her first trial when she ran third at that track on July 9 – she must have telepathy as she has improved out of sight since. Nash was delighted with her this morning.

THURSDAY, JULY 22

Well the AJC and the STC have succumbed to the pressure of the Government, which dangled an alluringly large sum of money – $150 million to go to Randwick for two new grandstands and a "theatre of the horse" parade ring, and $24 million to Rosehill, mainly for grandstand refurbishment and access improvements – on the basis of the clubs merging. Is the merger, which is subject to members' approval, good for racing? I am not sure. I am a great one for healthy competition such as that we see with Caulfield

(Melbourne Racing Club) and Flemington (Victoria Racing Club), and, previously, the AJC and the STC. But if it means that the money provided will pay to upgrade facilities so desperately needing improvement, then we have to move with the times.

With the committees merging, certain people will be stood down and others will form the governing body. I think the new body should govern racing in the State as it seems silly to have Racing NSW plus a new committee of the merged clubs. It would be bureaucracy on top of bureaucracy and dollars on top of dollars to pay this new body. Previously these committee positions had been filled by people who did it for the love of the industry, sometimes to the detriment of their own businesses.

I think things will happen very quickly now and hopefully it will prove uplifting.

The gallops this morning were great but cold, and when the dirt closed we moved to the B grass. It was a bit shifty, so I got the boys to hold their horses together. Young Amjad Ali Khan from India is new to riding gallops, but Mark Newnham gave him the thumbs up. I told him to put up his stirrups two notches and he immediately had a better seat and a better control of his gallop.

I went into town to have a look at a new bed because we are thinking of investing in a new nest as yours truly fights with dust mites. What might dust mites like? Well, I can tell you. They like us and flakes of skin – yum, yum. They like warmth, the bed, the carpet and the curtains. When I went to the doctor recently for my allergies, thinking it might be my equine friends causing it, my arm blew up like a balloon when scratched, with 'Mr Mite' present in it.

Anyway, I had a good work-out, jumping from allergy-free bed to allergy-free bed. Some were so high you needed a ladder, on others you could raise the head for night-time reading. Food for thought and something Rob and I can sleep on tonight.

FRIDAY, JULY 23

I have just installed two mirrors so the horses who fancy themselves can stand in front of them. I saw this in England at the stables of trainer Sir Mark Prescott, a gentleman who has a great ability to improvise with different devices to stop box-walking, crib-biting and the like. The More Than Ready colt Ten Seconds has no quirks, but it just so happened that his box was best placed to house the permanent fixture. He has always been a gorgeous thing and I think he might think so, too. Since the mirror has been installed he won't leave his 'new friend' and stands near 'him' all day.

This morning was great; very busy, but great. Mark Newnham, Steve O'Halloran, young Blake Spriggs, Johnny Livingstone, Darshan Prakash and a rejuvenated Nash

Rawiller got us through the work. Nash has found the extra energy through sleeping in a hyperbaric chamber with 100 per cent oxygen, which has helped the leading jock through a back injury that affects him at different times.

Concerned, I said to him, "Didn't Michael Jackson sleep in one of them, and look what happened." Nash said, "Seriously, it is great." He explained that at first it was an unusual feeling, but after about 40 minutes he started breathing at a much slower rate and felt remarkably better for it. He has suggested the chamber to Darley's No. 1 jockey Kerrin McEvoy, who is recovering from back injuries after his serious fall at Gosford on June 23.

Mark was taken by the work of Descarado, who was much more focused with blinkers on. He got his head down and stretched out, but his biggest assets are the way he relaxes and his remarkable stride. More Strawberries was yummy. She glided over 800 metres – she is the sort that runs time you would not believe, given the ease of her style.

Filly Joy Toy (Encosta De Lago-Sunday Joy) and colt Tuxedo Royale (Encosta De Lago-The Golden Dane) were just super. The blinkers on the filly made a huge improvement and she powered to the line with the colt in close pursuit.

The Strada yearlings impress me. The two gentlemen I have in work now do everything right. Steve said of the Wreckage colt, "He knows what he is doing and is a big strong colt." Boardwalk Dancer, from My Pirouette, was quite tiny when he first came in, but when he was gelded and spelled he grew a hand. He has the best temperament; he puts all his energy into his work.

Track-riders Johnny and Darshan showed the ropes to two nice sorts, the Redoute's Choice-Shamekha colt and the Fastnet Rock-Barawin filly.

A girl is allowed a couple of vices, and mine are my hair and nails. I have only taken up having my nails painted in the last year and there is nothing I enjoy doing more than working on my blog while I have my nails done.

Back at the stables, you pick up so much from the horses in the afternoon, especially with vets Percy Sykes and Leanne Begg by my side. Horses sometimes show lameness several hours after they work, so it is important that the whole team is watched over in the daylight hours. I make sure each horse is trotted daily.

MONDAY, JULY 26

What a devastating win at Randwick on Saturday by two-year-old Squamosa (Not A Single Doubt-Class Success). He was a colt that we all thought a lot of, and my comments from the Magic Millions Gold Coast sale in 2009, where we bought him for $140,000, read: "Strong, masculine; great forearm; racehorse." He sat languishing on Denise Martin's books at Star Thoroughbreds for several months before the astute Robert Tan purchased the colt. He later named him after an endangered clam (*tridacna squamosa*) and now is laughing all the way to the bank.

The win makes it two from two, with earnings already at $90,000, and in the process he answered the wet-track and distance questions asked of him. He was like a road-runner, scooting over the 1400-metre journey like it was a 1000-metre event. He made the opposition look ordinary. Squamosa is not overly big, but he is robust, much like his father.

AJC chairman Ron Finemore was grinning from ear to ear after the event, and he had every right to, as he owns a large amount of Not A Single Doubt, who stands for $13,750 at Arrowfield Stud. The son of Redoute's Choice is shaping up as more than just a bread-and-butter sire. He certainly passes on his speed and versatility, as Squamosa shows.

The two-year-old filly She's a Sure Thing, who Blake will ride at her debut at Wyong on Thursday, is another by Not A Single Doubt. She worked with Neil Paine in the saddle this morning and, on dismounting, Neil commented that, as her name suggests, she's a sure thing.[75]

It is interesting to see the huge fields the two-year-old races attract late in the season. Programmers at Racing NSW need to put on their spectacles as there are not enough races available for the youngsters. Why is there is no two-year-old race at Kembla Grange this Saturday? The fillies race at Canterbury on Wednesday has had to be split; the juvenile race at Wyong on Thursday has 48 nominations; Friday at Warwick Farm sees a 1400-metre event with 28 entered; and Saturday sees 21 in the $100,000 Rosebud at Rosehill. Yet, at Kembla Grange, they decide not to bother with a race for the young guns. Why wouldn't they? A two-year-old win in a horse's pedigree is much more attractive to buyers than a victory at three, four or five. The new season is about to start and it is time that Racing NSW became far more in tune with the needs of trainers and owners.

The babies are going great, with the Strada gelding Boardwalk Dancer the early standout. Mark Newnham quipped, "He's the best yearling I have ridden so far." Closely following him is Costa Serena (by Encosta De Lago-Merlene), named by my readers. She is big and fat, but she has natural ability to burn. Lady Vuvuzela (Hussonet-Fountain Joy) is a hoot of a filly. Her favourite trick is to jump the shadow created by the new light

---

75 She's A Sure Thing ($4.40) was fifth at Wyong on July 29.

at the furlong marker. I have mentioned this to course manager Mick Stanley and I am sure it is being addressed.

I made an interesting pairing with The Rosebud (1200 metres) at Rosehill on Saturday in mind. Crossbow (Redoute's Choice-Rainbow Bubbles) and Dal Dal (Encosta De Lago-Blab) matched strides and Nash asked me afterwards, "Which should I ride?" Neil answered for me, saying, "The one who has your weight, Nash." That's Crossbow (56.5kg); Dal Dal has 54kg.[76]

TUESDAY, JULY 28

What a day. 'Damo' arrived at home to pick me up and 'Batman and Robin' were off to the track at Randwick for the usual 4.30am start. On the way we were caught up with tunnel maintenance, which is always pain in the neck as you never get where you want to on time – and my mob is very punctual, always ready to start the gallops at 4.30. Dave Meijer and the boys had the horses walking around the tower and the jockeys queued patiently, the light spilling over it all quite eerily.

Best of the morning had to be Dance Idol. The Danehill Dancer-Distinctly filly worked a treat and I am delighted with her progress. Cups hope Herculian Prince delighted Neil as he flew along the back and then found the line with vengeance.

Pureness (Tale Of The Cat-Purespeed) has come through his debut win at Canterbury last Wednesday so well. He won't be seen again until August 18, as I want to keep him in his own class and let him work through the grades. Small fish are sweet for his owner, one G. Waterhouse.

Two-year-olds Upon This Rock (Fastnet Rock-Joleur) and Shakira Morn (More Than Ready-Dane Shakira) were stylish this morning, as were the Dancers, Chinkara Dancer (Danehill Dancer-Reem Albaraari) and Flamingo Dancer (Don Eduardo-Wonderer). Stratofortress (Stravinsky-Instantly) has a girth on him the size of a 10-tonne Tessie. I said to Glyn Schofield if he was not happy with Stratofortress' fitness he wouldn't start on Saturday. On return, Glyn had only positive comments, saying the gelding did not blow at all and that he was definitely ready for Saturday. We will all know then if Glyn is a good judge.[77]

The two Zabeel colts I wrote about after the New Zealand sales early this year, one out of Sarajay, the other out of Power And Grace, are real lads. They were jumping around the back straight like they were 'Beverley Hillbillies'. They formed a trio with the Fastnet Rock-Desert Ibis filly, who, at this point, is more precocious. This was

---

76 Crossbow finished seventh as the $1.80 favourite; Dal Dal did not accept.
77 Stratofortress finished eighth of nine over 1400 metres at Rosehill.

expected, as she is bred in Australia for the Slipper, while the Kiwi lads are bred for the Derby. The important ingredient in training the staying horses is time.

A nice couple from Perth enjoyed watching the training session. They commented that they had met my father quite some time ago, at which point the guy, Rick, produced a racebook from the 1979 Railway Stakes day at Ascot and inside was my dad's signature. He had signed it, 'Best regards, TJ Smith, 1980'. It was the perfect example of TJ, who was always looking forward.

Too often people worry about things they cannot change. Only the other day a Sydney journalist was told by a doctor that he was suffering from stress. The journo asked me, "How do I deal with it Gai?" I said, "Easily. I download every night on to a writing pad before I go to bed so that I have nothing lurking in my mind, and then I sleep well and am ready to fire in the morning."

Stress causes wrinkles, grey hair and ulcers. Other things I do to bust stress include my wiggly-worm exercises every morning and walking in the evenings with the dog, and the husband. These are all little things, but they make a big difference.

The trials at Warwick Farm were a pleasing event. Winners included the two-year-old colt Charing Cross (Fastnet Rock-Coogee Beach), who delighted owners Jeff and Trisha Sheehan with his effort. Ice Creme also delighted, as did Kiss From A Rose (Encosta De Lago-Comical Smile), Master Of Reality (Danehill Dancer-Palabiro) and Halekulani (Encosta De Lago-Flying Spice).

WEDNESDAY, JULY 28

Tullamore, a three-year-old by Savabeel, came out of 'zombie zone' this morning when matching strides with his equally dopey mate, Power Personified, a three-year-old son of Exceed And Excel and Jewelmer who I thought at one stage was a Golden Slipper horse, but was unplaced at his only two starts as a two-year-old. Tim Clark gave the Zabeel entire Show Dancer what I call a 'quiet stretch and extend' before Friday's Warwick Farm engagement, when Blake, now claiming 2kg in town, will ride him. Tim commented that Show Dancer, who won his Maiden over 2000 metres at Hawkesbury on July 8, stays all day, so 2400 metres won't worry him.[78]

After two-year-old filly Cinderellas Secret (Danzero-She's A Meanie) ran fourth in the first race at Canterbury today we had time to kill. I mentioned to 'Damo' that we should visit Trish Muir's antique shop. If there is something you need, Mrs Muir always has

---

[78] Show Dancer started at $5 when last of seven at Warwick Farm.

it – she has a very astute eye for beautiful things, and even her husband says that's why she chose him.

You would not find the shop, Architectural Decor, unless someone gave you the tip, but it is in Lewisham, only minutes away from the racetrack. It is run by Tony Healy. I called in to buy some urns because I wanted something lovely for the resting place for my parents and old Jock. The shop had exactly what I wanted, except they were attached to the sides of the most beautiful old clock. I had no place for the clock and, understandably, no deal could be struck.

The thing I took real fancy to was a little boat with the initials DR on its side. It once cost 20 cents a ride when the boat sat outside the famous Doyles Restaurant at Watsons Bay. As anyone who has ventured into Tulloch Lodge will know, it is, as my dad used to say, full of junk. I like to acquire bits of art and culture, but Dad never appreciated my artistic bent. "What the devil are you doing filling the stable with junk?" he would ask. The answer was – and still is – that I am trying to make the stables as interesting as possible. I'm still thinking whether I should add the boat to my collection.

THURSDAY, JULY 29

This morning started slowly, so I thought to myself, 'Oh heavens, how are we going to get through in the allotted time?' The dirt track was sealed (rolled to keep the water out), but somehow magic took place. The horses flowed in and out like liquid gold, and Neil Paine and Mark Newnham deserved gold medals – they are always so professional and are always in attendance. Neil said the work was 'hard yakka', as when you are riding at this pace over 1400-1600 metres the horse is putting weight on to the bit and pulling on the rider's back and legs. When it was all done, Neil and Mark said they felt they needed to join Nash for a nap in the hyperbaric chamber. Hopefully, it holds a king-size bed.

The filly More Joyous was just that. She is out to prove the critics wrong in two things: that she will get more distance – I am aiming her at the Cox Plate (2040 metres) – and that she can sustain a longer preparation. I really do have a filly to work with this time.

The search for a little party dress is always tricky, but David Jones kindly puts together a variety of ensembles and I can choose what will look best on racing's ambassador when she flies the flag for the opening of David Jones' Melbourne store on August 12. Glorious evening gowns by George Gross and Armani also were tested. I never cease to get over the great value George Gross gives to us. There are terrific designs at affordable prices, and it's hard to find both when you are looking for style.

I had an interesting afternoon looking at feet with vet Percy Sykes and farrier Kane Simpson, with them pointing out slightly different shaped feet, some chubby and others wider. How to correct this was also discussed, in terms of what type of shoe to wear and what needs trimming to ensure our horses stay sound and race for longer. Percy was insightful as ever. Young Kane is no slouch and was very quick to pick up the flaws.

FRIDAY, JULY 30

Owner Bob Scarborough was on deck at Randwick this morning. Bob is one of Australia's elite breeders, having a boutique broodmare band at Wood Nook Farm at Nagambie in Victoria, as well as being chairman of the Moonee Valley Racing Club. He has horses with a number of trainers and I feel privileged to be one of them. The horse he was viewing was Light Brigade, a tall, leggy son of Redoute's Choice out of a Stakes-winning Zabeel mare, Winning Belle.

As Dave Meijer said of the rising three-year-old colt, "He's a spitting image of his mother." Dave would know because he strapped Winning Belle, who won Group 2 and Group 3 races and was second to Makybe Diva in the Group 1 Australian Cup (2000 metres) at Flemington in 2005.

The fog was so bad you couldn't see your hand in front of you. Damien (Gaffney) and Dave (Fenning) did a great job spotting the silhouettes of the horses at the 1600-metre mark and as they passed the post. Given the conditions, I relied heavily on the jocks' thoughts of the gallops. Nash was extremely pleased with rising three-year-old filly More Strawberries and, with Bob listening, told me Light Brigade was his second best gallop of the morning.

This afternoon I really enjoyed spending time with my family. We all gathered for a stylish photo shoot, which will be used to promote Tom's new internet bookmaking business – *www.tomwaterhouse.com.au*.

It's been a busy week. Liz, my masseuse, said "Hasn't the week flown." I think it would be more correct to ask, "Where has the year gone?" Each day is filled with so many different tasks, be they interesting or mundane, difficult or simple. I have been hell bent on reorganising my stables; some might say I've been a little too zealous in my approach. I'm trying to get back to basics and put the show right back on the road again! Often the smallest detail can be overlooked and thought trivial or not important, but they add up and add to the success of the yard.

Many play a part during a three-year whirlwind

What a remarkable three years it has been since I started writing about my daily experiences as the unimaginable scourge of EI struck the east coast of Australia. What started out as a new mode of communication to my owners has become part of my life, my routine, and a great joy it has been.

Reading back through these mountains of words, I can see the whole picture as a mixed bag. There have been wonderful highs, disappointments, and the sad loss of my gorgeous mother Val and our marvellous house guest, and great mentor, Jock.

Through all that, racing goes on. A new season comes, then goes, then moves into another. It's an amazing whirlwind of observing young horses, choosing carefully, meeting owners and working with a varied group of people. The battle never ends, but, as with every battle, it is the team that puts it all together – and I believe I have the best team.

The introduction of Nash Rawiller as stable jockey was one of my biggest highlights in recent years. What a difference these years have made to this excellent young man. When he relocated from Melbourne to Sydney, Nash was shy and introverted and certainly not the man I work with today. He has a delightful personality and we all agree that he is one of the great jockeys of Australia. What a tremendous achievement to win the 2009-10 Sydney jockeys' premiership. He deserves every success that comes his way.

Denise Martin has been a constant support to me and the stable with Star Thoroughbreds blazing the way in quality syndication. Like her marketing says, "no one does it better". Her style, personality and dedication to her owners and to the stable is something one hopes for in any relationship. In nearly all the syndicates there are 10 owners so the people we deal with on a daily basis are many and varied. My owners – individuals and syndicates – are the entire reason I train. They are interesting, wonderfully different and are from across all sections of society. Every one of them is important to me and to the stable.

Of course my staff is paramount in our success. Jane Cully (née Abercrombie) and Steve Dennett have been batting with me since day one. They have seen the stable transform from a handful of horses into a major yard in the southern hemisphere.

Lofty (Brett Killion), Tania Rouse, Dave Meijer, Mel Norton, Fleur Blanche, Frank Fitchett, Steve O'Halloran, Crewy (John Brady) and his daughter Leigh, Scott Cleal, Nicky Matura, Johnny Livingstone, Ranjeet Singh and Motto Hoy have all worked with me for many years. Each of them contributes greatly to the success of the stable as they carry out the important never-ending tasks of stable life. The detail and the diligence make all the difference.

Emma Candy, daughter of the Queen's former trainer Henry Candy, is a most capable horsewoman, and for three years I had the pleasure of having Emma as assistant trainer (a position Tania took over in 2007). After Emma's visa had run its course, she returned to England to assist trainer James Fanshawe at Newmarket. She married Rupert Erskine Crum, who runs a horse transport business in England, and someone said to me that Emma was the only person they knew who had gone from a candy to a crumb. She is a sterling woman who has a wonderful eye for a horse and I enjoyed her assistance very much.

No business can work without a heart, and in the case of our stable, it's the office. Communicating on a daily basis to all our owners, transport companies, feed merchants, agistment properties, etcetera, the office takes a great deal of pressure off *The Lady Trainer* and makes the business run like clockwork. Jane Cully manages the office. Assisting her we have had Robyn Hartney, Alison Schofield and Tracy Clark (née Stockman), who of course married young Dan (Clark) who worked with the team for many years.

Steve Dennett floats between the stable and the office keeping all informed. You name it, he knows it, and all I can say is thank goodness he is around.

Susie Loewy is my coordinator extraordinaire. Every single function I attend, every plane I catch, every talk I do, every meeting I make she puts in the diary and drives me to be on time. Sometimes I do not know how she copes as there is always so much going on.

Pauline Blanche's father Bob Curran was TJ's most trusted foreman and her mother Myra (known as Becky) looked after the colours so caringly and kept the office immaculate. I can't remember Tulloch Lodge without Pauline as my father's secretary, friend and confidante. When Dad passed away Pauline became Mum's greatest mate. My mother-in-law Susie and Pauline ("Mrs B") so ably assist me at the Randwick races. It is great that this wonderful woman is still in the sport of kings.

My racing managers have been of highest quality. Steve Brem moved from his prestigious position at Haunui Farm in New Zealand to assist me for seven excellent years. Steve has the most remarkable knowledge of racing and breeding and was so professional in his approach. The owners and I adored him. After Steve left Richard Haynes assisted me. He was a delightful young man and a pleasure to work with.

Amy Austin also filled these boots. I met Amy when she worked with English bloodstock agent Amanda Skiffington. Then came Marrette Farrell, a quietly spoken Irish woman with in-depth knowledge of American and European breeding. I think Marrette found *The Lady Trainer* a little full-on.

Lofty, who is a man of few words but great observational powers, said to me, "What a wonderful person Marrette is". From Lofty that was high praise indeed.

Catherine Hudson spent a lot of time on the phone outside the office which made us all laugh. All of us knew she was going places; she has relocated to America and is doing very well for herself. When she went we were left scratching our heads as to who would fill the role, but Jane pointed out a bright young person and a star of the Darley Flying Start program. Enter Kate Grimwade, a girl from Newmarket (UK) whose father manages the Royal Studs now based at Sandringham. Kate lives and breathes breeding and racing, and we had an excellent period as she is such a natural salesperson.

Now the man of the moment is young Bruce Slade, who came to the attention of Rob and I in January when we were in New Zealand. When Kate gave notice Bruce asked, "Who will take over the job?" I said, looking him fair and square in the eye, "You, baby."

Race programming/managing positions have gone from Sandy Almond to Robyn Hartney, who comes from a line of racing folk deeply involved with the thoroughbred. When Robyn moved on to assist Patinack, I needed to find someone super. I have known Mark Webbey in a professional capacity through his work as chief handicapper for Racing NSW, racing manager and chief handicapper for the Singapore Turf Club, his role with Patinack and, lastly I hope, with *The Lady Trainer*. Mark is wonderfully adaptable and has fitted in well in the hectic Tulloch Lodge office.

In the accounts office sit Louise O'Halloran, Carolyn Steinberg and Arthur Buxton. Louise is an exceptional woman who assisted me so capably at home when Mum and Jack were alive. I then asked Louise to join the team at Tulloch Lodge with her brother Steve, who you have read plenty about. Without Louise's support and knowledge in acccounts I would be far worse off.

Arthur came to me after 20 years in the public service. He is a mate of Dave Fenning, who I've also written about, and I could see Arthur was not happy in his previous job so I asked if he would like to join the team. He specialises in occupational health and safety and wears many different hats. Carolyn, a charming and reserved lady, looks after the payment of yearlings and is often put in a difficult position – companies have to be paid and, as I "speck" so many yearlings, she is often chasing the dollars.

Also in accounts is Errol Chant, who is an unsung hero. Errol ran an accounting firm before he retired. His wife Marion said discreetly to Lea and me a few years later that Errol was lost in retirement, to which I said, "He won't be lost for long." I run all my financial problems by him. He is a wonderful asset and a lovely friend.

Damien Gaffney came into my life as my driver several years ago and plays Robin to my Batman. As I seemed to spend most of my time in my car when I wasn't with the horses, and used it as a second office, I had decided it was better if someone else drove, leaving me to phone clients and the office while going from A to B. Damien's job description has expanded to basically one of multi-tasking, including clocking the horses some mornings – put simply, he does whatever needs doing during a day with Gai.

My best friend Lea Stracey always provides wonderful support, and that extended to proof-reading this book, a task also undertaken with relish by Rob's friend Len Loveday. Because I'm an only child, Lea has been like a sister to me. We met in a birthing clinic 28 years ago and our bond was immediate and lasting. We talk the same language and laugh at the same jokes, yet we have totally different personalities. Thank goodness Lea does not have a personality like mine! She has wonderful warmth, is very caring and, in my eyes, is the complete woman.

In my personal life Mary Green has looked after all of us forever, watching over the kids, caring for mum and Jock when we have been away and now taking care of Baci and Bello. Mary was with my darling mum when she passed away and she knows the ins and outs of the Waterhouse family better than anyone. She can take it when I am stressed and overwhelmed and handles me like a mother with her child.

Sonia Dejager has been working with me at home for many years. With a heart of gold, she helps me get ready for everything and does all the things that most housewives do.

My children Tom and Kate are a constant source of delight. From the moment they tumbled into the world our lives have been filled with joy and happiness. When they were kids we always holidayed as a family and we still do this today. We admire each other's strengths and are accepting of our weaknesses – they are both stars.

My parents-in-law Bill and Susie Waterhouse have been important parts of where I am today. It could not have worked if we were not so closely aligned. The love Tom and Kate have developed for them is a joy to behold. Susie has carried on in great style the position Mum filled at races. She comes to every Randwick meeting and her charm and elegance draw great respect and love from my owners. She is an enormous help.

My darling sister-in-law Louise is more like a sister. She is the smartest woman I have ever met, she sees things so clearly with her crystal-like intelligence and is the backbone of the family. Her husband Guenter Raedler is a great strength for her but lets her have a loose rein – as needed by most successful woman. They love Tom and Kate like their own children and they are so helpful in the guidance of their careers.

If I am anything I am a product of my mum and dad, both strong people with determination their key attribute. They loved me, guided me and brought me up in the world of racing, little suspecting that it would become my chosen career.

Finally, to my partner in life 30 years this December. I have been with Rob longer than with my mum and dad. He is my inspiration and guidance. He is always there for me and cares for me more than anyone else. We are partners in the true sense.

Gai Waterhouse

BORN: September 2 1954.

MARRIED TO: Rob Waterhouse, on December 14, 1980.

CHILDREN: Kate and Tom.

TRAINING: worked with father TJ Smith from 1978 until licensed as a trainer on January 3, 1992.

STABLE COLOURS: dark blue and green stripes, dark blue cap.

STAR THOROUGHBREDS COLOURS: purple, white stars and cap.

FIRST WINNER: Gifted Poet, Hawkesbury Superfecta Hcp, March 15, 1992.

FIRST GROUP WINNER: Moods, Gosford Cup (Group 3), April 29, 1992.

FIRST GROUP 1 WINNER: Te Akau Nick, The Metropolitan, Randwick, October 5, 1992.

FIRST CLASSIC WINNER: Nothin' Leica Dane, VRC Victoria Derby, Flemington, October 29, 1995.

OVERALL WINNERS: more than 2000.

GROUP 1 WINNERS: 98, including Grand Armee (7), Desert War (6), Theseo (5), Juggler (4), Dance Hero (4), Tuesday Joy (4), Assertive Lad (3) and Bentley Biscuit (3). This places Gai fourth all-time, with Colin Hayes, behind TJ Smith (282), Bart Cummings (260) and Lee Freedman (125).

SYDNEY PREMIERSHIPS: 7 (1996-97, 104.5 wins; 2000-01, 153; 2001-02, 137: 2002-03, 156: 2004-05, 118; 2007-08, 70; 2008-09, 74.5). Seven crowns place Gai third behind TJ Smith (34) and John Hawkes (9).

AUSTRALIAN RACING HALL OF FAME: inducted November 26, 2007.

BUSINESS AWARDS: winner of the Westpac Business Owner Award and named the Telstra NSW Businesswoman of the Year in 2000.